ADDED VALUE

OTHER LOTUS TITLES

Ajit Bhattacharjea	*Sheikh Mohammad Abdullah: Tragic Hero of Kashmir*
Anil Dharker	*Icons: Men & Women Who Shaped Today's India*
Aitzaz Ahsan	*The Indus Saga: The Making of Pakistan*
Ajay Mansingh	*Firaq Gorakhpuri: The Poet of Pain & Ecstasy*
Alam Srinivas & TR Vivek	*IPL: The Inside Story*
Alam Srinivas	*Women of Vision: Nine Business Leaders in Conversation*
Amarinder Singh	*The Last Sunset: The Rise & Fall of the Lahore Durbar*
Hamish Mcdonald	*Ambani & Sons*
Kunal Purandare	*Ramakant Achrekar: A Biography*
Lakshmi Vishwanathan	*Women of Pride: The Devdasi Heritage*
Lucy Peck	*Agra: The Architectural Heritage*
Lucy Peck	*Delhi a Thousand Years of Building: An INTACH-Roli Guide*
Madan Gopal	*My Life and Times: Munshi Premchand*
M.J. Akbar	*Byline*
M.J. Akbar	*Blood Brothers: A Family Saga*
Maj. Gen. Ian Cardozo	*Param Vir: Our Heroes in Battle*
Maj. Gen. Ian Cardozo	*The Sinking of INS Khukri: What Happened in 1971*
Madhu Trehan	*Tehelka as Metaphor*
Monisha Rajesh	*Around India in 80 Trains*
Noorul Hasan	*Meena Kumari: The Poet*
Peter Church	*Added Value: The Life Stories of Indian Business Leaders*
Peter Church	*Profiles in Enterprise: Inspiring Stories of Indian Business Leaders*
Rajika Bhandari	*The Raj on the Move: Story of the Dak Bungalow*
Ralph Russell	*The Famous Ghalib: The Sound of my Moving Pen*
R.V. Smith	*Delhi: Unknown Tales of a City*
Salman Akthar	*The Book of Emotions*
Sharmishta Gooptu	*Bengali Cinema: An Other Nation*
Shrabani Basu	*Spy Princess: The Life of Noor Inayat Khan*
S. Hussain Zaidi	*Dongri to Dubai*
Sunil Raman & Rohit Aggarwal	*Delhi Durbar: 1911 The Complete Story*
Thomas Weber	*Going Native: Gandhi's Relationship with Western Women*
Thomas Weber	*Gandhi at First Sight*
Vir Sanghvi	*Men of Steel: India's Business Leaders in Candid Conversation*

FORTHCOMING TITLES

Shahrayar Khan	*Bhopal Vignettes*

ADDED VALUE

THE LIFE STORIES OF INDIAN BUSINESS LEADERS

Peter Church

LOTUS COLLECTION
ROLI BOOKS

Lotus Collection

First published in hardback in India in 2010
This paperback edition, 2011
Third impression, 2016

The Lotus Collection
An imprint of Roli Books Pvt. Ltd.
M-75, G.K. II Market, New Delhi 110 048
Phone: ++91 (011) 40682000
E-mail: info@rolibooks.com; Website: www.rolibooks.com

Also at
Chennai and Mumbai

Layout Design: Supriya Saran

ISBN: 9788174368676

Typeset in Warnock Pro by Roli Books Pvt Ltd
Printed in India at Repro India Ltd.

For my rapidly growing brood of grandchildren –
currently Daisy, Polly, Harry, Fox and Lily
and, most of all, for the long suffering Ginny

CONTENTS

Note
An endnote to each chapter provides a brief description of the subject's business or organization.

ACKNOWLEDGEMENTS

In any project such as this, the first and most important contribution is obviously made by the interviewees themselves and, as we all know, their extremely important secretaries and assistants, without whom there would be no book.

However, a number of other people contributed significantly. Most important amongst these by far are Anuradha Altekar and Dev Chandrasekhar at Ubiquus, who worked closely with me for the whole life of the project and whose expertise and experience were invaluable in so many ways, including identifying potential interviewees and arranging my meetings with them, in editing the stories, in designing the dust jacket and developing and implementing the communication strategy. Thank you, Anu and Chandra. My thanks also to their network of colleagues and friends and, in particular, to Devyani Khanvilkar, Dhananjay Mungale, Karthik Menon and Praveen Paul who, in turn, generously helped with their contacts.

It would also be remiss of me not to acknowledge and thank for the assistance given to me by many other people who helped me shortlist those to be interviewed. Amongst these were John McCarthy AO, the then Australian High Commissioner to India, Vinod Kumar, the then deputy High Commissioner of India to Australia and my colleagues Shiban Bakshi and Suresh Iyer.

I would also like to thank my long suffering personal assistant, Daphne Lim who, when I wrote a similar book to this one on South-East Asian businessmen and women in 1999, I promised it would be my last book. I will make no such rash promise this time around as I have thoroughly enjoyed the whole process from concept through to publication. I found all of the subjects to be easy to interview (with one exception – see if you can guess who that is) and to be both charming and generous with their time.

Finally, I would like to thank Pramod and Priya Kapoor, Nandita Bhardwaj, Neelam Narula and Supriya Saran of Roli Books for taking on the challenge and publishing the book and providing expert advice and assistance along the way.

The life stories in this book are the direct result of my interviews with the subjects over a three-year period so that they are not necessarily completely up to date as at the date of publication in March 2010. They are their stories and each of them approved the text for his or her chapter. If any mistakes remain then the responsibility rests with me.

INTRODUCTION

This is not a book about wealth but certainly, many of those interviewed are wealthy. It is more about the lives of Indian business leaders who have added value to their businesses or professions and, in many cases, to India as a nation. The book also focuses on their thoughts on success and its ingredients.

Through my involvement with the countries of Asia over the last forty years, first as a student, then as a lawyer and corporate adviser, I have met and observed a number of the 'movers and shakers' in the region. Usually, when I read about them in the press or heard others talk of them, what is reported is how much money they have, what huge deals they have done or the wonderful lives they lead. There seems little interest in their life stories which, for me, are far more interesting than speculating about how many dollars they have in their bank accounts. How did they do it? Was it luck? Was it just hard work? Or are there a number of factors or threads which could guide others to success?

Ten years ago I wrote a book[1] on the life stories of some sixty-five leading South-East Asian businessmen and women from the ten countries making up the Association of South-East Asian Nations (ASEAN). The book answered many of these questions and, by far and away, the most important ingredient to success so far as I could ascertain was timing. There seems to be a time to get into businesses, a time to grow businesses and a time to get out of businesses. For a number of older people interviewed, the right time came in the years following World War II and as their nations gained independence.

As my involvement in India has increased over the last decade it set me thinking as to whether I would find the same situation if I was to explore the life stories of Indian business leaders. This book is the result. Not surprisingly there are many similarities but, as you will read, the history and culture of India is different in many respects to the countries of South-East Asia. Certainly India, like all the countries of South-East Asia, with the exception of Thailand, was colonized by a Western power but India created some amazing twists and turns for many of those interviewed for this book.

What looms largest in the stories of many of these men and women is the long dark shadow cast by the 'licence raj' when one almost needed a licence to breathe. Even large industrialists suffered. How individual men and women prospered in that period is almost beyond belief. For those who did, I think the personal characteristic that shines through most is their grit and determination to never give in. Deepak Puri of Moser Baer described the situation as '(t)he government at that time wanted the Indian entrepreneur to go and box in a boxing ring with his arms tied behind his back and win the bout. An Indian businessman in those times had to find a way to win a boxing bout without using his arms.' Yes, grit and determination is a common element of every person featured in this book.

And again, as in South-East Asia, timing shines through as a key ingredient in the success of many of those covered in this book. They were in the right place at the right time when the 'licence raj' drew its last breath. But, of course, their success is far more complicated than this.

Apart from external factors like timing, what then are the characteristics one expects to find in successful entrepreneurs? Many psychologists have spent their careers trying to identify these. The precise definition of exactly what the word 'entrepreneur' means seems to be the subject of some debate and the definition I most enjoy is the one of Peter Kilby in his classic essay 'Hunting the Heffalump.'[2] He likened the search for an entrepreneur to be like hunting the Heffalump, a character from A.A. Milne's *Winnie the Pooh* that, in Kilby's words 'is a rather large and very important animal. He has been hunted by many individuals using various ingenious trapping devices, but no one so far has succeeded in capturing him. All who claim to have caught sight of him report that he is enormous, but they disagree on his particulars.'[3]

Fortunately, many psychologists such as Reg Jennings, Charles Cox and Cary L. Cooper[4] do agree on several key 'particulars'. As you read the life stories in this book I suggest you bear in mind the characteristics they identified from their research. Although their study was of Western entrepreneurs, I think you will be surprised to see how many of the following apply to the Indian subjects in this book:

- Assertiveness – the grit and determination I mentioned above, not surprisingly, tops the list and I think is exhibited by every person in this book.
- The Learning Curve – the ability to learn from setbacks or failures.
- Ambition – being highly proactive and responsive to challenge.
- Achievement Orientation – the need and belief they can succeed. GVK Reddy of GVK Group said, 'I think my most important attributes are a vision of the future and the courage to follow my convictions with persistence to achieve that vision. The Novopan business is an example of that. Many people thought that I would give up and fail but I persisted and the business has succeeded.'
- The Internal Gyroscope – a clear and positive view of where they are going. Professor Swaminathan of the MS Swaminathan Research Foundation exhibited this when he said, 'For me, it was blindingly clear that the most important thing for India after WW II was going to be

food.' Captain Gopinath of Air Deccan who lived for years in a tent on his fledgling farm told me, 'Each day I would get up at sunrise and walk around the fields and I had this vision of what I would do with the farm. I said I must really build a beautiful farm. And also the thought of being there with nature and working, I could read, and all these things were so exciting to me. So I was, like I said, so much into it that nothing else existed for me.' Raghav Bahl of Network18 similarly saw the future in his sector clearly, 'To me, it was clear that the tape would die, that the future lay in broadcasting.' And Dr Anji Reddy of Dr Reddy Laboratories also demonstrates this, 'One day, I was just walking past the lab and the thought suddenly struck me: I had to build my own Pfizer one day. The feeling was so powerful that, from that moment on, I looked at chemistry from the point of view of a businessman.'

- An Integrated Value System – clear values with one of the most important being dependability. Wealth and power rank lower in importance for most entrepreneurs than people and relationships.
- Effective Management of Risk – most take much bigger, and sometimes all or nothing, risks earlier in their careers which become more calculated later in their careers. Subhash Chandra of Essel Group told me a story of the risks he took in starting Zee TV. One night one of his brothers called him up and said, 'Subhash, I am here with our two brothers watching Zee and am alarmed to see there have only been three ads on the station this evening.' Subhash apparently replied, 'That's the "good news", do you want to hear the "bad news"?' Of course his brother said he did and Subhash told him all three ads were free. Subhash says, 'I think I heard my brother drop the phone!'
- Goals: 'do-able' lists versus 'wish-lists' – most entrepreneurs seem to focus on realistic goals rather than absolute fantasy. Harsh Mariwala of Marico puts it, 'Every person is born with certain strengths. I recommend that a young person determines what his or her strengths are and then leverage those strengths rather than merely aspire to be "something".'
- High Dedication – in terms of effort and time put in – every person in this book exhibits this characteristic.
- Intrinsic Motivation – most love what they do and have high energy levels in pursuing their chosen field. BN Kalyani of Bharat Forge said that, 'I can also remember as a small boy I had a mindset for mechanical things. I enjoyed doing such things as tightening nuts and bolts. Even when I was around eight or nine years old I could dissemble and reassemble my bicycle and repair it. I did this very often with many things.'
- Well-Organized Lifestyle – most have the unshakeable support of a spouse and apparently 'entrepreneurial duos' are not that unusual. GVK Reddy's wife was appointed as the managing director of Novopan while

he was in the US and successfully operated the business. 'She's my "speed breaker". Many of the businesses activities I have sought to enter were in her opinion a big risk and her questions forced me to think more clearly about what I was doing. I don't think she has ever stopped me from taking the risk or I would not refer to her as a "breaker" but it is important for me to have someone question me like this.'

- Pragmatic Approach – most entrepreneurs have a pragmatic approach to life rather than an intellectual approach. I asked Deepak Parekh of HDFC what he thought was the key strength he had brought to HDFC. His modest response was: 'I think it is that I am a practical man.' It is clearly far more than this but is indicative of his own assessment and its value to a corporation. Dr Anand Deshpande of Persistent Systems brought pragmatic skills to his studies at IIT Kharagpur. 'After the first three months of working hard, I realized I was not going to be the top ten,' he laughs. 'I also worked out that it was easy for me not to be in the bottom half and that I was looking to be somewhere between 11-40 per cent in the year. I found it was not difficult to make that percentage and have a good time as well.' Subhash Menon of Subex had a similar pragmatic approach to his studies, 'When I got to Standard 12 I thought I should pursue engineering. Once I had made the decision to do engineering I checked out what marks I needed to get. I found out with "x" percentage I would get into engineering. So that became my target and whether I came first or last in class was unimportant.'
- Sound Analytic and Problem-Solving Skills – and don't these have to be applied to succeed in India!
- High Level of 'People Skills' – to achieve their objectives entrepreneurs usually need the assistance of others. Most seem to operate an 'open and consultative' style but with strong authoritarian back-up. YK Hamied, the chairman of Cipla had as his mentor Lord Todd who was awarded the Nobel Prize for Chemistry. 'He was a humble man. He used to cycle to my digs and say, "Yusuf, you must be alone. Come and have X'mas lunch with me and the family". I am not seeing that nowadays among the so called politicians and the academics. That humility is not there. One of the many things I learnt from him is the importance of humility. Here my door is always open to any of our staff. Anyone in the company can come in and sit and talk to me about his or her problems.'
- High Level of Innovation – entrepreneurs are more at ease creating new ways of doing things rather than just adapting existing models.
- Parental Influence – interestingly most independent entrepreneurs have mothers who played a dominant role in their early childhood and career path. Few apparently reported poor relationships with their fathers.

- Social Origins – socio-economic background affects development and behaviour. In India it is well known that certain ethnic groups such as the Marwari produce a high percentage of entrepreneurs. It is also interesting to note that in the research done by Jennings, Cox and Cooper they found elite independent entrepreneurs in the main had working-class origins and did not have entrepreneurial parents. Given India's caste system I am not sure if India would bear this out. Vijaypat Singhania from the well-known Marwari family which owns Raymonds of which he is Chairman Emeritus, was brought up in a very traditional way – 'On 21 February 1951, at the age of twelve, I was engaged to Asha, then nine years old. She was from the illustrious Jalan family of Calcutta. She was brought to my home for the first time on the pretext of being given chocolates. Five years later when I was seventeen and she was fourteen we were married. We had our first child, a son in the following year.' Such experiences cannot but shape a person's character as Vijaypat Singhania's chapter reveals.
- Education – regardless of the education received the research indicates that successful entrepreneurs usually see any misfortune they may have had in not receiving a good education as just another hurdle to overcome in achieving their goals. AVS Raju of Nagarjuna Construction Company told me, 'You may have all the education in the world but what's more important is common sense which, despite its name, is not that common. Recently, I was invited as the chief guest to a meeting of auditors. I think they must have regretted inviting me because I told them that, although I did not know much about the auditing profession in my experience all one needs is common sense to understand how a company is doing.'
- Career Development Patterns – nearly all entrepreneurs have had to cope with failure of some sort and most see it as a positive to learn from one's mistakes and failures. Most exhibit extreme resilience and the ability to bounce back.
- Work History – most entrepreneurs did not spend very long as employees before taking the plunge in creating their own businesses. Shashi Kiran Shetty of Allcargo Global Logistics commented, 'In one sense I was delighted to be on my own at last; at the ripe old age of twenty-nine. But it was very tough as I had no financial support. It was a "hand to mouth" existence. I often had to avoid calls from creditors while I chased debtors to pay. To give you an idea of how little spare money I had, you should know I built up running accounts at the local restaurant just so I could eat! Deepak Puri of Moser Baer lasted only nine months as an employee before leaping into the unknown of being self employed.
- Philanthropy and Pro-Social Behaviour – the research suggests altruism stems from parents and religious teachings of moral obligations and a

strong work ethic, combined with internalized norms of behaviour and the concern for others' needs. Shahnaz Husain's father told her, 'You will never ever be happy if you only work for your own personal benefit and not give to anybody else. Remember you are sent to this world by God, so apart from the fact that you must justify your existence to him, you have an obligation every day to try and make somebody else's life worthwhile.' Professor Swaminathan echoed these words of advice when he told me as I left his home: 'He alone lives who lives for others.' And Arun Firodia of Kinetic Group told me, 'When we are doing a business we should make profit but at the same time we must also use the knowledge and insights that we have gained to make a difference in the lives of others. We should focus on other things besides making money. Today, money doesn't excite me.'

- Marginalization – Many entrepreneurs come from socially marginalized groups. Kiran Mazumdar Shaw of Biocon, one of a small number of very successful Indian female entrepreneurs, says at the time she founded her bio pharma company, 'At that time I just wanted to run a successful company. I was a bit of a rebel. I wanted to prove that a woman was capable of running a business and handling a plant, because some men had said women couldn't do this. I wanted to prove them wrong.'

There are also some unique aspects of Indian life which have touched many of the lives in this book. The most prevalent of these is the concept of a 'joint family'. Whilst Indian readers of this book will all too well understand exactly what this concept means, it may be helpful for others to have some explanation. Essentially a joint family is an extended family arrangement; particularly prevalent amongst Hindus and under which several generations will live under the same roof. All the male members are blood relatives and all the women are either mothers, wives, unmarried daughters, or widowed relatives, all bound by the common sapinda[5] relationship. The family is headed by a patriarch, usually the oldest male, who makes decisions on economic and social matters on behalf of the entire family. The patriarch's wife generally exerts control over the kitchen, child rearing and minor religious practices. A daughter cannot remain the member of her father's family after her marriage and the sisters, though they were once entitled to a share in the property, would lose their right and would be entitled to only maintenance until their marriage and their marriage expenses.

Six key aspects of joint family are:

- all members live under one roof;
- share the same kitchen;
- three generations living together (though often two or more brothers live together, or father and son live together or all the descendants of male live together);

- income and expenditure in a common pool – property held together.
- a common place of worship; and
- all decisions are made by the male head of the family.

The most critical element of the joint family from the point of view of an entrepreneur is that all money goes to the common pool and all property is held jointly. As you will see in many of the life stories in this book, it is this element that often leads to the break-up of the joint family. The common pool concept probably worked well in more traditional times and may still work well where the members of the family have few opportunities and little wealth. But in the India of today, and particularly urban society, one can see the enormous pressures this must bring. What if one member is lazy or incompetent? What if one member wishes to take risks and others don't? What if the patriarch lacks the skill and experience to manage the businesses? As you will see different entrepreneurs have handled it differently but there is no doubt that the entrepreneur only starts to 'fly' once he is on his own. Arun Bharat Ram, for instance, has seen his family's businesses break up several times during his own lifetime. He is now regularly consulted by others who seek his advice on overcoming joint family problems; almost always these relate to money and property. Uday Kotak found it difficult to remain in the joint family business. He told his father, 'Dad, I don't want to join the complicated family business. I love commerce; I love trading; I love everything which is being done, but I find it difficult to manage the family complexity. I would rather take professional employment at Hindustan Lever.' His father had known this was long coming and responded, 'Uday, what if I gave you an opportunity – on the family platform – for an independent business?' And so Uday's career as an independent entrepreneur peacefully got underway. Others such as GM Rao have sought to create family constitutions to overcome the failings of the joint family arrangement. What these families have done is to learn from successful European and US families which have not only survived, but prospered, over many generations. Rao says, 'I have decided to give more importance, not only to "corporate" but also to "family" governance. Without family governance, the circle is incomplete.' What is interesting too is that a number of these new Indian family constitutions treat men and women equally.

Inextricably tied up with joint families and the lives of many of the subjects of this book is how they 'handle' the next generation coming into the business they have built or inherited. In the time of the 'licence raj' it may not have mattered much. Indeed Rahul Bajaj says, 'During the socialist times in India, a brother or a son was put in charge of a company even if he was not competent as there were other professionals who were managing the company, the opportunities were limited and there was a shortage of supply in the economy. Given these situations, any one could have managed the company. Nowadays, with globalization, many MNCs have come into India and if a son is not as good or better than somebody else, you better not give him charge of the company because then nobody benefits, not even you and your son.' Most of the entrepreneurs seem to have views similar to Rahul Bajaj and, a number seem to be following the European and US concept of 'family offices' where the businesses are run by professionals and the family office acts more like a holding company.

There is one element not mentioned above which the psychologists I have read do not seem to touch on with respect to whether an entrepreneur succeeds or not. This is the concept of luck. Perhaps there is no such thing as luck or, as one hears from time to time, that people make their own luck. But most of the entrepreneurs covered in this and my earlier book on South-East Asia admit there is an ethereal element that defies description and could be called luck for want of a better word. Alfonso Yuchengco, one of the Philippines most successful businessmen (who incidentally was raised for a number of childhood years as a girl, but that is another story) said candidly in his interview, 'If you are unlucky, you may be the hardest worker but you will not succeed.' Timing could well be a part of luck but the entrepreneur still needs to seize the opportunity which he has identified.

I should mention how the business leaders were chosen. First, I sought guidance from my Indian friends and from Australia's and India's diplomatic and trade missions in asking them to provide me with a list of twenty names of Indian entrepreneurs who succeeded in their chosen profession or business and who have the respect of their peers and the wider community. In reviewing these lists it was surprising how many names appeared multiple times. I then set about approaching my shortlist and this book is the result. Some I approached declined to be interviewed but very few.

I conducted all the interviews face-to-face. Many of my friends and colleagues who knew I was writing this book asked whether I had 'grilled' a particular person on some event or rumour about their lives. I always replied that this book was not meant to be investigative journalism. Indeed, I sent a draft of my interview to each person for approval and, in most cases, only minor changes were made to correct mistakes in names or dates.

Some readers familiar with the lives of particular individuals may observe what they believe to be inaccuracies in the stories. Any such inaccuracies would be irrelevant to my overall objective of seeking common threads in the stories of their successful business and professional careers.

The relevance or importance of chasing wealth was something else which interested me and I was pleased to find that, for most, the key was doing something they liked and doing it well. The wealth followed. Most seemed to think that if one just chased money, then other important elements of success, such as ethics, tend to go out of the window. If one loses one's way ethically, then the general opinion is that, while a short-term gain may be enjoyed, one could easily lose one's name and reputation and that would affect the rest of one's life. This was summed up aptly by Narayana Murthy, the universally respected founder of Infosys who said, 'I strongly believe that people get into trouble when they become victims of money. As long as you are the master of your money, as long as you can live without a luxury there should not be a problem. Many of those who violate laws and behave unethically do so because they are victims.'

For me one of the most interesting things to come out of the various meetings and which should spur many young people from around the world is that not all of the people were brilliant academically. Certainly many are, but quite a number were not and were quite relaxed to say so. For example, CK Ranganathan of CavinKare told me, 'I used to play chess with my brothers and they would beat me in 7 to 8 moves. I was the kid who was always struggling, did not speak English and was not brainy. If I managed to pass in school, it was just barely. I was shy and had a terrible inferiority complex.'

And by no means all were compliant and well behaved. GVK Reddy said, 'I am told that one day, when I was a child, my parents went to a fortune teller. The fortune teller apparently told them about me up to the age of 14; and stopped after that saying: "I don't want to say anything more about this child as he will be totally useless".' And when I asked Kishore Biyani what part of his character was most responsible for his success. 'That's easy,' he says, 'rebellion. It's a very positive force. In fact, I remember the first ad I made when I started the business. I created the character of a black sheep of the family and he was successful in life. The ad was for trousers.'

All in all, I hope this book enables Indian and foreign readers, both young and old, to understand what makes these successful entrepreneurs 'tick' and to understand a little better the challenges they have had to overcome to achieve that success. In doing so I hope in particular younger readers who are budding entrepreneurs will realize that all is not lost if they do not stand first in school and university, but also clearly understand that the path of an entrepreneur is difficult, full of risk and rarely one of never-ending success.

---

1 PC Church, *Added Value: The Life Stories of Leading South East Asian Business People*, Sydney: Murmeli, 1999.
2 PM Kilby, *Entrepreneurship and Economic Development*, New York: Macmillan, 1971.
3 I wonder if this revelation could lead to some new nicknames of the entrepreneurs covered in this book by their children and grandchildren?
4 R Jennings, C Cox and CL Cooper, *Business Elites: The Psychology of Entrepreneurs and Intrapraneurs*, London: Routledge, 1994.
5 Sapinda relationship with reference to any person exists as far as the third generation (inclusive) in the line of ascent through mother, and the fifth (inclusive) in the line of ascent through father, the line being traced upwards in each case from the person concerned, who is to be counted as the first generation.

> Even if you have to take a decision which you know to be walking the edge between the right and wrong, don't try to fool yourself that you're doing the right thing. Remember that your credibility and your honesty is all you will have as you go forward. That's your biggest wealth. You've got to be honest – honest with your colleagues, partners, vendors and consumers.

RAGHAV BAHL

Founder & Managing Director
Network18

Raghav Bahl was born on 2 January 1961 in the small town of Saharanpur in Uttar Pradesh. His father served in the Indian Administrative Service (IAS) and his grandfather as the principal of a government college. 'We come from a family of civil servants and bureaucrats.' Though he was born in Uttar Pradesh, Bahl lived most of his life in Delhi growing up in what he describes as a 'very regular, middle-class upbringing ... that a lot of people you come across in India would have'.

His father, who belonged to the Rajasthan State Cadre of the IAS, spent much of his career there. Bahl joined his parents there on holidays but for a good part of his school years, if his father was not posted in Delhi, he lived with his grandparents in Delhi.

He studied in St Stephen's College and acquired an MBA from Delhi University and then proceeded to Columbia University, briefly as it turned out, to do a Master of Science en route to a doctorate. 'I had done well in the GMAT and got a scholarship to Colombia and it seemed only logical I take it up. But two things happened to me in quick succession. Firstly, my health deteriorated. I had developed a medical problem with one of my legs which got worse. So it became difficult living in the US as a single person with a little bit of a handicap. More importantly, I realized I wasn't cut out for further education. I wanted to be in the real world. As I sat through classes in my first semester, I was saying to myself: do I really want to spend another two years doing this – just sitting in front of a blackboard, writing term papers and writing tutorials? I decided I wanted to get a job and work with people.'

Bahl returned to India to join the corporate sector. 'I always enjoyed business. I thought I had a particular knack for finance and some strategic parts of business – I don't think at that time I was very good at marketing and brand building – but I enjoyed the finance and strategic bits more.' He began in the mid 1980s, working with A.F. Ferguson, a leading audit and management consultancy company and then joined American Express Bank.

All through his college days and school days, Bahl had been interested in public speaking and debates. He naturally gravitated towards television, more as a hobby. At college, he regularly anchored television shows like *Youth Forum* for Doordarshan. 'We would visit colleges, talk to students and generally do student-based or youth-based shows. I made a bit of pocket money and enjoyed it,' says Bahl. 'I was academically good at school and generally would have been in the top 10 per cent of my class. I was never number one. I studied, but never with the intention of being number one as I enjoyed all the rest of the activities school had to offer.'

He considers himself lucky that he was allowed a free reign by his father who would have preferred he join the Indian Foreign Service and become a career diplomat. 'I must say I flirted with that idea for quite a while. Somewhere along my college days, I figured that government service could be very constraining and I had seen a lot of it from my father's side having sort of vicariously lived a government servant's life through his.' The idea of living 30-40 years outside the country, travelling from one country to another and being at ceremonial jobs did not appeal to Bahl. 'It seems to me that it is only towards the end of your career that you end up doing anything significant.' The independent streak in him told him he was not cut out for a 'Yes, Minister's role'.

Bahl grew up under his grandfather's influence, particularly inheriting his love for sport. 'He was still actively playing tennis even six months before he died. I remember as a young boy going along with him to play. On the other hand my father was not so keen on sport. Being a man of letters, my father certainly influenced me on public speaking and language, particularly English. Certainly, they both had a major influence on me.' His mother too was an enormous influence on Bahl. It was from her that he learnt calmness and strength. She was for the most part a housewife except for briefly teaching in primary schools.

In the late 1980s, when Bahl was working with American Express, television was becoming more professional in India although it was not yet privatized. Satellite television was still to make its debut. What was interesting to Bahl was that a video cassette on the news of the day was being brought out by a very reputed media house – the India Today Group. 'They thought there was an opportunity since there was no private television. In state-controlled television, the news was extremely sanitized. They came upon, according to me, a very pioneering idea: why don't we approximate private television, capture what is happening, put it on a video cassette and distribute the video? It sounds anachronistic now, that people would actually want to buy a video tape of news events one week late, but imagine a time when there was no private television. Suddenly, the consumer did feel a need to see images of things that he read about which he could not see on state television.'

One of the producers, Vinod Dua, involved in that venture, *Newstrack*, knew Bahl from his anchoring days at college and invited Bahl to anchor the show. Since Bahl had a corporate job at that time, he offered to anchor the show over weekends and late evenings. 'Sure, why don't you do that?' said Dua. 'So I started doing that and one thing leads to another.' The producers liked his work. 'I could, in those days, work reasonably hard,' he smiles. As his involvement increased Bahl received as he says 'my first opportunity to be quote-unquote "well-known in the industry".' What *Newstrack* lacked in visibility and volume, it made up by making its mark on the "right" audience'.

Bahl continued anchoring the show for three years, part-time in the first year while he was still working with American Express. 'Then, I decided that I'm enjoying this; it's good.' The money was much less if he went full time with *Newstrack* but he decided it was good enough to survive on. 'I was unmarried, only twenty-seven or twenty-eight years old and doing things that I would never do in a corporate job. I think I added all of the positives up. I enjoyed the job, enjoyed the ... well, "fame" would be a very strong word ... but, at least, I enjoyed the recognition that came. I said to myself, "let's get into this more" and left American Express.' In his last two years with *Newstrack*, he was devoting nearly all his time to the show.

In the early 1990s, India got its first taste of satellite television, 'the CNN coverage of the first Iraq war' and 'it was very clear to all of us that tape would die, because you could put the same show on air – on a channel like BBC – who would then subscribe to the tape?' At that time, satellite television was "neither illegal nor legal"; it was just not regulated. It just spread like "wild fire". Before the government could figure out what happened, a few million households had it. That's the sheer entrepreneurial energy of small Indian business people. They strung wires across the street and across trees and got the signal into their houses. There was no licensing and there were no norms. In a couple of years there was a full, thriving industry that had grown up completely unregulated.'

For Bahl, the writing was on the wall. 'To me, it was clear that the tape would die, that the future lay in broadcasting. Suddenly the monopoly of the state had been broken, and broken completely by technology, not by the state itself – the state still continues to have one broadcaster. But because of this "thing" called "satellite TV" you could beam programming throughout the country and be as effective as any other television channel. This was the most seminal period of my life to that point.'

At this time, Bahl moved from *Newstrack* to Business India Television to help them bring out a similar video tape specializing in the business sphere.

Two things were clear to Bahl. One, as mentioned above, satellite broadcast would become large. Two, he had a skill in business news television gathered from debating, public speaking and anchoring. So Bahl brought his 'intellectual skills' and 'all the other wherewithal' to play in making the pilot version of the Business India Television tape a success, although the project was subsequently shelved when satellite took over from tape.

The turning point came when somebody approached Bahl to create some programmes for overseas Indian audiences. Bahl was clear that only local content would succeed in India. 'India would not survive on programming turned out from London by the BBC. That would be a very marginal thing. India would need its own local programming; being too large a country, with too much of an ethos of a functioning democracy of its own news and entertainment. So, it would not borrow from the West.' Bahl created two pilot shows along with the people who commissioned the assignment. One was a 30-minute entertainment programme called *The India Show* crafted for non-resident Indians (NRIs). 'I believed there was an audience for it in India as well.' Bahl offered them a deal which was, roughly to create the programme for them at lower rates for the NRI audience and use some of the content to make another pilot for local audience.

Bahl and a band of three or four 'very highly motivated and intelligent people' together invested their sweat equity and money to raise the initial capital of around USD 4,000 that they needed to produce the two pilots. While Bahl put in the bulk of the money the others brought skill. 'This was the only time that I solely put money, into the company. Ever since then all the shareholders have put in any capital required.'

Bahl and his colleagues made the tapes – *The India Show* and the *India Business Report*; the latter too being a 30-minute show. They mailed the lifestyle show to Star TV in Hong Kong and the business show to BBC World. 'Maybe the shows were well made and maybe they were at the right time' – Bahl believes it was a matter of the timing – 'but both of them got commissioned.' These were the two first shows out of India on satellite TV channels beaming back into India on Sunday mornings. Bahl anchored the BBC show for seven continuous years. The show became popular and the BBC put it on the world beam broadcast to Europe, South-East Asia and Africa, and 'wherever BBC World went'.

During the wait before the shows got commissioned by BBC and Star Plus,[1] Bahl used to report to work – a one-room place – at about 11 o'clock 'because there was nothing to do and at 3 o'clock there was still nothing to do. For about four hours, I used to just fish around for something to do.' Every morning, the high point of the day used to be whether there was an overnight fax for him from London, the US or Hong Kong?' 'We didn't have our own fax machine. There was a fax operator close by and I had his telephone number. The first call I used to make every morning was to him to ask "is there a fax for me?" Three days out of the week he'd say "no", but the fourth day he would say "yes". "Who's it from?", I'd ask, and he would say "BBC" or "Star". Then, "I'm sending somebody to pick it up immediately," I would say.' Fortunately, Bahl believes he has always been blessed with a lot of patience. His advice to business aspirants is that 'the world doesn't move at your pace. The world has got other things to do while your new business is your entire reason for existence. So you need enormous patience.'

Bahl's consultancy contract with Business India TV for the business news tape provided him with the sustenance he needed during the hard times that accompanied the wait. Bahl and his team also made 'ends, meet' by doing other work such as corporate films, script writing, voice-overs and television columns. 'It was enough for a single person. What was tough was the waiting, not the money. As I was living at home my needs were limited and I had enough odds and ends that I could do.

'I wouldn't say that there were intense periods of doubt,' but Bahl did have misgivings at times. Once, when travelling, he ran into a friend who was flying business class. 'I was flying economy and he was working in a multinational bank and he was talking about when he landed in Mumbai he was going to stay at the Oberoi. I was going to take an auto rickshaw, do my meeting and take the afternoon flight back to Delhi because I couldn't afford to spend the night at a five-star hotel. On days like those, you felt bad and you questioned yourself "am I doing the right thing?" I looked at this guy and I said to myself, "he is high up in this bank. If I had stayed there maybe I would have even been his boss". So whether it's business class travels or whether it's having a secretary – we never had secretaries – we used to handle our own phones and type our own letters, there was time for doubt. So many of my peers who I had grown up had these solid, multinational careers with all the perks.'

With these two products Bahl, in partnership with a few others, founded TV18. While he was personally involved with the business show, others were involved in the lifestyle one. 'We ran with these for a while', rolling income earned every week to survive and make the next shows. 'We were not wealthy by any standard, but comfortable.' TV18 grew and produced programmes for other broadcasters including Zee TV and Sony TV as well as more shows for the BBC. This led to a much wider client base. Continuing at this pace from 1992 to 1998, TV18 became the market leader in business news and well known for its English language feature programming in lifestyle, fashion and food and its forays into fiction and drama. 'We were growing as a production house.'

The TV18 team expanded its operations – rented offices, equipment and taxis. 'We had programme advances and so we didn't have to borrow too much money. From ten people, TV18 grew to sixty and then hundred between 1993 and 1997. Its revenue grew from USD 10,000 month to USD 100,000 a month.

Now was the real turning point; the 'big bet' as Bahl calls it. 'If you want to be a big business news player you cannot be a production company. Nowhere in the world can production companies make "news". News is about infrastructure; news is about broadcast; news is about being able to deliver it online and on television; news is about being able to cover breaking news as it happens. One weekly show is an anachronism, I believed the weekly show was going to die just like the tape died.'

At this time TV18 was stringing for a company called Asia Business News (ABN), a Dow Jones-Wall Street Journal promoted company. ABN was CNBC's predecessor. TV18 made three to four stories every week for ABN. This led to ABN approaching TV18 with an offer of a broadcast joint venture focused on India but with the rider that ABN would not be able to invest too much money in it. TV18 was required to make the programming for the evening primetime in India. This was the 'moment of reckoning', says Bahl. 'It was a conflict of interest with the BBC as I had become reasonably popular and well known with the BBC business show.' The stark choice was whether TV18 took the bet and went into broadcast with ABN thereby giving up the relationship with BBC which, until then, had been their identity. 'This was risk capital; with ABN this was not going to be a "we'll give you weekly payments" situation. This was a life and death situation. My colleagues and I decided we would give up the BBC and get into this joint venture with ABN. We would somehow raise the capital and take the risk of broadcasting because I reasoned that if we did not do this, we would go the way of the tapes. We're going to die because weekly television shows will die.' Bahl's prophecy came true as in due course BBC's show was taken off the air.

The decision was based on consensus. Bahl's team backed him fully. 'I've always been lucky to have a team that believed in me. We raised the capital, we made a placement, we borrowed and we took the bet.'

During the six months that it took to set it up, TV18 continued to make shows for other channels though, of course, they lost BBC. Though BBC's contribution to TV18's income at that time was only about 20 per cent, its value to the company was high in visibility and credibility.

More than raising capital, the challenge before TV18 was the absence of a definitive regulatory policy in this sector. Though they had approval and a term sheet signed with ABN, TV18 did not get the mandatory FIPB approvals from India's regulatory authority for foreign investment proposals for almost a year. 'India was going through uncertain years – we had three governments in three years – but in 1998-99 we finally got a stable government. I remember going to meet the relevant minister, Sushma Swaraj and saying, "I've got this term sheet with ABN and we're really stretched on debt. Please give us a decision – 'yes' or 'no' – because otherwise there are 150 people whose jobs I will not be able to guarantee."

'To her credit, Sushma Swaraj saw it. She said, "Give me 30 days and I can assure you of a decision". She was true to her word. She gave a decision and it was in TV18's favour. 'We got the money in but the next complication was that ABN and CNBC merged in Singapore in 1998.' CNBC had its own GE company making its content in India. ABN had TV18 in a 51:49 joint venture. 'So one of us had to go. Sometimes, your good deeds come to your rescue at such moments. ABN was so happy with the kind of partnership we had provided them that they almost insisted that we continue.' GE folded in their operations and TV18 was appointed the continuing partner. 'I remember going into that final decisive meeting; it was one of the most tense days in my life. I didn't know whether we would come out with the deal and, if we did not come out with the deal, I knew I had no option but to sack the whole business news division of the company.'

Then, according to Bahl, they 'got lucky, genuinely lucky'. TV18 did an IPO in 1999-2000 at a time when the world economy boomed and new media companies got fantastic valuations. Reflects Bahl, 'The markets gave us more value than I think we deserved. For the very first time in our life we got capital and plenty of it. From that day onwards, I don't think we've ever looked back. There was huge luck with the timing as the markets were in a frenzy.'

A fresh crisis came in a 2001 government mandate that all news channels had to uplink out of India, not in their case from Singapore, and be under Indian control. 'The government gave us three months. Not only did we have to technically do the uplift out of India within three months but as a consequence of the then different roles of the partners we had to redo our equity structures. For once, we had the capital to handle this crisis.'

Bahl's role is different now from that in 2000. From being chief of operations and finance to editing, fronting and anchoring, 'I was doing pretty much everything.' After completing TV18's IPO, Bahl felt he had to evaluate his own role, if the company was to grow further. 'I needed to step back and get in a solid, professional set of managers. We were a bunch of creative guys. I realized that creatives can only bring you up to a certain point and that now we needed commercially savvy guys.'

TV18 recruited a CEO and added more people. Bahl stepped back from the commercial side to let them run it completely. He continued to be involved in editorial work, which also he gave up about three years ago. Now he is focusing entirely on strategy, diversification, capital raising, and relationships with TV18's many partners.

'If we can pull this off right, we can be truly large. I'm excited about that leap now. One of the main strengths we've built over the years is that we have had very stable teams.' According to Bahl, people very rarely leave TV18 once they join. The company empowers its employees completely. 'I don't like to take decisions; I push decisions down. If it's your decision, you take it. I don't second guess anybody's decisions. I make my bet on the man. If he's a guy that I trust, that I've selected, then he has 110 per cent of my trust and support.'

Bahl's advice to young Indian entrepreneurs: 'Even if you have to take a decision which you know to be walking the edge between the right and wrong, don't try to fool yourself that you're doing the right thing. Remember that your credibility and your honesty is all you will have as you go forward. That's your biggest wealth. You've got to be honest – honest with your colleagues, partners, vendors and consumers.

'Take decisions on instinct. Don't get terribly trapped in IRRs and ROIs. That's important; you should know what you're up for. You should know if you're wrong you could be down this much, and if you're right, you could be up this much. But, having done that, go for it. Take risks up to the point that if this capital gets wiped off, would I still be able to feed my kids and live? If the answer is yes, go for it. If the answer is no, don't. One of the best definitions of entrepreneurship that I've come across is that "he is a risk minimizer".

'Before I got my handicap with my leg I used to play school and state-level squash, tennis and hockey. I used to be incredibly sporty – everyday for three hours, run five to ten kilometres, play squash. If someone asked me what is it that you would ask God for? I would say: give me a life where I can be sporty throughout. What losing full control of my leg at age twenty-three has taught me is enormous patience and to see things from the other person's point of view. That's one other piece of advice I give to my young TV18 colleagues – that when you take a decision or when you're negotiating with someone, if you can see the situation from the other person's point of view, you'll be able to pretty much resolve everything.'

Despite Raghav Bahl's successful climb to the top of the entrepreneurial ladder in India, I left the meeting with the feeling that there is still a lot of the 'anchor man' left in him. Perhaps, one day we will see him in that role again?

Network18 Group (www.network18online.com) is one of India's fastest growing media and entertainment conglomerates. Network18 is a leader in news broadcasting and has partnered with NBC Universal (CNBC) as well as Time Warner (CNN). Its network also includes:

- entertainment broadcasting with Viacom (www.viacom18.com);
- film entertainment with TIFC (www.theindianfilmcompany.com);
- IBN7, a leading Hindi general news channel in partnership with the Jagran Group, owners of India's largest Hindi language daily;
- WEB18 which is a leading player in the Internet space in India;
- Home Shopping Network (HSN) comprising a home shopping channel and online venture; and
- Newswire18, a real time news & data platform.

1 The first formal contract was signed with Star Plus but the first positive response came from the BBC. The India Show went live first with Star; within three weeks the other show too went live.

"During the socialist times in India, a brother or a son was put in charge of a company even if he was not competent as there were other professionals who were managing the company, the opportunities were limited and there was a shortage of supply in the economy. ... Nowadays, with globalization, many multinational corporations have come into India and there is severe competition and if your son is not as good or better than somebody else, you better not give him charge of the company because then nobody benefits, not even you and your son."

RAHUL BAJAJ

Chairman, Bajaj Auto & Head
Bajaj Group

I met Rahul Bajaj with one of my colleagues, Justin Shmith, in his suite at the Taj Palace Hotel, where he normally stays when he is in Delhi for meetings. This time, he was in Delhi to attend the Parliament. He is a member of India's Upper House, the Rajya Sabha.

The first thing one notices is that Rahul is a large man with an imposing presence. One can easily imagine his prowess as a boxer in his youth which he recounted during our interview. For me, the Bajaj name was well known before I had anything to do with India as I had used their three-wheeler taxis in Indonesia from the mid '60s. No one can visit Jakarta without seeing these unique vehicles (essentially a motorbike with a small cabin built around it) scurry to and fro.

Rahul started our meeting with describing some of the history of his family.

'Our family is Marwari originally from Rajasthan but who, like many other Marwari families, shifted to other cities in India due to the harsh climate and few economic opportunities existing in Rajasthan. In the case of our family they moved over a hundred years ago to Wardha near Nagpur in Maharashtra.

'Marwaris have been very active and successful in business in India so that it is difficult to pinpoint when my forebears became involved in business but there is little doubt it would go back over a hundred years. However, the Bajaj Group as it stands today was founded about hundred years ago by my grandfather, the late Jamnalal Bajaj.

'The world of my grandfather was an intensely spiritual and philanthropic one. He had a very close relationship with Mahatma Gandhi who treated him as his fifth son. In fact, for the last eighteen years of his life from 1930 to 1948 when he was assassinated, Mahatma Gandhi lived in Wardha at an ashram he established there on land given by my grandfather.

'Our family was also close to the Nehru family. My father Kamalnayan and Indira Gandhi went to school together for a time. It is said that Jawaharlal Nehru picked my name Rahul which he wanted for the sons of his daughter, Indira Gandhi. As it happened, she named her son Rajiv. Here, too, there is history as my wife and I named our first son Rajiv, and Sonia and Rajiv Gandhi named their first son, Rahul.

'With these close relationships with the Gandhi and Nehru families, you will not be surprised to learn that my grandfather and our family were ardent nationalists and many of them spent time behind bars for their support of the freedom movement. For example, my grandfather joined Mahatma Gandhi in 1930 on the famous 240 mile Salt March from Sabarmati to Dandi. Before he died in 1942, my grandfather was a supporter of the Congress Party and was its treasurer for a number of years.

'During the 1930s, my grandfather started sugar and steel mills but, when he passed away in 1942, he left little for my father and uncle in terms of wealth and assets as he had given away most of his wealth for Gandhi's constructive work. That said, the sugar mill near Lucknow had, over the years, become the largest in India. We lost the steel mill on India's partition in 1947 as it was located in Lahore in what became Pakistan. A new steel plant was built in Mumbai. Whilst my grandfather owned a lot of land in Wardha, he gave almost all of it away to a charitable trust involved with Gandhi's activities.

'My father, Kamalnayan, grew up in Gandhi's and Vinoba Bhave's ashram in Wardha. My father had his education in the ashram and did not have a formal school education. However, when he was twenty-two, Gandhi sent him to England with the instruction he should go to Cambridge University. Unfortunately, with no formal qualifications he had to go to Dublin in Ireland to sit for his matriculation.

'He then joined the Cambridge University where his studies were interrupted when the Second World War broke out. Everyday, he would sit outside the registrar's office and wait for a meeting. After a few days, the registrar said he would give him five minutes. My father managed to extend that to forty-five minutes. My father told him that he didn't care so much about getting into Cambridge and that he was mainly there to imbibe the English culture and observe India's struggle for freedom from the other end but that, if he was granted admission, he would study economics. The registrar is reported to have told my father, "Look, I have a quota under which I can only take three Indian students and already have applications from twelve, all of whom have first-class degrees from well-known institutions and colleges in India. Would it be fair to them if I accept you? On top of all that, your English is not even very good."

'My father's supposed response sounds vintage him. He told the registrar that he must do what he thought was correct. However, if Cambridge wanted to take a finished product and put its rubber stamp on it, then they should do that, but if they really wanted to train or educate somebody, then he should be considered. He told the registrar that he should also keep in mind his closeness to Mahatma Gandhi and India's freedom struggle. "Who," he said "of all your applicants would be best equipped to bring India and England together?" He went on to point out that India was fighting in a non-violent way for its freedom and there was no doubt it would succeed. No colony had until then won independence without bloodshed and if the registrar thought my father might have a role to play in pulling the two countries together, then my father should be selected. You can guess what the registrar decided. My father got in!

'When my father came back from Cambridge, he threw himself into the freedom struggle and business because my grandfather died in 1942. My father had a brilliant business brain for finance and any money matters.'

Rahul was born in 1938 in Calcutta. He spent the first few years of his life living in Wardha before moving to Bombay with his parents. 'At that time it was a joint family consisting of my grandmother and my father and uncle. My father, Kamalnayan and my uncle, Ramkrishna, who was eight years younger, were the ones who re-built the empire – first with Bajaj Auto and then came Bajaj Electricals and other companies. However, Ramkrishnaji was very much interested in social activities as well.

'When my father died in 1972 at the age of fifty-seven, my uncle became head of the joint family and businesses. However, whilst of course he remained head of the business and was Chairman of Bajaj Electricals and our sugar company, I became Chairman of Bajaj Auto which was the flagship of the family businesses.

'My father had been preparing me for the role for years. For ten years before he died, we used to live and breathe the business together. We would stay up until 2 or 3 a.m. discussing and debating. We would often disagree with each other and I did not hesitate in making him aware of the few wrong decisions he had made and he did the same for me. We had a very close relationship, in many ways, more than father and son. My relations with my uncle Ramkrishna were very close. A couple of years before my uncle died in 1994, I found out something he had said to my three cousins, his sons. It brings tears to my eyes even now.'

Rahul told me that his uncle had called together his three sons and asked them to make sure at all costs they maintained the joint family with his father's family. He is reported to have said to them, 'I normally never disagree with Rahul's decisions, but if I ever do disagree with him, I want you to support Rahul.' Rahul told me, 'Nobody in this day and age would say something like that. He was an amazing man who lived very much the Gandhian way of life.'

At this point I asked Rahul to take me back to his childhood. 'I stayed at the Gandhi ashram until I was about seven years old and don't really remember much of my time there. When I was seven years old, in 1945, we moved from Wardha to Mumbai for the family business. I went to Cathedral & John Connon Boys School in Mumbai from 1948 until I passed out in 1954. Cathedral was a typical convent school; if you stood first, second or third in class you were labeled a "bookworm" and if you were good in sports you barely scraped through in class. I must say I enjoyed school tremendously because I was lucky to be good at both studies and sport. I was the school boxing and table tennis captain and also played cricket, hockey and football. My classmates were astounded because I would stand first in class as well.' Rahul laughs, 'I guess they couldn't tease the school boxing champion too much for doing well at his studies.

'It was a pretty laid-back existence at school compared to what my grandchildren have to face these days. You didn't need to learn things by heart. We had classes during the day and then sport in the late afternoons. I guess we all studied a little before the exams but other than that we mostly played.'

I asked Rahul if he was treated differently at school because he was a Bajaj. 'No, I don't think so. Being a Bajaj only became something in the '80s. But back then, in the '40s and '50s, I was not treated differently.

'After Cathedral I moved to St Stephen's College in Delhi to do an honours' degree in economics. I could have done an economics degree in Mumbai but after senior Cambridge for some reason it took four years there whereas in Delhi it only took three years. Also, St Stephen's was one of India's top colleges. Many IAS and IFS officers graduated from there. I had the option of either living in the college hostel or with one of my three Delhi-based aunts and, in particular, with the one who lived close to the college. My parents wanted me to stay with her but I decided to stay with everyone else in the hostel. I am glad I did because they were fun years. I can remember we used to jump the hostel gates after midnight after a night out on the town. We also did harmless typical college stunts like setting off a cracker under a professor's window.

'I no longer came first in class but I had a wonderful time and graduated with an honours' degree in 1958. I then decided to go to Harvard to do an MBA. But as you probably know they prefer the applicant has work experience under one's belt before one enrolls. So, I went back to Mumbai and joined the family Bajaj Electricals for two years.'

I asked Rahul what he did in the family companies. 'In Bajaj Electricals, I worked in dispatch, accounts, marketing, and met salesmen and dealers. While I was working there, I decided to simultaneously do an LLB by attending morning classes at the Government Law College. Fortunately, the college was only five minutes away from Bajaj Electricals. Whereas I used to attend every lecture when I was in St Stephen's, my friends and I spent some of our time in the coffee shop instead of sitting in the law lectures. Nevertheless, we all scraped through by studying a month before the exams. So I got my legal qualification and moved on to my next job.

'I then spent 1961 and most of 1962 at Mukand Steel Mill. There I worked in the foundry, the machine shop, the rolling mills, the stores and in my last year I was one of their junior purchasing officers.'

So then it was off to Harvard, I asked. 'Yes. I graduated with an MBA from Harvard in the class of 1964. I am proud to say I am on their Global Advisory Board and in October 2005 received their Distinguished Alumni Award. Only 300 awards have been made out of a total of 75,000 alumni around the world. I am the first and, to date, one of only two Indians to have been so honoured out of the MBA contingent. Ratan Tata was also similarly honoured from the Advanced Management Programme. It was then back to India to join Bajaj Auto.'

I asked Rahul if there was pressure on him to join the family business or did he have other options. 'Our family is very open minded, mainly because of Gandhi's influence. I would answer your question with the following example. My father believed that at the age of sixteen, the son becomes the father's friend. My father didn't smoke, drink or even have tea or coffee. When I came back from Europe, I had started smoking. My father knew that although I wouldn't smoke in his presence out of respect. Not once did he ask me to stop smoking.'

I wondered whether Rahul had found time to get married and, if so, whether it was an arranged marriage. Rahul burst out laughing and said, 'How I wish it was an arranged marriage as it would have been a lot better. Rupa and I have been married for forty-six years but it was not easy to get married. As you know I am a Marwari, whereas she is a Maharashtrian. In addition my caste is Baniya; whereas Rupa is a Brahmin. On top of that, she comes from a family of civil servants and I from a family of industrialists. We met at a party during the time I was at the Law college. I guess I was a bit of a playboy in those days and one day my mother called me because she was used to seeing me with a whole range of short-term girlfriends. She noticed

I had been constantly seeing Rupa for more than two months. Call it "mother's intuition" but she sensed it was getting serious. So, she asked me if I wanted to marry Rupa. I told her that I would like to. This complicated things because I had made a deal with my father regarding marriage. He had agreed I could choose whoever I wanted to marry but the person had to be approved by him. I had warned Rupa of this condition. My mother was delighted at the news but said we would have to wait for my father's decision. He was still at the office and so my mother and I spent a nervous few hours waiting for him to come home. I told him about Rupa at dinner and he asked to meet her and invited her to dinner. Rupa was an intelligent and well-educated young lady. She had a BA in history and was studying for a master's. She definitely passed the test on that front and all of the other differences I mentioned earlier also did not present a problem. However, there was one that I had not foreseen. Rupa's father had worked for the British whereas my family had fought for our freedom and been jailed by them. My father did not use this as an excuse but relied on the old argument that we were both too young. His decision was that we stop all contact for a year, no meetings, no letters, and no contact at all. After a year, if we still wanted to get married, he would give us his blessings. He added if we did not want to abide by his decision he would not stop us from marrying but would not give us his blessings. Rupa was a very sober and mature person but when she heard what my father said she broke down. Her parents were surprised. Nevertheless, we decided to go with my father's decision. To his credit, my father invited Rupa to dinner a few times during the year when I was not around. We survived the year and married and have been happily married ever since.'

I knew that the Bajaj Group had grown enormously during his years at the helm and I wondered if Rahul and his father's styles of management were similar. Rahul responded, 'Quite different. He created the businesses but he was completely hands off. He didn't manage any company. He was Chairman of the group companies and managed them through CEOs. I am completely – or, at least, I was until I started stepping back – "hands on". People used to say – it's not correct – that I knew "every brick in the factory". Even my close friends such as Tarun Das who was the Director General of CII (Confederation of Indian Industry) used to say, "Rahul Bajaj signs every cheque – even for Rs 5!" That was just not true.

'But I do know the business. My wife and I have lived in the factory complex for four decades. Actions speak larger than words. I have never believed in absentee landlordism. In the beginning when we moved from Mumbai to Pune, we were living in a 10' by 12' room in a Bajaj guest house. The rest of that guest house was reserved for the General Manager of Bajaj Electricals. Eventually, in 1965, we did get our own house in the factory colony. I am not sure if my sons have the same view but for me to live side by side with the Bajaj employees gave me a close understanding of what made the business tick and gave people the confidence regarding my commitment and that I knew every brick in the factories.'

I asked Rahul if there were any particular experiences during his career he would like to talk about. 'One era which was very different was the socialism of the 1960s right up to 1990. During that period if you wanted to buy a Bajaj scooter you had to order one in advance. There were shortages for cars and many other products and, believe it or not, for Bajaj scooters there was a waiting period of ten years. We wanted to expand to meet the market demand but were not allowed. In 1971 we produced more than our licensed capacity and were hauled up before the Monopolies and Restrictive Trade Practices Commission for this breach. There were three people on the panel – all very anti-large industry. We could have easily been the highest priced scooter in the market but were, in fact, the lowest. Black marketers were the ones who made the big profits rather than Bajaj, by buying and selling our scooters at a big mark up in the black market. I pointed out to the panel that scooters were not bought by the rich but by the middle class, including students and women in particular. I told them that every one of my family, including my mother and father, had been sent to British jails fighting for the freedom of our country and that I did not mind going to an Indian jail for meeting the genuine demand of our people instead of keeping them waiting for up to ten years. "Nobody", I said, "Mr Chairman will wait for ten years. They will pay a premium and buy it in the black market." We were shocked when we learnt that the panel recommended we be allowed to expand; not as much as we wanted, but it was something. This panel was notoriously anti-big business; so it was a rare victory. Since I was only in my early thirties it gave me the courage to take on the government when I thought they were behaving irrationally. I will always remember that the official report of the panel complimented me on my mastery of the facts and figures of my industry.'

As many interviews with Rahul Bajaj indicate, he has an 'A+' personality and I could feel his 'larger than life' personality during the short time I spent with him. Gita Piramal, in her book *Business Maharajas*, records one such example of this. 'His innate restlessness is particularly evident when Bajaj sets off for work every morning at 10.30. The Bajajs live inside the factory complex. The journey is under 150 metres. After a heart attack in the August of 1984, the walk would undoubtedly do him good. Yet the left-handed Bajaj prefers to drive his creamy 1990 Mercedes 300D to work at top speed for all of one minute flat.'

By now, it may have become evident that traditional Indian business groups seem to falter during the transition of authority from father to sons and, particularly, in joint family situations. 'This is a difficult matter and I think I have done quite well with this although it is still not fully recognized. Owners, by and large, don't hand over charge that easily,' he says with a chuckle, 'and especially an owner like me. I love my work. I am now sixty-nine and my sons are now forty and thirty-seven. I started thinking about succession from the time I was fifty-five in the mid '90s. It is not just India but everywhere in the world there is an issue with succession. 95 per cent of the Bajaj family wealth is tied up in the equity of the Bajaj companies of which 80 per cent is Bajaj Auto. If the Bajaj Auto share price goes to the dogs then our wealth goes southward and so does our reputation. During the socialist times in India, the brother or the son was put in charge even if he was not competent as there were other professionals who were managing the company, the opportunities were limited and there was a shortage of supply in the economy. Given these situations, any one could have managed a company. Nowadays, there is globalization, many multinational companies have come into India and there is severe competition and if your son is not as good or better than somebody else, you better not give him the management because then nobody benefits, not even you and your son. I have made this clear to everybody.

'Both my sons have done their bachelor's of engineering in India with distinction. My elder son stood first in the university and the younger stood seventh. They went on to do their master's in manufacturing systems engineering in Warwick in UK. My younger son then worked for two years and then went to Harvard for his MBA. They are both outstanding but have very different personalities. My younger son, Sanjiv is outgoing and a lot like me in personality whereas Rajiv, the elder son is much more reserved. Rajiv spends his leisure hours learning homeopathy and practicing yoga. He says homeopathy cures one from the inside out and that one of its lessons for business is that one should not blame the competition. They both live for the company. Even today people say that they are very different. This is correct. We are not clones of each other. We disagree a lot; just like I used to disagree with my father. Provided the debates are constructive and not personal, in my opinion this is a healthy situation; not only for the family but for the business.'

I asked Rahul how they had specifically handled the handover in the joint family as well as in his immediate family? 'With respect to the joint family we decided that in my generation, which consists of five sons – three from my uncle, Ramkrishnaji, and two from my father, Shishir and me – one would get the sugar company, one would get Bajaj Electricals, one the steel interests, one who is less interested in business would get cash, and I would get Bajaj Auto. This is all done.

'With respect to my immediate family and Bajaj Auto, from 1997, I started a seamless and gradual handing over charge to Rajiv which was completed by 31 March 2005. From 1 April 2005, I am no longer Chairman and Managing Director. Rajiv became Managing Director of Bajaj Auto and I am now the Non-Executive Chairman. However, I have created a balance between Rajiv and Sanjiv insofar as Rajiv runs Bajaj Auto and Sanjiv runs Bajaj Auto Finance and Bajaj Finserv. They sit on each other's boards. I am the Chairman. Will it work after I am gone? Who knows? Like any father, all I can do is my best to teach them what I know and advise them that if they do have any personal differences they must not take them out on the company.' With such a punch line it seemed an appropriate time to bring the interview to a close and leave Rahul to rush off to dinner with friends.

The Bajaj Group (www.bajajauto.com) is amongst the top ten business houses in India. Its footprint stretches over a wide range of industries, spanning automobiles (two-wheelers and three-wheelers), home appliances, lighting, iron and steel, insurance, travel and finance. The group's flagship company, Bajaj Auto, is ranked as the world's fourth largest two- and three-wheeler manufacturer and the Bajaj brand is well known in over a dozen countries in Africa, Latin America, and Asia.

"I ask him if he knows which part of his character is most responsible for his success in business. "That's easy," he says, "rebellion. It's a very positive force. In fact, I remember the first ad I made when I started the business. I created the character of a black sheep of the family and he was successful in life. The ad was for trousers.""

KISHORE BIYANI

Founder & CEO
Future Group

I arrive at the Future Group office at Nariman Point after a 90-minute drive from my hotel, The Leela at the far end of Mumbai in Andheri near the airport. As I soak in the ambience, my eyes rest on some photographs mounted on the wall across the reception. I walk over for a closer look and find myself gazing at a dozen portraits of eminent people from all walks of life with a quote from each, including:

> *Sometimes, we are a nation of a billion people, thinking like a nation of one million people.* – APJ Abdul Kalam
>
> *Survival and success depend on speed and imagination.* – NR Narayana Murthy
>
> *Give till it hurts.* – Mother Teresa

The 12th frame contains no photo but is a mirror. I am intrigued and make a mental note to inquire about it.

I knew that Kishore Biyani is credited with revolutionizing the retail industry in India and was looking forward to the interview. I thought he would be larger than life and, like many Indians, would be a wonderful storyteller. I was surprised to find him quite a shy man and the interview would have to rate as one of the most difficult for the book. Not because he was not gracious with his time or open and forthright with his responses, but purely because I sense he is more comfortable with close friends and talking about business than his life.

I start the interview by asking him about the photos in the foyer. 'I think the quotes are very important. They're interesting quotes. For example, "Give till it hurts" by Mother Teresa; that's behind the Future Group policy to give huge discounts or promotions to the customer. I think the Future Group is all about ordinary people doing extraordinary things because normally people are ordinary. A grouping of extraordinary people finds it difficult to get together in any which way.'

I ask who the mirror is meant to be. 'The mirror is nobody. A lot of people have their own assumptions. The mirror is basically to make it interesting. It's a design.' So my thought that it had some deep meaning went out of the window.

Born on 9 August 1961 in Mumbai, Kishore Biyani went to a school a stone's throw away from his home in Napean Sea Road. Sports and the outdoors meant a lot to him as a child. 'I don't remember much; I am not a person of the past; I am a person of the future.

'It was absolutely a middle-class background' in the company of lots of children. 'We were a joint family. There was thirteen of us – eleven boys, two girls – everybody staying around each other.' His father and his five uncles were textile traders.

Kishore as a child nurtured few ambitions beyond some limited outdoor activities and the occasional family outing. As a boy, he was 'naughty and very active' but learnt how to care for himself from being in a joint family.

He has a lot of memories as a sports person in the apartment block where he lived. He was 'an average student, neither brilliant, nor mediocre'. The closest he came to topping his class, was the time when he stood third, which he waves aside. 'It was a fluke. I don't think I was a very good student, in any way.'

Biyani felt himself changing distinctly in his high school years. He took to literature and, as he became more rational, he became skeptical about traditional religion much to his family's chagrin. As devout Hindus, they considered Biyani's rejection as nothing short of sacrilege. Biyani was by then converting into an atheist. 'By the 10th or 11th standard I was questioning religion ... the existence of God ... rituals.' This also made him the only rebel in his family. 'It led to big arguments. I think this was the first contrarian in me which shaped up. I was questioning everything.'

Oddly, he displayed none of the same rebellion at school. There was no questioning of authority here. It could be that he has blanked out some of these memories or more likely because he doesn't 'remember learning anything much from school'.

Biyani's parents too, did not place too much importance on education or force him to study. They looked upon schooling as a routine for their three children – all boys – Kishore being the second. They wanted him to help with the family business because 'I was the one who knew English, I knew typewriting and I knew some other things which other family members did not know.' Biyani spent some time in the business everyday but, as yet, without any clear purpose or direction.

He took the lead in setting up a club to organize sports and festivities in the building where he lived. That was the first leadership role that he played and he loved it. He learnt a lot about people management from organizing recreational activities for his building's housing society of 65 apartments with 400-500 people. 'You had to manage everyone when you're hosting a big event in the building. I think I used to do that quite well.' It was at this time that Biyani became aware of his managerial ability. 'I didn't know I had it in me. I don't know why I have this ability or where it came from. I just found I could manage things. This ability aside, I don't think there was any other rebel even in the building; I was the only one,' he laughs.

Biyani did sufficiently well in high school to be able to pick the college of his choice, HR College of Commerce and Economics. He graduated with better than average marks. 'I don't remember that in five years of college whether I attended class for more than a day or two, but I never failed.'

If anything, college taught him more than his school, Manav Mandir which in retrospect he feels too restrictive. 'College was a formative period because of relationships, friendships, going out, understanding the real world, questioning things, looking at business and commerce and starting to understand what is happening around you.'

During college and after graduation in 1982-83, Biyani kept himself busy with a variety of activities, from passing his preliminary exam in chartered accountancy and taking a course in textile weaving, to export-import management and typewriting. He also spent two to three hours every evening attending to the family business. Biyani sized up any and every business opportunity, even in plastics and corrugated boxes. He learnt about laminated and un-laminated packaging at that time. 'I was learning what not to do, rather than what to do.' This was the phase of elimination for Biyani. One thing was sure: he was not getting into the family business, but, 'I knew they would be somewhere around there.' The rebel in him made him averse to joining and reporting to someone in the business, if only because he disagreed with their ways. 'I thought I'll probably do something on my own.'

Even now traditional education is not important for Biyani. 'Once you become quite educated, you become quite structured. Once you become structured, your flow of thinking starts with a particular system. That doesn't allow you to wander anywhere. Life is all about knowing everything and not about knowing one little thing.'

Marketing and advertising fascinated Biyani; so much so that he seriously contemplated making that his career after graduation. 'I started understanding what advertising and communication is all about.' He even took a course in marketing for a year and read related books. Then he got an opportunity with garment manufacturers to supply them with stone-washed fabric. He carved out a niche for this venture within the larger family business and managed it independently. If his family did not support him much, they did not oppose him either. They gave him some capital to begin his business, though it was 'not much.' The profits from that business, until today, go back into the joint family business but, as Biyani says, 'money was never a consideration for working.'

Biyani continued in trading and manufacturing for some time. 'I've never done one thing for more than two years.' In 1987, he started a company called Manz Wear, reincarnated as Pantaloon Retail. 'Whenever the family was not able to do anything with the property assets they had, I converted them into productive assets by using them for Pantaloon.'

Biyani was the first of his family members to get a bank loan. 'We were lenders, never a borrower.' Being financially conservative, the family was wary of raising capital to fund growth. Biyani shrugs off the reaction that followed. 'There was opposition everywhere; without opposition, nothing happens. It never worried me.'

He started many more companies at this time but did not remain involved with a number of them after they were established. For example, he backed his personal involvement out of one company he set up for yarn manufacturing. His argument: 'Once the other businesses become bigger than what you've created earlier then they (the first businesses) have no relevance.' As to the fate of the earlier business 'move on; life is all about moving on. You retain some part of it and keep moving on.' The yarn business is still functional and continues to be in the family's fold.

Biyani believes in the sanctity of the family as an institution. 'We are not hungry for money. There was never a case for breaking off with the family. I always thought family should be together.' So it was that two brothers, that is, his father and uncle and their families, stayed together, even as the others parted in the late '90s.

'If you look at the past, it's a problem. But I always say, whatever one does, that if you're not a contrarian but instead a conformist, you can't do much.' About the challenges that business people faced in the controlled economy, he says, 'I am in the new age, a product of the liberalized era. I can't understand and comprehend what they have passed through, but I had my own "licence raj" in my family.' He is sure that he would not have survived the control regime. 'I was not made that way. I'm a rational human being; that's my big problem. So, wherever I can't see anybody following reason, it's a big issue ... a frustrating issue, and government has its own agenda. They don't work with your agenda, as such.'

I wonder if this means he is a controversial character. 'I'm not at all controversial. I've been a conformist to nature. I'll never do anything against the flow of nature. I am a conformist out there. I'm not a conformist with the system. When you're conforming to nature, you can't go wrong.'

Future Group has an open-plan office in Express Towers, Nariman Point, the premium business and commercial hub of south Mumbai. 'We don't believe in hierarchies; we believe in seamlessness. It's again the flow of nature. You can't divide. The flow of nature has nothing to do with being, or not being, a Hindu. Nature is nature. Nature is not perfect. You can't be perfect. You can't predict nature so you should also not be so predictable.'

Although Biyani has paved his own way, 'there's nothing such as originality in this world, because there is always somebody somewhere who might be thinking like you in some form.' And so Biyani brushes aside the tribute that he has revolutionized Indian retail. 'I don't think so. The best is yet to come but the way we've done the business is interesting. It's not that I've revolutionized the retail business but the way we've gone about it is quite interesting. We've broken a lot of myths in retail: that one should specialize in doing one thing; you can't be a multi-concept retailer, multi-formatted retailer. We've changed every rule of the game. That's something interesting. Not the retail business as such, the speed of growth.'

Future Group has a lot of interests now. 'Every year there's some favourite,' he smiles. 'On the capital side everything has been done; now it's brands. We're building our brands. A lot of people in the retail sector build up private labels; we're building up private brands – that's the difference.'

Pantaloon Retail, the flagship company of the Future Group, earlier Pantaloon Knowledge Group, listed as a public company in 1992, the first time for any clothing company. It was Kishore Biyani more than any other member of the family who led the front in going public. 'The family was very traditional; they didn't want to do anything. It all happened and everybody followed. So that's the way it is.'

I wondered if this attitude made him an individualist. 'We've coined a new term called "collective individualism". We're all individuals but we've collectively come together. It's not a joint family; it's collective individualism everywhere because everybody's individuality has to be maintained. It's not difficult. It's a way of keeping everybody motivated ... charged up ... and make them happy.'

I asked Kishore about his management style because I had heard it was unusual. 'It is very different. My management style has changed every three years. Three years ago ... six years ago ... nine years ago, my management style was very different. Today, I'm playing the role of a chief strategist and a chief relationship manager more than anything else.' The previous roles that Biyani played have been handed over to others; to the many professionals that Biyani has hired. 'I think our ability to bring in talent has been unprecedented. All the talent is very different. We don't like anybody who's like us. We want, absolutely, a diversity of people.' He tells me Future Group has about 100 people in the management team. Total employees across the group are 25,000. A major part of the expansion has taken place in the last four years.

'Anybody who joins us, first of all, in the first ten days, we make him unlearn what he's learnt till now.' I wondered aloud how they did that. 'That's an exercise, a big exercise. I do spend a lot of time with key people. All our induction programmes are made to make people unlearn. We blank them out. We like to get people young. No IQ tests. We have to like him, that's it. The top 50-100 are all personally be interviewed by me – sometimes five minutes, sometime ten minutes, sometimes two hours. Most of the people are handpicked. Sometimes, I know he is a person who can fit in very well. Then we work on him and for one to two years we chase him and get him.'

I said it sounded like he often had to fight the system to succeed with his ideas. 'Everybody has to be a fighter but it's all about when do you give up fighting, and succumb to something. The best strategy is to maybe lose some small battle, but win the war. I might be seen to be losing something, but the ultimate game is winning because winning is everything. If we lose, it would be because we have planned to lose, it will never be losing as such.'

About his semi-autobiographical book *It Happened in India*: 'It was so difficult writing the book ... very difficult. Going back in the past is not me at all. I thought I'll never go back in the past, as I age, so it's better to record it now. It's very difficult to go in the past for me. Very very difficult. That's the reason why my co-author went to all the people I knew in the past and recorded the past from them. It never came from me as much. I had no memories. I'm a little impatient as a personality. I can't stay on a particular thing for a long time. You're finding me a little subdued now. Maybe three years ago, I would interrupt you and complete your sentence. I'm very, very impatient. Impatient in the sense that I've kept wanting to move ahead and ahead. For me, slow is a painful thing and the past is very slow. You have to think ... you have to go back ... you have to reflect in time .... It's quite a difficult exercise.

'It's not about your past. You have to go to the roots. We go to the source of everything and the design. We are design thinkers. So we go into the source of everything. For us, the flow of nature is understanding the source. In India, we pray to every source. We pray to the cow because the cow is a source of milk. We pray to the Ganges because Ganges is a source of water. So there's a reason behind it. Source is something that's very important.

That's the history. This is not traditional, this is not a ritual. It is basically understanding the source. I don't do prayer, but there's a reason behind it. One has to look at the underlying reason. So we do that everywhere. We go to the source of everything. We go to the source of human behaviour also.'

On the breadth of his business interests: 'We are generalists. The whole organization is like that. If you look at the history of the world in terms of disruptive innovations you have things like the locomotive, the radio, the television and the aeroplane. Disruptive innovation has transformed the world as compared to how things were before. The cycle used to be fifteen-twenty years, then it became ten years and now it's five years. So nothing is constant. All the business schools were created to look at organizations to last for more than twenty years. But today, you can't continue in the same firm for even five years. So for us, TQM, 6 Sigma and so on is all history. If you do that, in my opinion, your whole organization will be killed.

'There are an unlimited number of areas we're going into. We're into many things already.' Future Group verticals are retail, media, brands, space, entertainment and logistics. Insurance, financial services and capital are all separately held under various other entities – holding companies – within Future Group.

I mention to him that a number of the interviewees for my book have a vision to create or have actually created global businesses. I wonder what his view is. 'We have an Indian view. It's not different. To be very honest, our understanding is only of the Indian customer. Indian customers are behaving very differently because they're emerging in a different era at a different time. And our strength is only that; we don't have any other strength.'

Given his contrarian philosophy and views on tradition I wondered if that included the institution of marriage. 'Everybody thought I was a rebel and I will never marry within the caste or community – no I never learnt the ability to say "no". So I married the first girl I met. It was an arranged marriage, in a sense.

'I believe in a lot of tradition – but I don't believe in everything. I am still a conformist in family values. I have not gone outside the family, despite doing whatever I have done in business. It's very easy to break off. That's the simplest of things one could have ever done. If you look at the flow of nature, if everybody is happy around you, you will be happier.'

Biyani has two daughters. 'I'm quite patient with them. With your children, you have to be a little different.' I asked him if he felt his daughters should have the same opportunities as males. 'I think that's a very interesting point. What I did was, I created a family trust. All the wealth of the family got transferred to a trust, and made everybody the beneficiary, son or daughter, male or female. I am the managing trustee. We had to write a clause in the document that daughters will also have an equal right. That was forced by my daughters,' he smiles. 'I had forgotten about it. The lawyers who initially drafted the document behaved like lawyers behave, so they were more male oriented and I didn't think about it. When I showed the documents to my daughters they pointed this out to me. They were, of course, right.

'The trust has addressed issues of rights and shares comprehensively. The trust becomes the family office of tomorrow. We don't have a family council for our generation, but I have created a family council for people in the younger generation. The problems won't be with our generation now, because I have defined it already. For the younger generation, we have made a council where they decide what they have to do. That's a little futuristic because there are fifteen-year-old and sixteen-year-old members of that generation but they will have to learn quickly.'

Biyani's wife does not participate in the business. 'The trust doesn't allow spouses to come into the business outside our Biyani family. It can start a lot of comparisons. They can do anything on their own. We can fund it, that's not a problem but being in the same business can create unnecessary tension. Business has to be run differently because everybody will find their own way in doing business.'

I ask him if knows which part of his character is most responsible for his success in business. 'That's easy,' he says, 'rebellion. It's a very positive force. In fact, I remember the first ad I made when I started the business. I created the character of a black sheep of the family and he was successful in life. The ad was for trousers.

'That's not there any more. People are rebelling against government systems right now. There's no other rebellion. Nobody rebels. The new generation is born to democratic parents. We were born to socialist parents. We never got what we wanted so we rebelled. The younger generation gets whatever they want so what do they rebel for? They have a fear of losing what they are getting, so they don't rebel. We never had a fear of losing anything because we didn't have anything. As I say, rebellion is very important. My daughters rebel against me – rebelling, in a different sense. They fight for their work... they fight for their rights, as in the case of the trust.

'Their upbringing was a little different. My younger daughter is going to study in New York. I've told her only one thing: do what you feel morally good about. Whatever you feel morally bad after, don't do that. So she has to make her own yardstick of what she feels good and what she feels bad about.'

He had mentioned that his elder daughter had just started with the company. I wondered if he expected the other to follow suit. 'They're open to come into the business. I don't know – it depends. But I think they would come. I would encourage them to come. The option is open. They will have to work through the system. They can't come in anywhere. They know that. They'll all get salaries, but not from the company. They'll get salaries from my personal company. There are three people from the family, younger ones who've just started. Nobody works with me and there is no special treatment.

Actually, it's the reverse issue – for them. They feel they have to prove themselves more than others.'

Biyani keeps away from work on weekends and holidays. 'I'm not a workaholic. I used to be once upon a time, but not any more. He makes himself available 24 hours on the phone. He starts his day at 9 a.m. and is home before 8.30 p.m. Socializing is limited to invitations from close friends and associates. 'I would say out of every ten invitations, I would avoid nine and a half!' No cocktail parties for him either. 'Once you attend those you're not spending enough time with the family. Secondly, you're not spending time with yourself. It's all about discovering oneself also.'

I had a sense his attitude to social life would spill over into other areas. I was right. 'We don't encourage spending by anyone. I was forced to take a Honda Accord car because all our employees were getting a car which was more expensive. So that was a problem. Employees were feeling a little ashamed!' So it was clear material things were not important to Biyani. 'Not at all. The kick is in creating something. Material possessions are for people who can't create the kick by something else. People get a kick out of drinking because they can't get something else in life. I think we've got enough of a kick by other means. For me, intellectual stimulation is a kick which a drink or two can't give.'

About himself he says, 'In the last two-three years, I've started thinking that what one can do as a legacy is to build thought leadership in India because currently if you look at many of the people who are taking decisions in this country, they have graduated out of business schools in the West. Nobody is an Indian thinker. Nobody. Even our national political leaders have been educated in foreign universities. There is no Indian ethos in anybody's thinking. We are absolutely aping the West in every decision we have taken. And that happened when? The whole world has changed now. India doesn't believe in itself now. In all our policies, statements from people in New Zealand and Australia are quoted. We quote them when we make some of our policy decisions. This is ridiculous. Sometimes I wonder why we should not advance thought leadership in this country. India needs thought leaders. If our thoughts can be explained to a lot of people and there are followers which come about, I think it will make a lot of difference.'

When I read back over this interview I can see that, while it may have been one of the most difficult for this book, and at times it was like 'extracting hen's teeth', it contains some of the most profound and deep thinking that is important; not only to budding young Indian entrepreneurs, but to entrepreneurs anywhere in the world.

Future Group (www.futuregroup.in) is one of India's leading business houses with multiple businesses spanning across the consumption space. While retail forms the core business activity of Future Group with a number of well-known brands such as Pantaloons and Big Bazaar, group subsidiaries are present in consumer finance, capital, insurance, leisure and entertainment, brand development, retail real estate development, retail media and logistics.

“My brother said, “Subhash, I am here with our two brothers watching Zee and am alarmed to see there have only been three ads on the station this evening.” I said that was the “good news” and did he want to hear the “bad news”? Of course he said he did and I told him all three ads were free! I think I heard my brother drop the phone!”

SUBHASH CHANDRA

Founder & Chairman
Essel Group / Zee TV

My meeting with Subhash Chandra proved to be one of the more elusive of this book. We originally arranged to meet on a Sunday afternoon in Delhi, immediately following my interview with Professor MS Swaminathan. Subhash would, I was told, be arriving in Delhi on his way back from attending a wedding somewhere in North India. However, as I was about to leave for Zee TV's Delhi offices, I received a call from his office to advise that one of Subhash's grandsons was sick in Mumbai and so he had decided to go straight to Mumbai and would meet me there in the evening as he knew that I too was heading to Mumbai later that day. My flight to Mumbai was delayed by a couple of hours and when I arrived in Mumbai a car and driver were on standby to whisk me off to his home for the interview. Traffic was worse than normal and so an hour or so into my trip from the airport we received a call from his home that Subhash could not wait as he had to attend a family wedding and that we should reschedule for the following morning, as both of us were leaving Mumbai on Monday afternoon. Fortunately, the Monday morning meeting took place and this is the result!

Subhash Chandra was born on 30 November 1950 in a small village called Aadampur in Hisar district in Haryana. 'It was a joint family scenario where my grandfather and his two brothers were running the business together. My grandfather had formed the company in 1926 under the name Ram Gopal Indra Pershad, based on a business started by my great-grandfather and one grandfather. The firm carried on business as food grain commodity merchants and traditional bankers. They would lend monies against commodities, gold, and various things and had branches all over Punjab.

'In actual fact, for some reason, my father was adopted by my grandfather who, at that time had two sons. My father's real father was my grandfather's brother. Very confusing, I know and for me too,' Subhash says smiling.

'Sometime around 1962 the three brothers of my grandfather's generation split up the family business between them. In the divided business, my "adoptive" grandfather's business prospered whereas the others got into financial difficulties. To give you an example of how successful my grandfather had become, at that time in the Punjab there would not have been more than a dozen cars, and my family had one.'

Subhash says his father told his 'father' that he could not live in comfort when his real father and uncle were in trouble and that he would go and help them. 'I can still remember as a young boy listening to my father and "grandfather" argue about this. My grandfather told my father, "Who are you to settle them? If their actions aren't right and God wants to punish them for their wrongdoings and actions, who are you to try and help them? This means you are taking direct confrontation with destiny and God and nature. You are too small; any human being is too small to take direct confrontation with the laws of nature."'

His father ignored this advice and still chose to leave. However, his grandfather insisted Subhash's father could not take his wife or children with him. This led to Subhash's family, minus his father, moving to his grandfather's place in Hisar which, at that time, was a bigger town than Aadampur where Subhash was born.

'That's where my real journey started. I was twelve years old at the time we moved. I went to school and when I came home I would sit with my grandfather and assist him. In those days I would lift the phone and tell the operator on the other end at the exchange, a number and he would connect me and I then would hand the phone over to my grandfather. Each evening my grandfather would dictate letters to his 200 clients about the day's commodity prices. So I would help write the letters and get them off. And if we had a guest coming in the evening my grandfather would invite me to join them and to massage their legs. But, of course, I would at the same time listen to their conversations and learn.'

Subhash was also attentive to his studies and, after passing his 10th standard, got admission into Punjab Engineering College in Chandigarh, one year earlier than would be the norm.

But then disaster struck the family. Over a very short period of three months or so, speculation in the grain, cotton and oilseed extracts caused his grandfather to lose the family fortune. 'I had only been in college some ten months when I received a postcard from my grandfather which read something like "Son, I cannot afford any more your expense of Rs 300 a month which I send you regularly. You need to get the money from someone there or come home."

'So I came home in 1967. I was seventeen. In the first six months after I got back I worked with my grandfather to clean up the mess. Business was at a standstill and everything was in short supply. These were socialistic days so to speak as everything was controlled by government – you needed licences for everything. One had to be creative to survive. For example, we had boilers in our plants for oil extraction processes and our cotton ginning. Industry was entitled to a quota of coal and, even though our production plants were shut down, we continued to take our coal entitlement and sell it into the market. In a way this was wrong but it was what the "licence raj" forced people to do.

'After being back for six months I was frustrated as there was little money coming into the family. So one day I said to my grandfather, "Let me start one dal processing mill at least." That's a photograph of him over there.' Subhash gestures to a large photo on the wall in his office.

'In those days my grandfather was a prominent and respected leader in business and the community. He told me and it was the first time I had seen him cry, "Look my son, the time is not in our favour, don't do this. We will lose some more money because the time is not right." I said, "No, let me try." He then asked how I would start and told me we already had net debts of over Rs 6 lakh which was a lot of money at that time. I told him if he would give me permission to start I would stop in six months if it did not work out. So my business journey really started then and there has been no looking back.'

The two older of Subhash's three younger brothers helped him with the dal plant before and after school, the youngest being too young to help.

'I faced a lot of challenges. It was difficult. In the traditional sense, the agricultural commodity markets, mandis, as we called them, were controlled, so that the trader could not cheat the farmer who brought his produce to sell. There would always be a government civil servant to witness the bidding process.

'It was often frustrating because even if my bid was the highest, the shop owner would still not sell to me as he was not sure whether I could pay. So he would tell me that he could not sell to me but, no sooner had I turned my back, he would sell it to someone else at 20 paise cheaper.

'But they were also good days. The family had good relationships. In the markets in those days, if there was one hundred shops, we would have a relation of some sort with all of them. Call it a network if you will. If the owner was older than me as was usually the case, I would always respectfully call him "Uncle" and never "Mr so and so".

'I would say, "Uncle, why aren't you giving me supplies?" And he would respond, "Son, I am a small shop owner and I need to give the farmer his money immediately but can probably wait five days at most. I can't wait ten days or more." I would tell him not to worry and I would pay him within five days.

'So that's how we started, they trusted us with small amounts. I would buy the raw materials, process them quickly into dal and then sell it so I was able to pay the shop owner within the five days. Quite quickly the shop owners started to trust that we were sincere and could be trusted to pay.'

Life was still complicated for the Chandra household as it was still a joint family of his grandfather, his grandfather's younger brother and a nephew and their families bringing the total to around forty people. 'We had to support three kitchens at that time,' says Subhash, 'and not just food, but social obligations, such as getting the girls in the family married. The cost of weddings and presents for their babies all mounted up. And on top of all this we still had the business debt.'

After a few years Subhash came up with an idea; not only how to pay back the debt but to create some capital to grow the business. 'I suggested to Food Corporation of India (FCI) that their surplus crops left over after their auctions should be sold to the army. The district manager, with whom we were working, responded that their crops were not to army specification. I told him that was where we came in as we would process the crops into army specified food. In the ways of Indian bureaucracy at that time, the district manager took me to his higher up, who in turn took me to his higher up and so on until we got to someone who could make a decision. They liked the idea and it was subsequently approved by the Ministry of Food.

'What was good about this business was that it required no capital base as the FCI would just pay us a processing fee. There was, however, one complication in that I had to move the business to Delhi to avoid sales tax which was payable in Punjab.'

The year 1972 saw India with a bumper crop with little or no storage facilities where the crops were grown, as the British had built all the storage facilities at the ports as they imported grains. By coincidence Professor Swaminathan had mentioned the same thing to me in his interview the day before. Subhash and his family needed to create massive temporary storage using plastic sheeting. The result of the bumper crop and its processing by Subhash's family was that by the end of 1973 they had paid back all their debts.

'Only after we had paid our debts did I tell my grandfather, "Now I am ready to get married". In India in those days around twenty was the age to get married for the male and for the female around seventeen. I was married in

1975 and, as was the custom, I only met my wife half an hour before we were married.'

By the time Subhash was married his grandfather and great uncle had split their business and Subhash decided it was time to strike out on his own with his brother, Lakshmi. The old family company of 'Ram Gopal Inder Pershad' was reconstituted as 'Subhash Chandra Lakshmi Narayan' and, in due course, Essel. I asked how it eventually came to be known as Essel. He replied, 'That's easy: Subhash is me and Lakshmi is my brother. Our initials are "S" and "L". What happens if you say those two initials together? So the short form became Essel.'

From this point on there was no looking back. 'The food grains business and then the storage business introduced me to the plastics business and what plastics are used for. There were new experiments for new kinds of storage covers. Then we hired a lamination plant for laminating different kinds of plastics. That experiment did not work so we started producing packaging material out of laminating paper with plastic for the pharmaceutical industries and we have continued with that business to this day.'

Meanwhile, supplying of commodities to the army became very competitive and somebody suggested to Subhash that they look at the export of rice to Russia. However, it required significant capital which Subhash did not have. 'So this friend of mine said to me – this is a political deal, you get the order and I will get you the financing. So I started working on it and found out in order to get the order it was going to cost me something like Rs 3 million. I went to my friends and asked if they could help. They said, "What happens if we don't get the order?" I told them that was indeed the risk, but I was confident I was talking to the right people. They all backed out but somehow I managed to beg and borrow and raise the money. We got the order and were on the fast track.'

Subhash says this was the most crucial deal in his career. The business continued for about five years and was very lucrative. He laughs, 'All 500 members of Parliament wanted to be involved in the annual deal. My friends who helped me were also under pressure. So I told them, "Don't worry, I've made enough money, you can give the deal to whosoever you wish."'

The revenue from the Russian rice deals gave Essel the money to invest in packaging. Essel Propack is now the global leader. 'We have a 36 per cent market share. Can you believe 36 out of 100 people using toothpaste are using our tubes?'

The mid '80s were still the 'licence raj' era and Colgate or Hindustan Lever were not permitted to produce more than an agreed amount of toothpaste. So when Subhash went to them with this new packaging which was more flexible, more hygienic and much better overall, they were interested. But Essel Propack was about to learn an expensive lesson!

These new tubes had apparently been developed by Proctor and Gamble and American Can in response to a multi-million dollar law suit Proctor and

Gamble lost when an American child chewed the metal toothpaste tube and got ulcers. The response was to produce a laminated tube which would revolutionize the toothpaste market.

Hindustan Lever signed up to an agreement with Essel Propack indicating it was prepared to buy Essel Propack's entire capacity for a period of years. While Essel Propack thought all its dreams had come true, the reality was different. Subhash says, 'We were naïve because we had no clause creating an obligation on them to purchase our whole capacity. Their real objective, as it turns out, was to stop us selling the tubes to their competitors and so they came up with every reason under the sun as to why they could not buy our tubes. This hurt us so badly that Essel Propack's capital was wiped out. But since the rice business was doing well it supported the company. In due course we were free of the contract and were able to start supplying a local brand of toothpaste. This brought the big boys back to the table and by 1987 Essel Propack was back rocking!'

At this point Subhash then handed over the Essel Propack business to his youngest brother. 'I was unemployed again and looking at what to do next.'

Around this time we started building an amusement park, Essel World which was located on Gorai Island in Maharashtra about three hours from Mumbai. The first phase was opened in December 1989 with the estimate of 3 million guests by the end of the first year of operation. Only one million came. 'We asked ourselves "what's the reason?" People want to be entertained, but they don't want to spend three hours commuting and then not have much time to enjoy the entertainment before they head home. As you know infrastructure is bad in India and it was even worse then. By 1991 we were wondering what is the alternative to get entertainment closer to the homes of people. That's how Zee TV was started in October 1992.

'At that time there was no possibility of getting the licence. In fact the then secretary of information and broadcasting told me that it would be "over his dead body" as he said we would start consumerism in this country and he would not allow that to happen.' I suggested to Subhash that the secretary was probably correct. Subhash laughs and says, 'Yes, indeed he was probably right.'

But Subhash was not to be stopped and decided if they could not set up a channel in India they could set one up in Hong Kong and broadcast back to the cable operators in India. The Indian side provided programmes and sold ads. He found the money from NRI friends and others in London and Hong Kong. 'In fact not many people know that Kerry Packer was one of the initial investors in Zee along with Sir James Goldsmith. Sir James Goldsmith apparently frequently asked Kerry Packer's views on potential investments. Packer had liked the idea and told Sir James he would invest with him. A couple of years later in 1994, I met Kerry Packer in London at the Ritz Carlton where he was gambling in the casino. He said to me, "You know I am your shareholder," and I said, "No. How?" He told me he had invested with Sir James Goldsmith.'

But Zee was not an overnight success and it drained a lot of funds from the other Essel businesses. Some of his overseas investors lost heart and Subhash bought them out. Subhash laughs remembering a particular evening when one of his brothers rang him. 'My brother said, "Subhash, I am here with our two brothers watching Zee and am alarmed to see there have only been three ads on the station this evening". I said that was the good news and did he want to hear the bad news? Of course he said he did and I told him all three ads were free! I think I heard my brother drop the phone!'

As we both needed to leave for the airport, Subhash concludes our meeting with a few comments about his current 'pet project' – the Indian Cricket League (ICL). 'One-Day Cricket was Kerry Packer's creation but I feel he somehow gave it away when the Australian Cricket Board pressured him to relinquish it in exchange for the telecast rights. In India that is not the case. The Board of Control for Cricket in India (BCCI) offered me the telecast rights after I announced the creation of the ICL but I told them, "No" I want to continue and I think ICL will continue for a long time.' I said I understood that one of the reasons he had set up the ICL was because the BCCI had refused over several years to provide Zee TV with the broadcast rights, despite Zee TV's protestations in some cases it was the highest bidder. 'That's true,' Subhash said, 'they denied us content and so we created our own. Having created our own, I am reluctant to hand it over to the BCCI which essentially is what Kerry Packer did with his One-Day Cricket.' Given Subhash's track record who would want to bet against him not succeeding in his tussle with the BCCI.

Like most, if not all, of the subjects of this book, Subhash has also put his talents and resources to good effect in charitable activities. He has, for example, established TALEEM (Transnational Alternate Learning for Emancipation and Empowerment through Multimedia) to provide access to quality education through distance and open learning. He is also the Chairman of the Ekal Vidyalaya Foundation of India – a movement to eradicate illiteracy from rural and tribal India. The foundation provides free education to nearly 8,00,000 tribal children across 27,000 villages through one-teacher schools.

Essel Group (www.esselgroup.com) is one of India's largest business houses. The core businesses of the group are media, packaging, entertainment, technology-enabled services, infrastructure development and education. The publicly listed enterprises are Zee Telefilms Limited, Essel Propack Limited and ETC Networks Limited. In India, Zee TV is the first satellite channel, Siticable is the first multi-system operator, Essel World is the first amusement park, Water Kingdom is the first theme park and Playwin is the first online gaming company. Essel Propack is the global leader in packaging.

"The company was basically driven on my personal and individual aspirations to be a high-tech programmer. That perhaps was the reason why we did not grow so fast in the early years. However, I eventually realized that if the company was to grow, it could not be "my" or "our" family company any more."

DR ANAND DESHPANDE

Founder, Chairman & Managing Director
Persistent Systems

Suresh Iyer from our Chennai office had met me in the morning in Mumbai for the three-and-a-half-hour drive to Pune where Anand Deshpande lives and works. Although it is only a distance of 191 kilometres, it takes almost two-thirds of the time just to get out of Mumbai and onto the six-lane highway leading up into the mountains on the Deccan Plateau where Pune is situated.

It was a Saturday and, not long before Persistent's annual results were to be announced, so Deshpande was bunkered down with his finance and other senior executives, from whom he took his leave to meet with us.

Deshpande was born on 7 May 1962 in Akola in Maharashtra. He was schooled at Campion School, Bhopal, which is a Jesuit school up to 11th standard. Bhopal is the capital of Madhya Pradesh where his father worked as an electrical engineer for the state-owned Bharat Heavy Electricals Ltd. 'Bharat Heavy Electricals was a very large manufacturing company, like GE at that time, which made steam engines. We lived in a company housing estate which housed around 30,000 employees. My parents and their work colleagues were more or less in the same age bracket as were their children. I must say it was a very nice and comfortable place in which to grow up. Everybody knew everybody as it was a fairly self-contained and secluded area.'

Deshpande is the eldest of three children; his sister is a couple of years younger and his brother, thirteen years younger.

Coming from a professional family, I wondered if he and his siblings were pushed to follow suit? 'Not a whole lot. I was never a topper in class but was usually among the top three, a pretty decent student.

'At that time everybody who regularly came in the top half of the class either went to engineering or medicine. Coming from an engineering township, most of the kids went to some engineering school or the other. In my case, on leaving high school in 1979, I went to IIT Kharagpur to study aeronautical engineering. Just as now, it is a pretty big deal to get into an IIT and I was extremely happy to have been accepted.

'After two years I switched to computer science as it was a new area and I was in only the third batch. Whilst aeronautical engineering was interesting, I realized there were not too many job opportunities. Just like at school I never topped my class but I was always in the top half which, so far as I was concerned, was fine. I graduated in 1984 with a Bachelor of Technology.'

I wondered what life was like at an IIT in those days and whether it was all work and no play. 'No, it was not like that. The first year starts out like that as it takes a while to get used to the system. But once you know what you want to do you know exactly where you're going to end up. The top ten in the year probably work all the time. After the first three months of working hard, I realized I was not going to be the top ten,' he laughs. 'I also worked out that it was easy for me not to be in the bottom half and that I was looking to somewhere between 11-40 per cent in the year. I found it was not difficult to make that percentage and have a good time as well.'

Like almost everybody else, after IIT, Deshpande headed for the US – 'States-side' as he calls it – on a scholarship from Indiana State University.

'Of course I could have stayed in India but going abroad seemed to be more sensible as I got to study in the US without paying for it and to also see the world. It was great. I was lucky as there wasn't any pressure from my family to get a job and contribute to the family income. My father was just twenty-four when I was born; he was thus only in his late forties when I went to the US and had many years of employment left to support my mother and siblings.'

Deshpande did both his master's and PhD at Indiana. 'Just like at IIT, it took about six months to get used to the system. I found it was pretty easy to beat the class. I had good grades and after the first two semesters I was being tracked for a possible PhD. Within a year I had pretty decent credentials to be noticed in the class.

'At that point I had two options to either leave after my master's or continue and do a PhD. It was a time of recession in the US so I also knew there were not too many jobs if I left after my master's. I cleared my PhD qualifier in the third semester of the second year so I knew for certain, before I graduated with my master's, that I would get into the PhD programme.

'As I had always known that I was not going to be the top student, I worked out to maximize my opportunities I would need to "work smart". For example, I knew that Indiana was good but not one of the top universities in the US. However, I knew I had a very good chance of getting a scholarship to do a PhD from them, whereas it might have been difficult for me to get a scholarship to Harvard or MIT. It is a question of optimizing.'

For his PhD topic, Deshpande chose databases and I wondered why. 'It just happened that my undergraduate project was also in that area. A professor assigned our topics and it just happened that I liked my topic. It wasn't luck but it wasn't necessarily strategic either.

'I was also particularly fortunate because my supervising professor, Dirk van Gucht had just joined the faculty at Indiana and for a time I was his only grad student. He was only a couple of years older than me and we worked closely and well together.

'In the first year of my PhD in 1987, Professor van Gucht was invited to a conference in Germany and he kindly arranged for me to be invited too. This conference was a very special one funded by Volkswagen where a German professor who specialized in databases invited around fifty of the top people in the world who were also working in this area. While I was in Germany, I had the good fortune of spending a weekend sight-seeing with Dr Umeshwar Dayal who is very well known in the field of databases. I spent the weekend with him discussing my thesis and asked him to be on my thesis committee. The conference was a great networking opportunity and gave me access to the top 40-50 people in the world in an environment that was completely non-threatening, both from my standpoint as well as theirs.'

In the last year of his PhD, Deshpande presented a paper at a conference in San Francisco. While there, he took the opportunity of visiting the Hewlett Packard Research Laboratory. 'It was one of the top places in the world working on databases. I also knew they were looking for some database specialists. I sweet talked them into offering me a job.'

From 1989 Deshpande worked happily at Hewlett Packard for eighteen months when he had to make a decision. 'I had a J1 student visa which meant I could work in the US for 18 months after I graduated, at which point I had to decide whether to apply for a green card or return to India. I decided to return to India and was back home in October 1990.'

I wondered why he had chosen to return to India. 'It was something I had always wanted to do. I was at a point in my life where I had decided that I would either return to India or stay in the US for a long time. A lot of my friends were in that mode, where they were debating on buying a car, because they did not know if they were going to return home or not.'

He was twenty-eight when he returned home to Pune, where his parents were by then living. He was engaged within seven days of coming home and married within two months. 'If I had stayed in India my parents would have pressured me to be married by the time I was twenty-five. As I was away I was able to fend them off. But they had been planning for my return and had lined up a number of prospects. As it happens, Sonali was the first "candidate" I met. I liked what I saw and that was it. She was at that time a hostess with British Airlines based in Delhi where she lived with her parents.

'So I was married but had no job. I was not worried as I had decided to strike out on my own with my father who by then had just retired from working for the Kirloskars in Pune following his time with Bharat Heavy Electricals in Bhopal and Delhi. Actually, on retirement my father had planned Persistent Systems for his own consulting purposes but we pretty quickly switched that to our family company.'

I tell him I had heard fate and luck played a part in him getting the company up and running. 'Yes, the government was in the process of setting up three Software Technology Parks (STPs) in Bangalore, Pune, and Bhubaneshwar. The Secretary of the Department of Electronics, N Vittal, had visited the US and had spoken to a number of Indian postgraduate software students, including me, about these software parks. He exhorted us to come home and set up businesses in them and export. As the Indian software boom had not yet started, most people did not take up his offer.'

As it happened Deshpande's business in India didn't take off as he would have liked. Within a week of his return in 1980, the Opposition leader, LK Advani, went on a 'rath yatra' (a motorized chariot symbolic and redolent of ancient Indian martial practice) mission to rebuild the Ram temple in Ayodhya where a Islamic mosque had been built by Babar a few hundred years earlier. A week later the government collapsed and Chandrashekhar became prime minister for a few months.

'It was chaos. I was waiting for approval to obtain space at the Pune STPs. The government had set up the STPs with a total area of 8,000 square feet. The area had somehow been allocated to fourteen companies; eight were given 300-400 sq ft and the rest were given "table spaces". None of the companies which had been given space were software developers but were mere marketing fronts for products made by others. The management of the STPs said that they did not have space for Persistent Systems as all the fourteen slots had been taken, but asked me to be patient as they would be setting up another park.

'I waited four months but nothing happened. I lost my patience and sent a stinker of a letter – I remember it was 10 March 1991, a Sunday – to N Vittal who was still Secretary of the Department of Electronics. He would have received the letter on the 12 March. That very evening I received a telephone call from him. I hit him with both barrels. I told him I had attended his lecture in the US and had come back based on his assurance the government wanted specialists like me to return to India and export from one of the STPs. I told him nothing had happened for four months other than being told there was no space. I told him I already had two foreign companies ready to give me work but was stuck twiddling my thumbs. He clearly felt bad about the situation because two days later I received a call from the head of the STPs in Pune. He told me, "Secretary Mr Vittal has told me to vacate my office and give it to you."

'That Friday, on 15 March 1991, one of the STPs personnel came and gave me the keys to the office. By Sunday, 17 March, we were working in the office. As it happens, it was the most auspicious day of the Maharashtrian calendar, Gudi Padva or New Year's Day. We did a Satyanarayana puja; that was the real start date of Persistent.' I said it seemed he and his father had chosen the right name for the company. 'Seems so,' he chuckled.

'I had about USD 10,000 savings from my time in the US and used it all to buy a nice computer with a 386 GHz processor, 8 MB RAM, high-end for that time. I had also applied in the previous January for a bank loan of around Rs 500,000 (approx USD 22,000) from The Bank of India's local branch. The bank manager told me that he had authority to approve up to Rs 10 lakh (approx USD 44,000) but since the IT sector was marked as a priority sector he had to send my loan application to the head office in Mumbai. It took me six months to clear that loan. Every week I used to go there to move the application from one desk to another.'

The groundwork more or less done in India, Deshpande now had to get customers from Europe and his biggest market, the US. It didn't help his cause much when, on 21 May 1991, the day before he boarded his flight to the US, Prime Minister Rajiv Gandhi was assassinated. 'It was not the best advertisement for the political situation in India, but I had no choice but to plod on.'

Deshpande prepared brochures for all of the leading database people he had met at the Volkswagen German conference in 1987, as well as to database companies in the US and Europe. Before he returned to India he met someone during his time with Hewlett Packard, a Frenchman – Francois Bancihlon. He too had attended the database conference and had started his own company, Object Oriented Technologies, in France. They had talked about their respective plans. Deshpande said that he would be returning to India to set up his own company working on databases and other software products. Bancihlon told Deshpande that he did not believe him, but assured him that, if he indeed did set up shop in India, work would come his way. 'I sent him my brochure; believe it or not, he delivered on his promise – that was our first contract.'

Around the time that Deshpande was a graduate student at Indiana State, one of his classmates, Tim Bridges, had written a number of applications for Small Business Incubation Reports (SBIR). These were US government grants of USD 25,000 to develop software prototypes, followed by another USD 25,000 grant to small companies to incubate successful prototypes.

'Tim and I liaised and we wrote an SBIR application where we would combine our database expertise with his in-chip design. We were successful: that was Persistent's second contract.'

Deshpande returned from his trip to the US and France in June 1991, hoping his loan would have been approved, confident that, come July, work could begin on those first two contracts. There was, however, no end to the twists and obstacles.

'The week I came back Narasimha Rao was appointed prime minister, with Manmohan Singh as finance minister. The first thing Manmohan Singh did was to de-value the Rupee and increase the bank IRR ratios. Because banks had to deposit more money with the Reserve Bank of India, that brought down the amount of money available for loans. It was also the time of the first Gulf War with oil prices rocketing up. Our loan had been approved but the bank had no money to lend. I had a computer sitting at the docks for which I had to pay demurrage. We really had to scramble for cash at that time. Fortunately, I had been registered as single on my income tax forms in the US and managed to get a refund of 2 lakh (approx USD 9,090). Not much, but it all mattered!'

Persistent exported its first software in September 1991, the first to do so from any STPs in India.

I asked Deshpande to explain some of the other practical issues facing software exporters in the early 1990s. 'Well, for a start, there were no communications to speak of. The government offered a scheme called PAD that was a 9.6 kbps link, through VSNL. It used to take us six minutes to send a 30 kb file. Fifteen per cent of our expenses were on telecom. It was actually cheaper to go to Bombay and check the mail than to dial into Bombay and check the mail. I had a monthly train pass and I'd go to Bombay every week.

'Even getting a phone was a big problem. We had to wait for about four months. I used the fact that I had brought in some US dollars so that we could get the line on a priority basis. Without priority it could take up to two years to get a phone line. Those were the bad times and I am pleased to say India is now a completely different country.'

The next big opportunity for Persistent came in the form of Microsoft from which they got a small contract of USD 20,000. 'The contract was mission critical to Microsoft; we had to repay the monies if the product did not perform. It must have performed as they've been our customers ever since', Deshpande says laughing.

'From that point on we have not really looked back. We grew from four people in 1989 to about 500 people in 1999 and 4000 by 2008.

'In the beginning I did both sales and the detailed writing of code. From 1989 till about 1997 it was "my company". Around 1997, it became more "our company". And then I started to turn down work because it would mean more stress for me. The company was basically driven on my personal and individual aspirations to be a high-tech programmer. That perhaps was the reason why we did not grow so fast in the early years. However, I eventually realized that if the company was to grow, it could not be "my" or "our" family company any more.'

In 1999, Persistent received a venture capital investment from the Intel 64 Fund and in 2005, Norwest Venture and Gabrielle Venture invested further funds in the company. 'We could have done an IPO several times but our focus right now is to scale the company correctly, and bring in the best of managers and technical talent.'

And in closing our time together I asked Deshpande what he felt the future had in store for him. He did not respond directly but I could see from his eyes that, whilst Persistent is no longer 'his' company, he strongly believes his and Persistent's future are inextricably tied. As it was by now late Saturday afternoon, we left Deshpande to get back to finalizing his annual report.

Persistent Systems (www.persistentsys.com) is recognized as an award-winning technology company specializing in outsourced software product development. With over 4,000 employees, innovative business models, and reusable assets and frameworks, Persistent helps its customers increase revenues and margins, and enhance brand value. Persistent Systems has delivered over 2,000 software product releases to their 170+ customers in the last five years. It has developed proven processes for the entire product lifecycle which reduce time to market.

"My philosophy of life is that man comes and goes. Man doesn't carry anything away with them when they part this life. I am definitely not driven by money alone. Yes, we all need money, we all need to enjoy luxuries of life, but once you have enough, there is no point in clinging to it."

RANJI DUA

Founder & Senior Partner
Dua Associates

I have known Ranji Dua longer than any other interviewee in this book. We met more than twenty years ago when he had just started his law firm and I was the Regional Managing Partner of an international law firm based in Singapore. He had 'big' plans for his firm from the beginning and which, on any assessment, he has achieved. But like many of the other interviewees in this book, there is no self satisfaction and he continues to focus on the future which includes not only the law firm but Dua Consulting, an independent practice engaged in government and regulatory affairs and strategic advisory services.

Ranji Dua was born in Simla on 3 November 1951. His father practised law in Simla. 'Actually my father came from the NWFP which is now in Pakistan. Pre-partition he practised law before the Punjab High Court which at that time was located at Lahore. After the partition we remained in Simla for a few years before we moved to Chandigarh.'

I wondered about the family name and whether it indicated anything. 'No, it is a family name. Duas originally hailed from the Punjab region. Of course, now Duas are spread all over India although my father told me when he lived in Simla we were the only Duas in the phone book.'

Ranji's mother came from Lyalpur also in Pakistan but was born in Calcutta where her father had investments in some mines and other business interests. 'Many people in my parent's generation were completely caught unawares by the partition. Some could not even make it back to their homes.' I said I thought there had been many warnings of what was likely to happen. 'Yes, there were warnings but it is human nature to think the status quo will remain. Even educated people like my family were surprised as to the timing. My grandfather on my mother's side, owned many houses in Lahore but lost the lot. So I think many in that generation really had to re-build themselves from scratch all over again. A lot of them were hard put to it because they were well-off and used to a certain way of life. I guess because of the experience of my parents they instilled in me the importance of living within one's means and to "respect money". That was one of their catch phrases "you have to respect money". The current global meltdown is a pointer to where "all greed" and "scant respect" for money can lead the world to.'

Both his mother's and father's families were involved in the Quit India Movement for Indian independence. During its fight for independence three Indian Army generals were brought to trial at a special hearing in Delhi which became known as the Indian National Army Trial (INA). Some of the most prominent Indian counsel defended the accused under a team led by Bulabhai Desai who was perhaps the leading lawyer of his time. 'My father was one of the counsel working closely with the defending team. The trial was held in the Red Fort in Delhi where the army was garrisoned at that time. The trial went on for nine months from Monday to Thursday each week. Fortunately the Chief Justice of the Lahore High Court, an Englishman had agreed that all my father's Lahore cases could be listed for Fridays only. For that nine-month period, my father would work on Saturdays in Lahore and leave notes for his clerks to attend to during the week, take the train on Sunday from Lahore to Delhi during which he would prepare for the Monday hearing and then take the train back to Lahore from Delhi on Thursday late afternoon to arrive in Lahore, in time for his court appearances on Friday.

'Pre-partition many people who lived in Lahore, like my parents, used to holiday in the summer months in Simla and some were stuck there at the time of partition. They could not go back. And so my father had no option but to start working as a lawyer in Simla, as he of course had to earn a living. He told me his first brief was to act on the transfer of the banking system of the Punjab region from Pakistan to India. The bank is today, the Punjab National Bank, one of India's leading and profitable public-sector banks. His fees from that case enabled my father to rent a house, get some clothes, buy a suit and ties,' and Ranji laughs, 'get cracking again.'

After three years in Simla, Ranji's father was appointed a Judge of the Punjab High Court and, as that was to be located in the new capital city of Chandigarh, the family moved there in 1954. It was in fact the first planned city in modern India designed by the famous French architect, Le Corbusier. 'I loved my childhood in Chandigarh and have watched it grow to become the city of today. But when we moved there it was small. I remember our telephone number was 19 and then 327. I did all my primary and secondary schooling there.

'I went to St John's School run by Irish Christian Brother's for the better part of my schooling. In my last year I had been appointed the "school leader" and was due to receive a prize for my role at the Annual Day. As it happens my father and mother were Guests of Honour that year and so I ended up leading the parade to salute my father and receiving the prize from my mother. It was a very emotional moment.'

I told Ranji I remembered hearing from his mother that there was a plan for Ranji not to go all the way through the Christian Brother's school in Chandigarh, but for him to be sent as a boarder to the then famous Doon Public School in Dehradun. 'Yes, my parents registered me for Doon soon after I was born and, when the time came for me to go, the headmaster of St John's came and met my parents. He apparently said, "Look, why are you sending him to a new school? You have such a happy home here and he is doing very well at our school so why move him?" My parents had already purchased my uniform and were putting my school number on all my belongings that I was to take to boarding school. As you know I am an only child and I think this, plus the headmaster's plea, saved me,' Ranji chuckles.

I then turn the conversation to his career and whether his father put pressure on him to 'follow in his footsteps' and become a lawyer. 'No, he never put any pressure on me and never even expressed a desire that I should do law – although I am sure in his heart of hearts he hoped I would.

'I actually got into law by accident. At St Stephen's College I had studied economics and then moved to the Delhi School of Economics to do my master's. That was a wonderful time to be a student there as we had leading world economists teaching us. We had professors like Amartya Sen, Jagdish Bhagwati, Sukhomay Chakravarty and KN Raj. Our current prime minister, Dr Manmohan Singh was also a teacher there.'

At that time the Delhi School of Economics was seen as one of the half dozen leading educational institutions in the world for the study of economics. Even though Ranji had been admitted to study economics at Trinity College in Cambridge to do his Tripos, he chose to stay in Delhi. 'There were two reasons. Firstly, the Delhi school was first rate but secondly and, perhaps more importantly, I wanted to continue to be close to my parents.

'At that time I thought I was heading for a career as an academic economist but one event changed all of that. What happened was that Nani Palkhiwala, one of India's most prominent and respected lawyers who subsequently became ambassador to Washington and a well-respected senior director of Tata's, came into my life in an unexpected way.

'One of the things for which Nani Palkhiwala became known by virtually everyone in India was his annual critique of the government's budget. He was one person every man and woman in India could trust to be independent and tell them the real economic position rather than government "spin". In the years before television was widely available he used to hold a public meeting at a stadium in Bombay and to which thousands would come and hear his address.'

In a strange twist of circumstances, one day Ranji read Nani Palkhiwala's cover story that appeared in a well-known magazine, the *Illustrated Weekly*. The cover set out the headline of Palkhiwala's article, 'If I were the finance minister.' Ranji did not agree with certain propositions made by Palkhiwala. As Ranji had just finished his master's exams, he was sleeping in late on Saturday morning a day or so after the article was published. On waking, he received a message that Palkhiwala had called and asked Ranji to ring him. 'Apparently, unbeknown to me, my father who knew Mr Palkhiwala had met a day or so before, when Mr Palkhiwala inquired of my father if I was going to join the legal profession. My father had replied that I was not. I did not know any of this at the time. I went to my father to tell him I had received a call from Mr Palkhiwala and that he wanted me to call him. I asked my father whether there was any background to this call. Being the disciplinarian that he was, my father, just told me to return the call. With fear and trepidation I rang Mr Palkhiwala and ended up that evening having dinner at the Oberoi Hotel in Delhi with him and his wife. At that time Mr Palkhiwala would have been one of the most famous and respected Indians and here I was as a young man having dinner with him. It was like a dream. I could feel everyone's eyes on him. It ended up being a long and friendly dinner and, as I relaxed, I challenged him on his article and we entered into a vigorous, but need I say, respectful debate.

'As we took our leave of each other, I can remember we were standing in the lobby of the hotel, I felt him put his hand on my shoulder and say, "Have you ever considered becoming a lawyer because, if you do then you must come and join my chambers in Bombay." I was stunned because I knew of his fame as a lawyer and that the reason he was in Delhi that weekend was due to a case of national importance he was arguing on the Monday. This was an unbelievable offer.

'I was exhilarated and could not sleep for two days and, on the last day before applications closed for the Delhi Law School, I lodged mine. I was on my way to becoming a lawyer.

'My father had by then revealed his earlier meeting with Mr Palkhiwala and not surprisingly said, "If you are going to practise law I cannot think of a better person for you to learn from."'

But that was not to be as fate again played a hand. 'In my second year of law I attended an International Bar Association conference in Delhi. Justice Rangarajan who was then Chief of the Monopolies' Commission introduced me to Jimmy Dadachandji who was a leading lawyer in Delhi at that time and for many years to come. He asked me to go and see him.

'Mr Dadachandji's firm, Dadachandji and Co. was the most respected firm in the Supreme Court of India and was a leader of the big corporate work at that time. He acted for them all – IBM, Coke and so forth. He was extremely well respected, articulate, cultured, and a man of great philosophy and integrity. And so I started with him in my second year of law school and remained with him until I founded Dua Associates.'

I asked what happened to Nani Palkhiwala's offer. Ranji laughs and says, 'In 1976, if I'm not mistaken, when I appeared in my first Supreme Court case with Mr Dadachandji, we had Mr Palkhiwala as our Senior Counsel. After the hearing, as Mr Palkhiwala and Mr Dadachandji were very good friends, both coming from Mumbai, and originating in the Mumbai High Court, Mr Palkhiwala invited me to have tea with him at Tata House. He asked me if I was happy with Jimmy and when I replied that I was, he said "that's good". I am sure he was not miffed that I had not joined him and particularly as I was with his dear friend, "Jimmy".'

I knew Ranji was not all work and no play and asked him about the latter. 'I played a lot of sport; I played football and cricket for the school and was in the representative teams for Punjab schools. I also played table tennis at the national level. But when I came to Delhi I switched to lawn tennis and also played competitively. Later, I led Delhi University to the All-India Inter-University Championships.'

I wondered if this was around the time of Vijay Armitraj. 'It was around then that Vijay had already moved onto the professional circuit, whereas I was an amateur. But even as amateurs we got to play in a lot of international tournaments. We even got paid sometimes.'

I ask Ranji if he ever considered a career as a professional tennis player. 'No I didn't, for several reasons. Firstly, I don't believe I was good enough to make a living out of it and secondly, coming from a traditional and conservative family, sport was not considered a career. That said, tennis was a great education for me because I made friends all over the world. In fact I met a lot of lawyers who were into tennis in the US and the UK. I think playing tennis helped me internationally in my professional career because I built a network of friends, especially in the UK, more than the US, and so my first clients were UK companies such as Rolls Royce and British Aerospace.

'I stayed with Jimmy Dadachandji for about five years and left in 1981 to start my own firm in one room in my family's home in Sagar Apartments.' I asked Ranji what the drivers were for him leaving Dadachandji and Co. 'Essentially, I could see that there was no chance of a real career partnership in the firm. Sadly at that time, and the practice continues today in many Indian law firms, the owning partners are unwilling to open up the ownership of the firm to anyone. This, no matter how deserving. And if they do "open up" and invite you to become a partner, it is usually in name only. You are paid a pittance and are really a "salaried" partner with no equity in the firm. This has changed greatly in the last decade and I am proud to have pioneered this change.

'I started with one phone, no fax, no telex and, of course, faxes were not around then. I borrowed someone else's telex machine. So I used to ring them up and find out if any messages had come. I had a part-time stenographer who worked in a government department in the day because I couldn't afford anything else. I remember when I got my first major client, which was Chevron Oil, and I had to write opinions for them I used to pretend I was extremely busy and could only give the opinion to them the next day or in two days' time. Actually I could have done the opinion that day but I had to wait for the stenographer to come in the evening and type up my handwritten opinion. I would then correct the draft, my stenographer would then re-type it and so on until I was happy with the opinion. This usually took a couple of days. I did no typing and, believe it or not, still don't know how to now. So it was fascinating times. I was also the messenger boy and would go our client's pigeon holes in the hotels and leave the opinions. It was a 24-hour job.

'It took me about three or four years until I was actually able to start paying my bills, as they say. And then I thought probably it was going ok and, as happens in many service sector businesses, once you get your first, second or third big client, and if you're hardworking and conscientious, work starts to flow. I then started to engage part-time lawyers and then full-time lawyers.

'One of the things I was most keen to do was to provide appropriate facilities and career paths to the young lawyers joining me and I am proud we have continued to do this over the years; albeit office space in Delhi in particular is getting to be a problem. As I suspect at all other leading law firms at that time, when I was with Jimmy Dadachandji, not only didn't I have a room, I didn't even have a desk, I didn't even have a chair! I used to sit and work on visitors' chairs until I found an empty seat.'

I wonder if Ranji saw it as a big risk opening a law firm. 'I'm actually very conservative, but if I see an opportunity or an opening, I am prepared to go in. But first of all I would assess the risk. As you know, besides the law firm, Dua Associates there is another organization – Dua Consulting. Needless to say, for Bar Council and other regulations, Dua Consulting is owned and run independently of the law firm.

'In the case of Dua Consulting I saw in the early '90s, when the Indian government liberalized a lot of the regulations and the economy, that our clients would need some help more than pure law, and lawyers also need to work with people from other disciplines. And that has proven to be absolutely true as we know on the regulatory side of the law practice. So Dua Consulting actually works in the area of government and regulatory affairs, public policy, and today I find that the consultants and the lawyers have to work together often, whether it is insurance, whether it is the competition commission, whether it is civil aviation, in any field ... oil and gas, you have regulators in every field. So I think that was right, it was the correct decision, although at that time, nobody agreed with me. The same is now true in the area of mergers and acquisitions. Foreign companies want to find Indian companies with which they can joint venture, merge or acquire. On the other hand Indian companies, as you know, are currently scouring the world for just the same. The clients do not just need legal advice.'

I asked Ranji if he had achieved his dream of opening up ownership of Dua Associates on the basis of a meritocracy. 'Yes, we now have 53 partners, over 200 lawyers and operate from eight locations in India. The firm is definitely not run by me but by a seven-man executive committee. My philosophy of life is that man comes and goes. Man doesn't carry anything away with them when they part this life. I am definitely not driven by money alone. Yes, we all need money, we all need to enjoy luxuries of life, but once you have enough, there is no point in clinging to it. I would be very delighted if one day my partners say, "Ranji, look we don't need you everyday in the office." I look forward to that day.' Ranji adds with a chuckle. 'But I would still come and say hello to them and have a cup of coffee.'

In drawing our interview to a close I say there is one thing quite unusual about Ranji in terms of Indian culture. 'I imagine you are referring to the fact I did not get married until I was forty-four. Naturally, my mother was extremely anxious for years but I think she understood that with the hours I was working building the firm it would not have been fair to my wife or family. Not only that, but I don't think I could have built the firm to where it is today as I was, in a sense, married to the firm right up to the day I married Amrita. I did not take a holiday for over twelve years. Can you imagine any wife putting up with that? By marrying late and at a time where many of my responsibilities in the firm have been delegated, I now have a much better balance in my life so that I can spend time, not only with Amrita and our daughter Shreya, but also with my mother who lives with us.'

As we part I tease Ranji that, with his permission, I plan to publicly disclose one aspect about his life that many people do not know and will not believe. 'What's that?' he enquires. I reply, 'That you have never had a mobile phone.' He laughs. Maybe, just maybe, the publication of this book will encourage him to get one.

Dua Associates is one of India's premier law firms.

> When we are working we should work but we must also use the knowledge and insights that we have towards benefiting others as well. We should focus on other things besides making money.

ARUN FIRODIA

Chairman
Kinetic Group

I had arrived in Mumbai early on a Saturday morning from Delhi where I met Suresh Iyer from our Chennai office at the Leela Hotel. We rented a car and driver and embarked on the three-and-a-half hour trip to Pune where I was to interview Arun Firodia of Firodia Group and Anand Deshpande of Persistent and then drive back to Mumbai in the evening. It was a long day as both interviewees were extremely generous with their time and it was not until very late in the evening that we arrived back in Mumbai. I can remember Arun getting anxious calls from his wife as she was worried he was going to be late for a dinner party they were attending.

Arun started the interview by telling me he was born in 1943 and was an only child in a middle-class family. 'We were reasonably well off, but mainly because of the Gandhi influence, we believed in simple living and high thinking. Our family was involved in the freedom struggle. From both my mother's and father's side thirteen members of our family went to jail during the independence movement.'

I knew Arun's father was one of the pioneers of the Indian auto industry and he explained how he had got into it. 'My father graduated in 1947, the year India won her independence. He then went to the US to Syracuse University where he studied industrial engineering after which he returned to India.

'At the time my father came back there were not many private sector industries where he could use his industrial engineering skills so he applied to work for the State Transport workshop in Pune as a trainee engineer. This workshop had started manufacturing bodies for buses as the transport industry had just been nationalized.

'My grandfather was the Speaker of the Bombay Assembly and when he heard my father was applying for a government job, he wrote to the Public Service Commission asking them not to employ my father. He did not want people to think that it was because of him my father got the job. Fortunately, they overlooked that note and my father got the job on his own merit and started working with State Transport in 1951.

'The workshop was about ten kilometres away from my father's home and, like everyone else at that time, my father cycled to and from work. Shortly after he started, he learnt they needed someone to live at the workshop and manage the second shift. Being young, my father volunteered and within seven years became the Works' Manager which was an extremely short time in a government organization.

'Around 1958, my uncle NK Firodia, wanted to start something in the automobile industry. He had entered into agreements with a German company called Tempowerke and with Piaggio from Italy. He asked my father to join him and my father agreed. But it was not that simple as the chief minister of Bombay, YB Chavan did not want my father to leave government service and tried to lure him to stay by offering him the extremely important role of General Manager and Chief Mechanical Engineer. However, my father did not accept the bait. Even when he told them he was leaving, they offered him one year's leave of absence in the hope his private sector venture may not do well and he would come back.

'And so my father and his brother, NK Firodia in collaboration with the Bajaj family started the manufacture of "Tempo" three-wheelers and Vespa scooters.'

I asked how the Bajaj and Firodia families came to get into business together.

'The Bajajs were our family friends. Rahul Bajaj's father Mr Kamalnayan Bajaj was a member of Parliament. As you know in those days of the "licence raj" it was extremely difficult to get a licence and one needed political connections which Mr Bajaj provided.

'In fact, the relationship between our two families goes back even further. Mr Jamnalalji Bajaj, Rahul Bajaj's grandfather, was also a follower of Gandhi. For a time, both Jamnalalji Bajaj and my mother lived in Wardha as disciples of Gandhi. Apparently Jamnalalji Bajaj wrote to my grandfather in glowing terms about my mother and suggested for his son to marry my mother. So without Mr Jamnalalji Bajaj I would not be here today,' Arun laughs.

Around 1969, the Bajaj and Firodia families decided to split the business in two with the Bajaj family having control of Bajaj Auto and the Firodia family having control of Bajaj Tempo which is now called Force Motors. Force Motors is now controlled by the family of Arun's uncle, NK Firodia although there is a close commercial relationship between Force and Kinetic with the latter providing parts for Force vehicles, three wheelers and tractors.

We then turned back to Arun's life. Following secondary school, he was in the first five year batch that attended IIT Bombay where he studied electrical engineering. He then went on to study at MIT in the US but, before leaving, married Jaya, who he met at Fergusson College.

'While I was at MIT, I worked on a very interesting project involving the design of the control system of a torpedo. It was a classified project for the US government. The Vietnam War was on at the time so they insisted I take up US citizenship. As the control system worked both on analogue and digital systems, they needed a special computer to be used. As it was top secret, they would take me to the lab through a secret passage, give me false data which another American would then convert into the right data.'

After MIT, Arun worked for a time for a company that designed the first microprocessors in the US and which was subsequently taken over by Intel. 'While I was working in the US, my father told me that he wanted to develop a vehicle for the common man. So he asked me to come and work on the project. In those days, obedience was a virtue,' he laughs. 'However, on the way back from the US, I stayed in England for six months as my wife, who is a doctor, wanted to do a diploma in children's health. While I was studying at MIT, she was working in the Harvard University's Children's Hospital.

'When I got back home in 1970, my father told me he wanted to set up a new company, now Kinetic, to design a vehicle for the common man. It had to be light-weight – about 50 kilograms – and the cost should be below Rs 2000 (about USD 160 at the time). The vehicle had to be easy to maintain and economical to run. The design should also be such that it could be dismantled in two hours and be reassembled in two hours.

'We started working on the project, assembled a team, brainstormed and came up with a moped called "Luna". It hit the market for the first time in 1973 and proved to be very successful. We made five million of them.

'What was different about Luna was that it was built using no imported machinery or equipment and without foreign collaboration. My father wanted us to think on our own whereas in those days everybody would import knowhow, components and machinery from abroad and set up factories in India. My father did not want to follow these norms. He wanted an affordable vehicle made from Indian components using Indian machinery.'

As with many successful entrepreneurs, timing plays an important role. Just after the Luna was launched there was the 1974-75 oil crisis which propelled fuel prices sky high in India. The 'common man' in India needed a vehicle that would give them sixty kilometre to the litre and the Luna did just that.

'The company grew rapidly but in those times of the "licence raj" there were always problems. Our licence said we could only make 24,000 Lunas in a year. We went far above that and the Monopolies and Restrictive Trade Practices Commission started proceedings against us. We advised them that we were using only local material and no foreign components. I knew the law at the time stipulated that the only reason the government could interfere was if we needed foreign exchange to produce more than the licensed number of vehicles. We didn't. There was no doubt we were in a monopoly position as our market share of scooters was above 25 per cent but there were few alternative suppliers of mopeds at that point and so the Commission did not take any further action against us.

'The lack of alternatives and the huge demand for cheap transport put pressure on the government to liberalize the two-wheeler industry. It shortly thereafter made an announcement encouraging tie ups with foreign companies for the manufacture of vehicles below 100cc. Honda, Kawasaki, Suzuki and Yamaha announced their plans to come to India. Kinetic tied up with Honda Motor Company to make scooters and Hero tied up with them to make motorcycles. We started selling Kinetic Honda scooters in 1986.'

But it appears that the joint venture faced problems in the early days. 'Our project ran into difficulties due to the heavy import content. At that time the Japanese exchange rate shot up to 100 Yen to one US Dollar and our costs went through the roof. We quickly had to heavily indigenize as many of the components as possible. We knew how to do this but to get it through Honda's R&D was not easy. However, we persevered and, in due course, succeeded.

'I believe in our small way Kinetic contributed to the industrial and social revolution taking place at that time in India. We gave mobility to the "common man" with the Luna and did the same for Indian women with the Kinetic Honda scooter. People still write to us about how these vehicles transformed their lives. At the end of the day, it is mobility and communication that helps in the progress of a country.'

I wondered what Arun considered were the important elements of their success. 'Luck and timing definitely play a part but strategy is very important; without a strategy you will flounder. Along with this, you must have the ability to associate with people who can help you, seek their advice and make decisions to move forward. I also believe in listening to a dozen opinions before making a final decision. But when I make a decision I stick to it.'

Like most of the interviewees in this book Arun radiates energy. Despite being sixty-four at the time of our interview it was plain to me that the thought of retirement was far from his mind. He agreed. 'My father worked right up to the end. As for me, I am about to embark on the most important project in my life. We call it "Dreamland" and it involves the development of a cluster of 100 villages. We are going to finance the education part of this project by asking people to adopt a school child by paying USD 100 a year for ten years. Imagine what we can do for the 10,000 school children in these 100 villages if we get these contributions. But it is not just about education it involves the total development of 100 villages by using modern technology. Through satellite pictures, aerial mapping and by studying the topography of the land, we will know exactly where to build dams to store water, where to do watershed development and so on.

'I have no doubt in my mind that this project will be a success but we will need to be persistent. We started our community initiatives about twenty years ago when we built a hostel and opened a school for destitute children. Many of them have graduated from the school and feel fortunate to have had an education. Some of them have gone on to work in cities and some have even gone abroad for higher education but half of them are still living in the villages. They are the committed volunteers who will help us in the project.'

Apart from the Dreamland project, I knew Arun and his wife were involved in many other charities, 'Yes, we work with a leprosy home. Kinetic started a workshop for them. We give them machines and they work for us. We pay them well and arrange loans for them so that they can build their own homes. We have also employed blind people for which we got the Helen Keller Award. People think that a factory is no place for the blind but they have an excellent sense of touch. We have set up a separate department for them.'

At this point in the interview it is already 7 p.m. and Mrs Firodia rang and pleaded with Arun not to be late for the dinner party they were to attend. But he had not finished telling us about his family's charitable work. I could feel his passion for these was as great as that for Kinetic.

'When we are working we should work but we must also use the knowledge and insights that we have towards benefiting others as well. We should focus on other things besides making money. Today, money doesn't excite me. I know of a story where this Indian man is sitting under a tree and an American comes up to him and asks him to go to work and grow more food and then make more money. The Indian asks why he should do this and the American replies "so that you can relax and sit under a tree". To this the Indian man replies, "why should I do that when I'm already sitting under a tree?"

'Everyone should sit under the tree, but not for twenty-four hours.' At this point, Mrs Firodia calls again. Suresh and I decide it is time to take our leave as we can sense Arun would be happy to talk for hours about Dreamland and Kinetic's plans for the future, which include developing an inexpensive vehicle for farmers to take their produce to market.

The main company in the Firodia Group of Companies is **Kinetic Engineering Limited** (www.kineticindia.com). Kinetic was established in 1972 and has a diverse product portfolio including: the manufacture of (i) transmission components (gears, shafts, axles); (ii) engine components (crankshafts, cylinder heads, camshafts); and (iii) complete gearbox & engine assemblies for auto & non-auto products. It also assembles complete vehicles for some of its customers.

> I needed to get the cost down. We did two things – rationalize on all costs and optimize revenues purely by innovation. We innovated at every phase, from operations to marketing and distribution. To bring down costs of distribution, I needed to eliminate the middleman. So we tied up with post offices, petrol gas stations and grocery shops to make buying a ticket as easy as buying shampoo.

CAPTAIN GR GOPINATH

Founder, Air Deccan & Chairman, Managing Director
Deccan 360

Captain Gopinath was born on 23 April 1951 in Gorur which is a very small village of some forty houses in the rural interior of Karnataka, about four hours west of Bangalore. Gopi (as he is known) told me, 'My father was a local teacher and a farmer. Not a farmer in the typical peasant sense but, of course, he used to work with his hands. He was a very austere person and very frugal. I think he was inspired by Gandhi and that is where his discipline came from. So a large part of my life was steeped in that village life and its associated values. We were not rich, not even middle class, but I think our ethical values were sound.'

There were eight children in the family and Gopinath was the second oldest. He has lasting memories of how difficult it was for his father to make ends meet on a teacher's salary, how the village had no electricity until he was nearly ten and walking bare foot to and from the local school in the village.

It was, however, all in all, a happy childhood. 'I can particularly remember summers in the village when my father would take us to the river and teach my friends and me to swim. We didn't have a scooter or a motorcycle or car or refrigerator or any other thing but that did not worry us. Most people in the village didn't have any of those things. Of course there were rich landlords and average landholders and poor landholders. We were not poor, but we were not even middle class – we were lower middle class in terms of income. But I think we were aristocratic in terms of values. But if there was poverty, it was full of sunlight. I think it was Albert Camus, the French philosopher, who said, "my poverty is full of sunlight because there is no envy".

Like many of the other interviewees in this book Gopinath's father was a strong disciplinarian. Being a teacher he insisted on them studying, which none of the children wanted to do. 'My father didn't put me into school before the fifth standard. He told me there was not much they teach in the earlier grades and that he could teach me to read and write at home.'

Gopinath says he often reflects on his childhood and that of his own children. 'There's so much of restlessness amongst us – in terms of getting this constant need for entertainment – this constant need of having something to occupy our minds, either you need to go to a party or a restaurant or watch TV, you want activity around you all the time because there is a sense of boredom. I did not have that restlessness as a child. And I remember long ago my father read to me a passage from a Bertrand Russell book where Russell stated that a large part of education must be how to teach people to face boredom, because a large part of most people's lives is boredom. In that sense, if you want to create a great work of art, a great work of literature, research – it can't be all excitement everyday. It requires a lot of ability to be by yourself, to have silence, to have solitude, which is normally construed as boredom. So when I look at it today, my children for example, sometimes myself, I think about my father. Every day for twenty-five years he would get up at seven in the morning, go to the fields and then take the bus to his school some ten miles away. He would teach there until 5.30 in the evening, take a bus again and come back home. Then he would sit and teach us. What comes through to me is his sense of commitment and dedication. I never ever saw him depressed about money issues or his "boring" life and then I contrast that with my life and those of my children and our friends.

'I think I had a lot of dreams. I remember the local headmaster one day came to our school and said there is a competitive exam for a military boarding school where the fees would be paid by the state. He asked who was interested. So I just raised my hand and found I was the only one who raised my hand; not because I wanted to be an officer or join the army, it was just that I wanted to get out of the confines of the village. I just had dreams to maybe go out, beyond the village. There is a line in a poem in Kannada which I have always remembered. It goes, "guddiyache giddayache gaddiyache pawana baniyo" which means – "guddi" means "temple" so "guddiyache" means "beyond the temple", "giddayache" means "beyond the woods", "gaddiyache" means "beyond the borders" and "pawan baniyo" means "let's go". So it was more than a sense of seeking beyond, rather than seeking a particular thing.' There was one problem in getting into the military boarding school and that was passing an exam – all in English. Needless to say he failed the exam. And here fate played a hand, as the headmaster wrote to the authorities to ask them to give Gopinath the exam in Kannada as, if the military wanted smart people, then knowledge of English was not a fair way to select them. "So I took the exam again, passed it, was selected and my life changed forever."'

It was a tearful departure with his mother crying and the whole village coming to see Gopinath off. His father took him on the first trip to Bijapur and many others over the next five year period. It was a long trek eighteen hours by bus and train. 'In particular I remember my father sitting next to me and reading passages from the trial and death of Socrates and talking to me about Gandhi.'

Only three people in Gopinath's class at Bijapur passed the All-India exam to entitle them to join the prestigious National Defence Academy in Pune, the equivalent of Sandhurst or West Point. Gopinath was one. He spent three years at the academy before moving to the Indian Military Academy in Dehradun, an old-style institution from British times, which turns out young army officers and from which he graduated at the age of nineteen as a second lieutenant. The plan was for him to go on to artillery school, but the India-Pakistan-Bangladesh war broke out in 1971 so his training was cut short and he, with many others, was dispatched to the front.

'I went straight to my unit, which was in Sikkim in the Himalayas, and the day I reached my unit, the unit had got orders to mobilize, to move. I saw first-hand what mobilization is. There is a sense of excitement, a sense of tension in the air. The whole of my first night was full of the movement of guns, the sound of boots running, and loading and unloading equipment. Running through my mind was the thought that "I'm supposed to be a young officer and this is what I have been trained for". We went into the night, literally into the night, to avoid detection that our troops were moving and mobilizing at the Bangladesh border. And then I was there for a few months through the war.'

I asked whether he saw action. 'Oh yes, I was there right through the thick of it as there were intense battles. Being in the artillery I was not right in the frontline, as some of my other colleagues were, but we were directly supporting infantry and there were lots of stray bullets landing all around us. And, of course, in the artillery, the officers go with the infantry for the attack. I saw a lot of dead bodies and lost a number of friends.'

The war had a profound impact on him. 'I saw the senselessness of war – war bruises everyone, both the victor and the vanquished. I literally boarded that train for the military college as a kid,' and Gopinath laughs, 'but I couldn't get off the metaphorical "train" for a long while. But the army was a great life in the sense that, barring this deep scar in me, it satisfied my adventurous character and love of the outdoors.'

Gopinath then spent the next eight years with the army in the Himalayas, Gujarat, Assam, Kashmir and Rajasthan. During his holidays he did a lot of trekking and mountaineering and drove a motorcycle all over north India. Finally, he took a leave of four months from the army and hitchhiked around the US.

When he came back he was a changed man. He was twenty-seven years old and by then a Captain with a very prospective military career ahead of him. 'But I thought there was more to life than the army as I did not feel intellectually challenged.'

However, it was a not a simple matter to resign from the army. A permanent commission such as Gopinath held was not for a period of years but 'at the pleasure of the President of India.' His first application was refused but he persisted and finally got the release he sought. He had managed to convince his superiors that his heart was no longer in the army. But whilst he knew what he did not want to do he did not know what he did want to do. Gopinath laughs and says he remembered someone had told him that 'it is better to be a dissatisfied pig than a satisfied Socrates.'

So Gopinath returned to his village. His father was shocked and said, 'What have you done? You don't have a job now and you had the best job that one could possibly have at your age.' Naturally his parents had been extremely proud of him; even more than they might normally be, as he was the only officer from the village.

But what had happened to his village and the surrounding villages during his time away also deeply affected Gopinath. The government had built a large dam across the river in which he used to swim as a child. Luckily, for his family, the village itself had been spared but they lost their farming land and more than sixty villages nearby were totally submerged. 'Wherever I went in the village, the temple, the bus stand, the village central courtyard with its peepal tree where people sit and smoke and chat, I found that everyone had become refugees overnight. They had become refugees, both in a physical sense and in an emotional sense. Physical in the sense they were physically displaced. Emotional in the sense, you know, you're cut off from your village, you lose your house, your village, your culture and your roots are suddenly taken away from you. There was this deep sense of insecurity, of the unknown, and the only talk was "what will we do?" and "where will we go?" Someone might say "I will go to Bangalore because I have an uncle there" and another would say that they would take the land which the government was giving in lieu of the land which was taken. I found I was really affected by what had become of the villagers.

'A village is a living thing. It doesn't exist in isolation, it lives in a symbiosis of other villages. For example, over the centuries, a village blacksmith has a brand which has been built up, as his father, grandfather, great-grandfather were blacksmiths. Both by caste and profession, he is a blacksmith. So people from surrounding villages will bring their bullock carts to be repaired by the blacksmith. Now when you dismantle this village by taking it apart, it is like taking the limbs of an animal, right? It dies.

'Even though India is predominantly an agricultural country with a lot of rural unemployment, it is nevertheless often difficult to get labour because there is a constant movement of people away from agriculture. I asked my father about the land he and his brothers had lost under the dam waters. He told me that, even before they lost the land, it was uneconomic to farm; principally due to the lack of labour and that many villagers were leaving to make the fortune (usually illusory) in the cities and encouraging their children to become doctors and engineers.'

In Gopinath's view, whilst dams obviously have positive attributes, the effect on the environment is often overlooked. He believes valuable forest land is frequently lost twice over because of a dam. 'Firstly, the dam will frequently submerge forest areas and secondly, when the villages are resettled it is often in a forest area which then has to be cleared.

'So I asked my father where was the land the government gave him and my uncles in lieu of the land submerged by the dam. He told me they had given them 40 acres in some other place, about 100 miles away and which they had not seen as it was so remote. They wanted to sell the land as he said his home was in the village, the temple was there as was his school. In short they were not interested in this land. So I went off myself to look at the land which was located beside a stream and about five miles from the nearest village. Whilst the land looked barren it was a picturesque setting with the stream running through it. Something passed through my mind. It was very romantic and beautiful. I found the aloofness and remoteness, romantic. It came to me all of a sudden that this was what I had been looking for – to live on this land. And the thought that I could work on the land with my hands, live in the open air, read in peace. I was extremely excited. So in that moment, the idea got planted. I thought it was a great idea. So I walked back to the village and took a bus home. I went straight to my father and said, "Let me buy this land from you and your brothers."

'My father thought I was absolutely demented. In Kannada there's a proverb, about a man who has fallen from the roof and is then hit with a stick. My father thought I was doing that to him. First, I had resigned my commission in the army and now I was coming to him with a harebrained scheme on what I was going to do with my future.

'He thought I'll come to my senses. That I would start and get into debt and, as I would not be doing well, I would give up half way. All these things were going through his mind – that I would live in poverty, become unhappy in due course, get dispirited and all those kind of things – what is my son doing? He's aimless. But I was not aimless. I was full of dreams and full of aims. But he was a man who had worked all his life for a salary. That night we slept side by side in our house and the whole night he was trying to persuade me not to do it. I remember some time around 5 a.m. he gave up and started to talk about what crops I should put in. The next day I signed a deal with my father and uncles on the land. The following day I went to Bangalore, bought a Doberman, a tent, provisions and other items. There was a Harijan boy in my father's house and I invited him to join me to be free and share in my dreams which he agreed to do. So I went and pitched a tent on the land and started living there. Each day I would get up at sunrise and walk around the fields and I had this vision of what I would do with the farm. I said I must really build a beautiful farm. And also the thought of being there with nature and working, I could read, and all these things were so exciting to me. So I was, like I said, so much into it that nothing else existed for me.

'I decided first of all I needed to have a dairy. Cows would be where I would get my daily income, milk for myself and manure for my fields and for a gas plant to provide power for lighting and cooking. Then I said to myself that I would grow seasonal crops from which I would get income every three months. I knew I also needed a monthly income so I thought that could come from poultry and raising silkworms. I also thought I would grow bananas because they would give me income once a year. And I also thought I would plant coconuts because, although they take about eight years to start producing, once they started, they would continue to provide income for the next 100 years. In the meantime I needed to hang on for dear life. So I conceived all this and wrote a paper that it would be an integrated farm with all these activities. And I went to all the banks in the area to ask for a loan but no bank would give me money. They said established farmers were not paying back their loans. They all said to me something along the lines of "how will you, a new guy, a young guy, who has come from nowhere, with no experience in farming, this is barren land – how are you going to pay the money back?"'

And then like so many other stories in this book, fate played a hand. One day Gopinath was cutting undergrowth and felt someone looking at him. This was rare as the farm was so remote that even a motorcycle could not reach it because of the stream. But there was indeed someone there. He came over to Gopinath and said, 'I'm Chandrasekhar, the manager of the local bank about ten kilometres away. I heard there was some ex-army officer who is living in a tent. I thought it was a joke but, as I was going by, thought I would walk in and see for myself.' Gopinath took him to his tent and cooked a meal for him after which Chandrasekhar invited him to come to the bank the next day. Gopinath says, 'So I went in the next day and he typed up my ideas into a business plan with a cash-flow statement and sent it off for approval. After a month he told me that my loan had been approved but that due to the amount of the loan they needed a guarantor. I thought I was so near but so far from succeeding. I didn't despair. I didn't fall into depression, like somebody said, "cynicism is slow suicide". And in the Gita, it is said, "you must not lose yourself in despair, you must lose yourself in action". So I was so much involved in the action, or in the job at hand, I never for a moment had bitterness, or despair or anger or cynicism against anybody, including the bankers. My whole time was spent in looking for solutions, rather than brooding over the problems. One day, a neighbouring farmer, Manje Gowda came and told me, "I heard that you need a guarantee", which I confirmed. He said he was always telling his children to look and learn from what I was doing in introducing ecological farming to the district. He said, "Look, Captain, if the bank is ready to accept me as a guarantor, I'm ready to give a guarantee. I've got ten acres of land, I'll give that." I just couldn't believe it. I resisted but he told me the title deed was lying in his cupboard and he really wanted to support me as an example to his children. I was really touched and have never forgotten his kindness. And so I finally had some money!'

One issue that puzzled Gopinath was why farmers were always in debt. The more he thought about it, the more he came to the conclusion it was their farming methods and over-dependence on fertilisers, chemicals and pesticides. The input was usually more than the output. He explained, 'Farmers would borrow money from the local moneylender for seeds, chemical and pesticides and repay the moneylender by selling his crop back to him. So the moneylender was making money all the way down the line.'

More importantly, Gopinath was concerned about the damage pesticides and other chemicals were causing. Not only would the pesticides kill the intended pest, but many other insects as well and many of which did good work. He says, 'I felt it was mindless agriculture. When in Kannada you say, "the earthworm is the farmer's friend," it is not just the earthworm, it is all the life in the soil which is your friend. So if you take it out in isolation and say earthworm is your friend and the termite is the enemy, so you should kill the termites. How does a farmer kill termites? Through pesticides. But when you kill the termites, you also kill the earthworms because the pesticides then go into the soil.'

With his strong belief in the benefits of ecological farming, Gopinath scaled up and, in particular, focused on silkworm farming. Within a relatively short time he became the largest silkworm producer in Karnataka and in 1996 won the prestigious three-yearly Rolex Award for Enterprise based on his ecological farming. By now he was making money but, more importantly, he was well known and that gave him access to important civil servants, bankers and businessmen.

This takes us to the next chapter in Gopinath's life, but first I wanted to know if he ever had time to find a wife. Sometime around 1978 Gopinath's father wrote him a letter indicating he was looking for a suitable wife for him. Gopinath takes up the story, 'I never wanted to have an arranged marriage and, in fact, I did not want to get married at that time with all the problems I had. Not only that but I figured no woman would want to marry a chap who lived in a tent. My circumstances indeed dissuaded the first few candidates found by my father, but one girl persisted and so I decided to meet her. I instantly liked her but told her marrying me would be crazy and that she would have to rough it out. She told me that was fine. I wanted to make sure, so I invited her to come and see my home. So she came with her mother and father, and my neighbour, Manje Gowda, sent his bullock cart to bring them the final kilometre. And you know, she still said she was prepared to give it a go. And so we married.'

Shortly before wining the Rolex Award, Gopinath and his family moved to Bangalore so his daughter could go to a good school and he could divide his time between the farm and an agricultural consultancy company he founded, Espak Agro which focused on advising farmers on ecologically sound farming methods.

One day in the late '90s an old army colleague, Colonel Samuel, who had been a helicopter pilot came to see him. For about a year the two of them regularly played squash and tennis together. Each time they met, his colleague told him he was looking for a job. He told Gopinath he had a job as an administrative clerk in a courier company. He was clearly depressed about this but needed the money for his family. Gopinath was shocked. 'He was an outstanding pilot, an army colonel and a leader of men. And now he had become an administrative officer. Suddenly it hit me like a ton of bricks that in the whole country there was not a single private helicopter company. The Ambanis and some other corporate magnates owned their own helicopters for their own use or for political patronage, but there was no helicopters available for charter. There was not one private helicopter in the whole of Karnataka, Tamil Nadu, Kerala or Andhra Pradesh. There were a few helicopters in each of Delhi and Maharashtra, but the rest of the country had none. No wonder there were no jobs for helicopter pilots in the private sector. Reform was just coming to India and so I said to Colonel Samuel and a few friends, "Let's set up a helicopter company". I knew there were many uses to which helicopters could be put such as oil support, tourism, medical evacuation, aerial photography, aerial mapping, geophysical surveys for mining and that, given the state of India's roads at that time, there would be great demand. I knew that each of these sectors would get privatized, if not today, then tomorrow. I felt in my bones that either we were already late or that we were a good year ahead of time. I said to myself that if I can get a helicopter by scrounging every rupee, live in a tent like I used to do, and hang on for dear life, this venture could not fail. And so Deccan Aviation was born although it took almost three years to put the team together and get all the licences and, of course, the funding. So I mortgaged our land, our property, everything we had. I got the best people from the army, navy and airforce to join us. In about five years we had about ten helicopters and became the largest helicopter charter company in India. And, more to the point, we were in profit from day one.'

My interview was taking place at the head office of Air Deccan, which was an airline and so I knew Gopinath's helicopter company did not bring me up to date in his entrepreneurial pursuits. I asked what came next. He told me that one day he was flying in a helicopter over the mountains and valleys and villages and noticed below many small airports. He knew one could fly from the first one he came across to Delhi and the second one to Hyderabad but there was no airline connecting the two rural airports. He explained further, 'It seemed to me that if all these people are buying TVs, motorcycles and refrigerators why aren't they buying air tickets? Somehow aviation was outside this consumption boom. And then I realized that it was not accessible to them because planes did not go to their villages or to where they wanted to go. Even the prices were too high. 800 million Indians live in small towns and it is these people we sought to reach through Air Deccan. I discovered that there were 500 airports in the country and many of them were small or medium sized and either not visited at all or were under utilized or in disrepair. I realized to create a viable low-cost airline I needed to go to the government and ask them to spend a little money to repair or ready some of these airports for Air Deccan. If you go and ask the government to spend a billion dollars it won't happen. I just asked them to initially spend a small amount of money on two unconnected airports. Our first flight was from Bangalore to Hubli which is a very small town in our state. But, getting the airports to fly into, is only part of the answer. I needed to get the cost down. We did two things – rationalize on all costs and optimize revenues purely by innovation. We innovated at every phase, from operations to marketing and distribution. To bring down costs of distribution, I needed to eliminate the middleman. So we tied up with post offices, petrol gas stations and grocery shops to make buying a ticket as easy as buying shampoo. And we launched, and from that one flight on the first day, today we're doing 350 flights a day which is the largest number of flights of any Indian airline.' Not too long after completing my interview with Gopinath, Air Deccan merged with Kingfisher Airlines in a 'win win' for both.

As I completed writing this book I heard that Gopinath is getting ready for his next venture – a comprehensive logistics setup along the lines of Fedex. 'Retirement' is clearly not a word in his vocabulary.

Kingfisher Red (www.flykingfisher.com), formerly known as Air Deccan, is based in Bangalore. It is India's first low-cost carrier and merged with and became a subsidiary of Kingfisher Airlines in April 2008. He recently founded **Deccan 360** (www.deccan360.in), an express transportation and logistics company.

"So I did two things. Firstly, I rolled up my sleeves and said I must know everything there is to learn about the pharmaceutical industry. So I taught myself how to make tablets and how to make injections, ... Secondly, my father was a voracious reader, we had a wonderful library on pharmaceutical subjects and I devoured them."

YK HAMIED

Chairman & Managing Director
Cipla

Just before I started interviewing Yusuf Khwaja Hamied on his life story he showed me a grainy old black-and-white photo of two young boys standing side by side for the photo. He asked me if I knew who they were. I didn't. He pointed to the smaller boy and told me that was him. The older boy was the world famous conductor Zubin Mehta who lived next door and became a life-long friend.

Some Indian families (like most families located anywhere) can trace the family tree back a couple of generations. Others, such as YK Hamied's, can trace back much further. Yusuf's father was born in Aligarh in 1898 as the fourth child of well known, but not very prosperous, parents. His father's ancestors were descendants of the reputed Saint or Sufi Khwaja Ahrar of Iran. When and how his grandfather's ancestors came and settled in India is not known, but his great-great-grandfather Khwaja Syed Ahmed Ali was given the title of Naqibul-aulia (member of a Saintly Order) during the time of the last Moghul emperor, Bahadur Shah Zafar. His great-grandfather Khwaja Yakub Ali also received the same title.

Sir Syed Ahmed Khan, his grandfather's uncle, was the founder of the Mohammedan Anglo Oriental College (MAO) which is now the well-known Aligarh Muslim University. It was in the middle of the nineteenth century, that his grandfather Khwaja Abdul Ali shifted his residence to Aligarh from Delhi.

Yusuf's grandmother on his father's side was a direct descendant from Shah Shuja-ul-Mulkh Durrani, Amir of Afghanistan. Prince Mohammed Farrukh Durrani and Prince Mohammed Ahmed Durrani, his grandmother's uncles and many other members of the family, including his great-grandmother, were brought to India as prisoners during one of the British-Afghan wars in Iran in 1839. They lived in Delhi on a pension from the British government. His great-grandmother, Princess Anjum Sultan married Khwaja Mohammed Yusuf who, at that time, was a well-known advocate of Aligarh with a lucrative practice at the Bar.

His great-grandparents on his father's side thus made Aligarh their home, so this was where Yusuf's grandfather was initially educated, including being one of the first students of the MAO College, Aligarh. He then graduated from the Calcutta University and, after qualifying in Law, started practice as an advocate of the Allahabad High Court. Government service was considered a great honour in those days and every educated man had the desire to become a government servant. Yusuf's grandfather gave up his growing practice at the Bar and joined the UP Provincial Service as a Munsif Judge. Government servants were transferred every few years from one town to another so his grandparents, along with all the other children thus had the opportunity of living in several towns in Uttar Pradesh.

But back to more recent times and the story of Yusuf and his parents. The most interesting part of the story started in 1921 being the year that Mahatma Gandhi had given a call to all Indian students to boycott British universities.

'My father had just finished his master's degree in science. He left Allahabad University when Gandhi gave this call and went to Sabarmati Ashram in Gujarat to stay with Gandhi. There he met another young man who had a master's degree from Aligarh University and had also heeded Gandhi's call. My father and this young man became "bosom buddies". His name was Zakir Husain and he went on in later life to become President of India.

'After six months in the ashram, Gandhi met with the two of them and said, "I want you to start a national university." Of course they heeded his request and together established the Jamia Millia University in Aligarh.

'But after a couple of years there, my father said to Zakir, "We can't get ahead in life unless we educate ourselves further, so we had better go abroad and study". Zakir agreed with him and around 1924 Zakir left for Germany to study. My father also wanted to go abroad to study but initially the British would not issue him a visa as they saw him as a left-wing activist closely linked with Gandhi. However, using the connections of my grandfather, they managed eventually to persuade the ambassador to issue a visa.

'In 1925, a year after Zakir, my father left on a boat bound for the UK. However, when the boat stopped in Genoa, my father changed his mind about studying in Britain and thought it would be nicer to join his friends in Germany. He went to the German Consulate in Genoa and somehow persuaded them to issue him with a visa.

'Not long after arriving my father was invited one weekend to join a group of his Indian friends on a picnic to some lake outside Berlin. His friends had told him to meet at the wharf at "halb neun". My father, whose German was still at that time rudimentary, turned up at the lake at 9.30 a.m. Unfortunately "half neun" is actually "8.30". So when he arrived, none of his friends were there.

'He had come all the way to the lake and decided to take the next boat by himself and see if he could catch up with his friends. Now, one of my father's hobbies was card tricks, at which he was pretty good. As he was bored on the boat he started showing a few tricks to the other passengers. After a while quite a crowd had gathered. After doing one of these tricks, a young girl pointed a finger at him and said, "I know how you did that." That woman later became his wife and my mother!'

Like Yusuf's father, his mother also has a very interesting history. She was a Jew from Vilna, Lithuania. Her parents sent her to study in Berlin where her aunt lived. Her aunt had married Arthur Tanzler, a German from Munich who was not only, not Jewish, but he had been an ace pilot in the Luftwaffe in WW I.

'My mother who was an activist at the time, like many Eastern Europeans, introduced my father to communism and the two of them regularly went to the then famous Lenin Club in Berlin. They met in 1925 and got married three times in 1928 – in a mosque in Berlin, in a synagogue in Vilna and a civil ceremony in England!'

I asked Yusuf what his grandparents thought about his father marrying a Jewish girl. 'My grandfather, who was by then a judge in Aligarh, apparently told his friends, "If my son has selected a girl, I know he is right". But you are correct, it was very unusual and my mother told me when they returned to

India in 1928 to meet my father's parents she was "as nervous as hell". What is even more remarkable is that, at that time, all the women in my father's family wore burkha. She changed it all and I can remember my grandfather telling me that my mother became the most loved woman in the family.'

Yusuf's older sister was born in Bombay in 1934 and, in 1936, 'when my mother fell pregnant with me she decided to return to Vilna where I was born on 25 July. The previous year my father had founded Cipla, following some years when he made good money importing sewing machines and typewriters from Germany. But his father's biggest money spinner was importing the drug "Okasa"'. Yusuf told me 'This was the original Viagra – "Okasa silver" for men and "Okasa gold" for women.'

Cipla was not an instant success and in fact it lost money for a number of years. And business was not his father's only passion. His father had been an active member of the freedom movement since he was a young man and Yusuf can remember as a young child meeting famous Indian freedom fighters such as Sardar Patel, Jawaharlal Nehru, Sarojini Naidu, Morarji Desai, and Subhash Chandra Bose who used to come to their home. Politics was in his father's blood and, in 1936, a year after starting Cipla he stood as an independent candidate against a Muslim League (Jinnah) candidate in Mumbai and won. 'My father was a member of the Bombay Legislative Assembly from 1936 up to the day he died in 1972.

'In 1938, my whole family went on a trip to Germany where my father had business. My father saw the "writing on the wall". He tried to persuade all his Jewish friends to leave. He had many such friends as Professors Nearst, Haber and Rothenhiem, all famous scientists. Most of them apparently ignored him by saying something like "Us? We are the elite here. Who is going to touch us?"'

But a dozen or so families did listen to his father. His father stood guarantor for them and arranged visas for them to come to India. 'There was Dr Weinberg, Dr Konarski and Dr Rothenheim as well as my mother's aunt Bertha Tanzler from Berlin.' A few were put in an internment camp in Pune by the British but all survived the war. Following the war, Arthur Tanzler came to India and joined his wife. Somehow he had managed to avoid punishment or death from having married a Jew; probably protected by his reputation in WW I.'

Yusuf then points to a large photo of Gandhi which is in his office. He tells me it is a photo of Gandhi visiting the Cipla factory in Mumbai in 1939. In the picture are Gandhi, his father, Sardar Patel and Sushila Nayar, who later became health minister of India. He tells me, 'Sushila Nayar was responsible for India changing its patent laws in 1972 and which was prevalent till 2005.

'Apparently Gandhi told my father, "I have come to see you because the British have approached me and promised they will give India independence if we help them in their war efforts." Gandhi apparently went on to say that it was getting difficult for the British to get medicines to India and he thus wanted Cipla to supply the British Army with part of its medicinal requirements.' This, Yusuf tells me, 'was the real start of Cipla or, as it was known at that time, Chemical, Industrial and Pharmaceutical Laboratories.'

One of the big product winners was Vitamin B12. Many soldiers became anemic and the treatment for which was B12. B12 is made from liver extracts and at that time the only product was one produced by Bayer called 'Campalon'. Clearly, that could not be used and so Cipla produced liver extract from buffalo and cow livers. The product Cipla produced was called 'Cipalon' and became one of its biggest sellers. Cipla was the largest supplier of anti-malarial drugs at the time – the lead product Qinarsol becoming a household name in the '40s.

We then turn to Yusuf's childhood. 'It was an extraordinarily happy and interesting childhood,' he tells me. He went to the 'Cathedral School' where, despite being a Muslim, he participated in all the Christian services. 'In the late '40s and '50s few were concerned about the differences between religions as it seems so many do today.'

I asked him if he had any particular memories from his childhood. 'One was in 1944 when there was a huge explosion at the docks in Bombay. I was in Kindergarten as I was only eight and I remember vividly how vehicular traffic was immediately banned and I had to walk miles alone going home past blown-out windows in building after building.

'Another story which I cannot forget is the day Gandhi was assassinated in 1948. I was playing cricket in the street with Zubin Mehta whose photo I showed you. Suddenly, one of the servants from my home came running to me and told me to return home immediately. I could tell from his voice something serious had taken place. When I got home my father, mother and sister were gathered around the radio listening to the news of the assassination. We did not know for an hour that he had been actually killed by a Hindu. If, God forbid, he had been killed by a Muslim, can you imagine what would have happened in India? You have no idea.'

I learnt that Yusuf was a serious student. 'Actually I was serious about everything I did. I played seriously. I played cricket for the school. I played football for the school. I played hockey for the school. I was a prefect and a house captain.' I wondered aloud if, coming from a prominent family, meant he felt pressured to be serious and succeed. 'No, not at all,' he assured me 'it was just in my nature.'

A turning point in Yusuf's life occurred in 1953. 'That year my father had become what was known as "the Sheriff of Bombay". The job of the Sheriff was to meet and greet prominent visitors to the city. If the prime minister came to Bombay, it was one of the duties of the sheriff to receive the prime minister. And so that year Lord, then only professor, Alexander Todd came to Bombay and was introduced to my father. He was then professor of Chemistry in Cambridge University.'

At this point Yusuf handed me a speech he gave in 2007 in Lord Todd's honour and asked me to read out the first paragraph. It read 'Lord Alexander Todd was my mentor, philosopher and guide. No person has played a more significant role in directing my life or helping to shape my destiny.'

Yusuf explains these words. 'Professor Todd was already in 1953 one of the world's leading scientists and who later won the Nobel Prize for Chemistry in 1957. Armed with my "O" Level Senior Cambridge results I was taken to a meeting with him by my father. My father asked if there were any special qualifications required for admission to Cambridge University. I can remember him replying to my father, "We have no rules. We admit anyone whom we consider suitable to be a student." He looked at my "O" level results and said, "I'd like you to come to Cambridge." As a young man I did not understand the significance of what he had offered me as very few students are invited to study at Cambridge with only their "O" Levels. Naturally, my father and I accepted his offer although, even though my family was relatively well-to-do, it was extraordinarily difficult for my father to find the money to send me to Cambridge.'

In 1954, Yusuf was admitted to Christ's College at Cambridge where his first introductory meeting to the college was with Dr Lucan Pratt who was then the Senior Tutor. 'Dr Pratt was a remarkable man. A medical doctor. He had been in the British Army during the war. He was above all a great sports lover. If you were a sportsman he would get you into the college. All the leading rugby, football players and cricketers were in Christ's College.

'I met Dr Pratt not so long ago, almost forty years after my last meeting with him in 1966. We used to send each other Christmas cards over the years but never met. How did I come to meet him after all these years? Well, last year I started a charitable foundation called the Farida and Yusuf Hamied Foundation. The young English solicitor who was given the job of drafting the trust deed could see that Christ's College was mentioned in the document and told his law firm partner that his grandfather had been Senior Tutor of Christ's College. He was Dr Pratt's grandson. I asked the grandson, Ben Habershon, to arrange a meeting with his grandfather last year. He was 100 years old. He lived on his own as his wife had died. He cooked for himself. He washed his own clothes. He took me around his garden and he could still remember every plant by its Latin name. I thought he looked completely unchanged in forty years. Believe me, the two or three hours I spent with him was like going back in time forty years. Following my meeting with him, I hosted a dinner for him in Christ's College, Cambridge and I invited over 100 of his old students who came. It was a nostalgic but memorable evening.

'And later this year [2008] I am hosting a dinner for over 100 people honouring the birth centenary of Lord Todd because I am very friendly with his family and I donated a room in the Chemistry Laboratory in Lensfield Road which is called the "Todd Hamied" seminar room.'

I asked him what it was like studying in Cambridge in those years. 'What helped me was, when I joined Cambridge in 1954, I was eighteen whereas all my classmates, the English, were twenty. They had all done two years' compulsory National Service after leaving school. When classes started, the teachers went back a little to help them because they had not been studying for two years. That's what saved me. And believe me, the first two years I found very difficult.

'But by the grace of God when the final results of the Natural Sciences Tripos, Part 2, came out in 1957 I had come in the top ten which entitled me to a "First Class Honors" degree. That was when I was invited by Lord Todd to continue my studies and do a doctorate in chemistry under his supervision. This I agreed to do and I was among the first research students to work at the then new Lensfield Road laboratories. It was also in 1957 that Lord Todd was awarded the coveted Nobel Prize.

'He was a humble man. He used to cycle to my digs and say, "Yusuf, you must be alone. Come and have X'mas lunch with me and the family." I am not seeing that nowadays among the so called politicians and the academics. That humility is not there. One of the many things I learnt from him is the importance of humility. Here my door is always open to any of our staff. Anyone in the company can come in and sit and talk to me about his or her problems.'

Yusuf worked with Todd and was awarded his PhD before he was twenty-four years old. 'Then in 1960 the college offered me a fellowship but I had come to the conclusion there were many more able chemists than me and that my future lay outside academia. However, I was still interested in doing some post-doctoral research. Lord Todd met me and asked me what I wanted to do. I told him, "Sir, I am still young, I do not want to go home and work." So he asked me if I would like to go and work in Germany as my father had done. I replied that that seemed a wonderful idea.

'I remember it today as though it was yesterday. He picked up the phone and rang Germany and said, "Adolf, this is Alexander." The "Adolf" he was speaking to was Professor Adolf Butenandt who, prewar had been Germany's leading scientist in Steroid Chemistry, and at this time was director of the Max Planck Institute in Munich. It was as simple as that. No interview, just Todd's one phone call and all was arranged.'

Shortly after Yusuf left for Munich to meet Professor Butenandt, Butenandt had won the Nobel Prize in 1939 and so it was a great honour to be invited to work with him. However, the meeting took an unexpected turn. 'He told me I would be working with him on the colouring matter of butterflies' eyes. He took me to the lab and showed me my bench space and told me the lab opened at 8.00 a.m. and closed at 6.00 p.m. and he expected me in the lab during those hours. My research life in Cambridge was very different. We could come and go as we pleased having a key to enter and close the lab where we worked. I asked Professor Butenandt what would happen if I came at 9.00 a.m. He told me my bench space could have been utilized by others. I asked him whether I could work late at night as was my preference and habit at Cambridge. To this he emphatically replied in the negative. I really don't know why but this really upset me so I said to Professor Butenandt, "Thank you very much, Sir but I have decided that I don't want to work here." I turned and walked out. I rang Lord Todd to tell him what I had done. I don't think it shocked him and it certainly did not affect our friendship. That's when I decided to come home and sent a telegram to this effect to my father. Believe it or not my German experience lasted two days. In retrospect, I feel sorry because I didn't learn German and perhaps the German training might have done me good. I really don't know.'

If Yusuf had been put off by the bureaucratic inflexible approach of Professor Butenandt he had a shock waiting for him in India. Cipla was a public company and in that time of the licence, if one was related to a director then the government set one's salary. 'Cipla put in an application in 1960 for me to be employed as a Research and Development Officer. The approval came back a year later in 1961! So, for one year I worked in Cipla without receiving any salary.

'You have no idea of what the conditions were like in those days. One went through hell. My approval letter said my salary was to be Rs 1500 a month for three years and that the company should apply again in three years. This was a salary of about USD 40 per month.'

I wondered how easy it would have been for him being the founder's son. 'It was indeed a difficult period for me. The employees looked at me suspiciously not knowing what to expect. Cipla at that time was very small and, given the experience I had had in Cambridge, there was no one in the company to teach me. In the pharmaceutical industry, I was self-taught. Genuinely, I am not boasting or bragging.

'So I did two things. Firstly, I rolled up my sleeves and said I must know everything there is to learn about the pharmaceutical industry. So I taught myself how to make tablets and how to make injections, which is what Cipla was doing. Secondly, as my father was a voracious reader, we had a wonderful library on pharmaceutical subjects and I devoured them.'

I asked him about his relationship with his father. 'My father had many interests outside Cipla, such as his membership of the Legislative Assembly and membership of the governing body of the Council for Scientific and Industrial Research which he himself had founded in 1942. He left a lot of the senior management in Cipla to run things as they wished. This upset me as I had different ideas and a different work ethic. I would have got rid of these people but my father said to me, "Son, in my lifetime they have been with me. In the last few years of my life please don't change things." Being the dutiful son, I complied with his request.

'But I had to find ways to release the tension and grow the business. One of the things was the manufacture of raw materials for the pharmaceutical industry. In the few months of learning after I joined Cipla, I came to the conclusion that the backbone of the pharma industry was not making tablets but producing the active raw materials that go into the tablets. So we started doing that.' Cipla were the pioneers of the basic raw material manufacture in the Indian pharma industry.

Secondly, in the early '60s the pharma industry was totally dominated by the large multinational houses. India in 1960-61 followed the patent laws of Britain of 1911 whereas Britain had significantly changed and updated its patent laws in 1949. 'Everything I wanted to do was blocked. The only window was steroids and hormones because they were discovered much earlier in 1940s and the patents had expired. And that's what I started manufacturing in India. The hormones – sex hormones – because India, even at that time, needed family planning.'

The same year of 1961, Yusuf and a number of like-minded Indians started the Indian Drug Manufacturers Association with one single purpose in mind – to change India's patent laws. It took them eleven years and Indira Gandhi to do so. 'The big multinationals looked down upon us. Even at that time we said, "Look, we respect patent laws but we don't respect monopolies. We need a patent law which is based on the needs of India."'

We had not yet talked about whether he had ever found time to marry. 'Yes I married a girl from Bombay.' He proudly showed me her photo. 'Her family was in the film business. Her father was AR Kardar who was the leading film producer and director in the '40s.' I asked him how he met her. 'Our parents were friends. New Year's dinner was always at my family home and they told their friends to bring their daughters with them. We met in 1961 and were engaged and married in the same month of April 1963. My mentor, Lord Todd, announced our engagement on 31 March 1963 and my father's old friend, Zakir Husain, the then vice president of India, came for the wedding on 12 April 1963.'

My meeting with Yusuf continued for several more hours with him regaling me with wonderful stories of his life experiences. Unfortunately, there is not enough space in this small book for them all but I have set out a couple more.

The first relates to the patents. Sometime in 1967, Yusuf went to see Mr Ramachandran, who was not only a close friend, but was also the head of India's FDA which controlled drug usage. When he arrived he was told to wait as his friend had guests. 'Shortly after, I saw four English gentlemen leave his room. On going in I found him in a foul mood. He said to me, "Yusuf, what do you know about ampicillin? The four gentlemen who I just met are directors of Beecham and they have come to seek a licence to import ampicllin which, as you know, they invented and for which they hold a patent in many countries. Our country desperately needs ampicillin given it is a life-saving antibiotic but, when I asked them what price they wanted to sell it in India, they told me Rs 8 per tablet. Yusuf, I was shocked because I know they sell these tablets for Rs 2 in England. I asked them why should India pay more than what the English paid for the drug. They then gave me some "cock and bull" story about recovering the cost of research and so on. I told them I would give permission for it to be imported by them if they sold it at Rs 2 per tablet. Yusuf," he said angrily, "they turned me down. Can you import ampicillin? If you can import and sell it for Rs 2 per tablet I will give Cipla the licence." I asked him to give me some time to investigate. I quickly found an Italian company, Ankerfarm, which produced ampicillin in Italy which, at that time, did not have any patent laws. I found I could import and sell it for Rs 2 per tablet but would not make any money as we had to pay 100 per cent duty on the imported raw material and Cipla had no brand name in the market for this drug. However, I believed this was a big opportunity and went back and told Mr Ramachandran that Cipla would do it. We got the licence. Predictably not long after selling the drug under the generic name ampicillin I received a legal notice from Beecham threatening action for breaching their patent rights. With this legal notice I went to meet Mr Ramachandran. I was young in those days, lots of energy and said, "Sir, this is a legal notice, what do I do?" He told me I should tell them to come and see him. "But what can you do?" I asked him. He replied clearly, "If they come to me I will tell them that if they pursue this legal notice I will revoke their manufacturing licence in India for McLean's toothpaste, for Eno's fruit salt and for one or two other drugs that they make."

'So I replied to Beecham that I was coming to the UK in a few months and that I would like to meet them to discuss their letter. That summer in 1968 I went to Beecham's head office in Great West Road in London and met with a number of their directors. They told me in no uncertain terms that I had to stop the manufacture of ampicillin as I was breaching their patent.

'I suspected one or two of the people in the meeting were amongst those who had met Mr Ramachandran on the day I did and asked if that was so. It was. I told them I had been to see Mr Ramachandran about their letter to me and that he had asked me to convey to Beecham he would like to see them again. "Why?" they asked. I said that he had told me why, but it was better it came from him than me. They pressed me to tell them what Mr Ramachandran would say to them. So I told them. I then went on "Gentlemen, we can do two things."

'I said, "I believe there is a solution. As you know I am legally buying ampicillin from Ankerfarm. They are selling this to me at USD 450 per kilo. I am willing to buy from you for the same price and, if you agree to supply Cipla on an ongoing basis, I will never try and stop you from coming to India to sell ampicillin as and when you wish to import and sell it." I left the room with an order for 200 kilos of ampicillin and the threatened action was withdrawn.'

I asked him what involvement the family now had in Cipla. 'The family currently controls 40 per cent of the shareholding of Cipla but it is run by professionals. You may not believe me but until 1996 we were really paupers. Prominent, well respected, but really paupers personally. I could sit and invite 1000 people to an office function but, until 1996, the highest salary an individual could be paid was Rs 15,000 per month, say USD 400. This amount was fixed by the Company Law Board. You were taxed more than 40 per cent on that salary. Worse than that was a 2 per cent wealth tax paid on whatever you were worth on 31 March each year even though this may not have been realized. Until I was sixty, I had a negative income as I was paying 2 per cent wealth tax on my shareholding value in Cipla which was a lot more than Rs 15,000 a month.'

I asked him how he survived. 'It was very difficult. One had to rely on the company paying for as many expenses as legally possible. In addition, we were allowed to draw around USD 200 per day when we travelled for exports. So I lived on that USD 200 per day. This led to me becoming a non-resident Indian later and to maintain this I need to spend more than six months outside the country. As my wife and I have no children this is not difficult for us to do.'

The final story relates to AIDS. It started in 1991 when Dr Rama Rao came and saw Yusuf. He was Research Head of a government laboratory in Hyderabad, as well as being a consultant to Cipla. He said, 'Yusuf, I have developed a synthesis of AZT.' AZT at that point in time was the only monotherapy drug for HIV. Yusuf went to see Dr Tripathi, then the head of the Indian Council of Medical Research (ICMR). Dr Tripathi told Yusuf the government would like Cipla to manufacture AZT.

'I said, "Why us?" He told me, "Because I know you are the only person who will take up the challenge." So we started producing in 1991 and marketing it in 1993. At that time, the only people making AZT internationally was Burroughs Welcome. Their price was USD 12 a day. We put it on the market in India at USD 2 a day. For six months we had zero sales. I went back to Dr Tripathi and told him we had no sales. I asked him if the government would distribute it. He replied that the government only had money for detection and prevention but not for treatment. I turned around and semi abused him. I said, "Why on earth didn't you tell me that two years ago as I then would not have invested?" We stopped the project in 1993 and had to throw away about 200,000 capsules. I forgot all about it until a few years later in 1995-96 while doing some reading, I came across a report called the "Haart" report indicating that a cocktail of drugs retarded HIV. That rekindled my interest. On 28 September 2000, I was invited to give a talk at the European Union on the HIV/AIDS issue. As I knew the meeting was also being attended by thirty health ministers and half a dozen ex-prime ministers from African countries I decided to make some bold offers. I told the delegates I would offer the cocktail at USD 800 a cocktail if private sector distributors bought it, USD 600 if governments bought it and, if any government wanted to produce their own anti-retroviral drugs, then Cipla would give them the technology for free.

'At that time multinational companies in Africa were marketing the cocktail at USD 12,000 to USD 15,000 so I thought my offer would have a huge impact. For five months nothing happened. No requests from anyone. Then one day, one of my friends from America who is an activist, sent me a message, "If only you could market your cocktail at a dollar a day." This set me thinking and so I called my brother Muku and Amar Lulla and said, "Let's do our homework again. Can we sell our cocktail at USD 1 per day?" We decided we could and on 6 February 2001 we sent an email to Medecin Sans Frontiers to tell them we could supply the cocktail for USD 1 per day. That night I was at a dinner party. At midnight my telephone rang. It was Donald McNeal from the *New York Times*. He has since become a good friend. He asked me if the story was true. I told him it was. He said at the end of our chat, "Yusuf, from tomorrow your life won't be the same." The next day, 7 February 2001, the story was on the front page of the *New York Times* and I can genuinely say that my life has not been the same since.'

As Yusuf walked with me to the lift, being an Australian and knowing Indians' love of cricket, we chatted about the game. Watching test cricket is one of Yusuf's hobbies and he visited the West Indies for the last World Cup where he bought at an auction a cricket bat signed by the then legendary Don Bradman. He told me he was giving it as a seventieth birthday present to that small boy who was in the photo he showed me at the beginning of our meeting and who remains one of his closest friends, Zubin Mehta.

Cipla (www.cipla.com) is one of India's largest pharmaceutical companies in terms of retail sales. Cipla manufactures an extensive range of pharmaceutical & personal care products and has presence in over 170 countries across the world. Cipla's product range includes pharmaceuticals (e.g. for cardiovascular disease, arthritis, diabetes, weight control, depression and anti-AIDS drugs), animal health care products, flavours & fragrances and agrochemicals. Cipla also provides a host of consulting services such as preparation of product and material specifications, evaluation of existing production facilities to meet GMP and definition of appropriate plant size and technologies.

‘Everyone has a God they worship.
I had mine – my father – I worshipped him.
He taught me to have total faith in my capabilities.

He always said you can make your own destiny; your life will be exactly the way you will it to be.’

(Dedication by Shahnaz Husain to her father in her book on health)

SHAHNAZ HUSAIN

Founder & Chairman
Shahnaz Husain Group

I met Shahnaz in her home, in an up-market residential area of Delhi. We met in her drawing room, which I have to say was one of the most striking I have ever been in. Everything in it seemed to be white and, as I looked around, I could see the room contained an absolutely amazing array of objects from sculptures, paintings, masks and even giant stuffed teddy bears.

Shahnaz started by telling me she was born on 5 November 1941 in Hyderabad and, looking back, she realizes what a privileged and happy childhood she had. 'My father became Chief Justice of the Allahabad High Court and had been educated in Cambridge and came from a family of lawyers, whereas my mother was from a conservative and influential Hyderabadi family. My grandfather on my father's side had been Chief Justice of the Hyderabad High Court in Vizag and was then Governor of Nagpur for many years. My father's brother, my uncle, became Chief Justice of India's Supreme Court. On the other hand, my mother's family was a scion of the royal family of the Nizam and was thus well-to-do. My grandfather on my mother's side was a General in the army and, at one time, had been in charge of the Indian Army stationed in Hyderabad.

'My father always said "I do not want the influence of wealth and Hyderabad to tell on your life. I want you to be a normal child. You are a government officer's daughter and must be brought up as one". There is one story which illustrates this.

'My father always made me feel special, but he brought me up in a very strict way. I was very fond of danglers for my ears; just small danglers. I went shopping once and saw a lovely pair of earrings with lots of coloured beads hanging from them. I must have been about twelve years old. I asked my mother whether I could buy these. She said, "go and ask your father". I went to him and said. "Daddy, can I buy these earrings?" His response was to ask me "Baby, do you really need them?" I replied of course that I did not. So he said, "Then you should not buy them. Buy only what is necessary." That lesson has always stayed with me, even though I have not always followed it,' Shahnaz says, chuckling.

I asked Shahnaz to tell me a little about her childhood. 'Not long after I was born, we moved to Lucknow, because of my father's judicial role. As my parents moved back and forth between Lucknow and Hyderabad, my parents put my elder brother, my sister and me into a weekly boarding school in Lucknow, called La Martiniere. All I can remember of it was that it was very British and that most of the children and all of the teachers were British. Another strong memory of my early childhood is that my mother was very much into "purdah". She never prayed five times a day or read the Quran but she was a very good woman. She was very principled and tough, with a strong view of "right and wrong". For example, she felt little girls should be brought up in a very conservative way and should not be exposed to boys until they were married. Never a party could I attend.'

I asked Shahnaz whether this meant she never went to children's parties. 'No, I would go, but my mother would come with me. And we would leave before the party started because my friends might have boys coming. Essentially my mother would take me to the party and I would hand over the present and then we would go home. We were brought up like that – very rigid.

'My only regular outing was walking with my father. There was a long drive from the main gate to the house and I vividly remember chatting with Daddy on those walks to and from the gate and on the little road outside.

'I also remember the wonderful long summer holidays when the whole family would move to Kashmir for two-and-a-half months and sometimes three months each year. During that time, all of us got to spend a lot of time with my mother and father, which made up somewhat for the fact that we did not see a lot of him during term times, as all three of us were boarding.'

I remarked to Shahnaz that with her father's education and her mother being brought up in 'purdah', they seemed like 'chalk and cheese'. Shahnaz agreed that they were very different but 'they had a very lovely balance'. 'He was tough and very British and principled. And she was very Indian, principled and very conservative. She wore a veil when she got married and continued to wear it afterwards until a particular event my mother told me about. She said my father had always been against "purdah" and the wearing of the veil. He told her it was bad for her health as there was no fresh air to breathe,' Shahnaz says, laughing, 'One day, my mother was travelling with my father in my grandfather's train carriage. You see, as my grandfather was the Governor of Nagpur, he had his own white train carriage when he moved about the state. Just before they reached Hyderabad where my grandfather and grandmother were waiting to greet them, my father threw my mother's veil out of the window. So, when she got down from the train she had no option but to be without "purdah". So, that's the day she broke the "purdah" and went into the world.

'There is another lovely story about my grandfather during the time he was Chief Justice. He was a great friend of Motilal Nehru. Whenever Motilal Nehru came to Hyderabad he stayed with my grandfather. At this time Motilal was seen by the British as a revolutionary as he wanted independence for India. My grandfather frequently gave parties in his home to which all the local dignitaries would come, including the British Governor of Hyderabad. Motilal would, of course, attend if he was staying with my grandfather. After one of these parties the British Governor reported to the Delhi government that Chief Justice Mirza Yar Jung, my grandfather, was keeping revolutionaries in his house as guests and that action should be taken against him. In due course he received a letter from the British government in Delhi accusing him of harbouring revolutionaries. This annoyed my grandfather greatly. He immediately wrote a letter to the Nizam of Hyderabad saying, "I understand that you have taken objection to my friend the Honourable Motilal Nehru staying in my house. I herewith attach my resignation because he is my friend and will continue to be my friend and continue to stay in my house. If as Chief Justice I cannot give hospitality to my friend, then I would like to resign." This shocked both the British and Indian establishments as they could not imagine my grandfather would resign over such a thing. A short time later, my grandfather received a letter from the Nizam advising, "you can continue to keep the guest in your house and you need not resign".'

When Shahnaz was ten her father was appointed Chief Justice and the family moved to Allahabad where she attended an Irish convent called 'St

Mary's by Sister Bernard'. 'My father was very concerned about our education as he had had a privileged education himself and wanted to make sure we all had the same opportunities as he did. As you will hear he made a major mistake with mine, that I believe he regretted to the day he died.

'He often used to give me stanzas of Keats and Shakespeare to learn or ask me to compose my own poems. My job was to stand behind him in the bathroom as he was shaving in the morning and recite what I had learnt or written. And he'd say "good" or "bad". He might say "your rhyme is no good, please go and improve it and let's do it again tomorrow morning". I have such happy memories of those times and I know there was a very special and close bond between us. Why he then did what he did has always puzzled me.'

I asked Shahnaz what she meant. 'Oh,' she said, 'Don't you know? He arranged my marriage and at the age of fifteen, I was married. That was the minimum age at that time. I am told, not long after we moved to Allahabad, my husband-to-be came to my Irish school to pick up his friend's sister and saw me come out of school. The next day again he asked his friend if he could again go to pick up his sister. His friend apparently asked him "Why?" to which he replied, "I saw this little girl come out and I think I like her." He then made it a routine to pick up his friend's sister. Subsequently he went to his father and told him, "I have seen a young girl and I want to marry her." His father told his son that he would do some checking. They found out my family's address from the maid who took my sister and me to and from school as my family lived quite a private and conservative life. Most days, as soon as I came out of school, I was put in the family car which had curtained windows and was whisked off home.

'Years later my husband told me how he remembered me staring out through gaps in the curtains. This was true. My sister always sat properly in the car but I always wanted to tear open the curtain so I could clearly see the hustle and bustle of the road. And I always wondered why I could not be part of this outside life.

'The next thing that happened was that my father-in-law brought the proposal of marriage of his son with me, to my father. This was the custom at that time and still remains to this day for many families in India. My father apparently told him, "My daughter is very young and has not completed her education" as I was only in 8th standard. My father-in-law is said to have replied, "She can get all the degrees she wants after she gets married." My husband to be was ten years older than me.

'There was an added complication, as my elder sister who is five years older than me, was not married and I believe my father tried to persuade my father-in-law to have his son marry her and not me. He declined, but my parents made sure my sister was married before me.

'The problem was my mother. She was very particular and told my father, "I know if I don't get her married on time, you will not let her get married and you will take her to London. She will get so educated that she will not come back and will settle down there." And she also realized my father was not a committed Muslim. He always said, "It doesn't matter who you marry or what religion you marry into as they are all the same. Religion is no reason ever for you to think about what to do in life." He was totally into the philosophy of "Deen-E-Ilahi" which believed in the goodness of all religions. To my mother who came from a conservative Muslim family this must have seemed a terrifying prospect. I strongly suspect when this Muslim family wanted me to marry their son she must have pestered my father until he agreed.

'So, my father went to see the Mother Superior and asked her to allow me to sit for the senior Cambridge as soon as possible. Apparently you had to be sixteen to do the exam but somehow my father and the school arranged for me to do the exam when I was fifteen. The results came out six months after I was married. I had stood first in my school.

'From the day I was married I know my father suffered guilt. He told me not long after I was married that, if I had not got married at that time, he would have sent me to London to do law and I can still remember his words "One day you would have become Chief Justice of the International Court in the Hague". And I said to him, "If you didn't educate me how would I have achieved this?" My father only laughed and told me that "Now you are married you need to start some sort of education".'

Shahnaz had a daughter within a year of being married. Her father and Shahnaz were desperate for her to continue with her education. Courses like law and medicine were out of the question. 'I decided that beauty was the best because it gave some kind of relief treatment for falling hair, dandruff, pigmentation, scars and burns. I could be like a paramedical doctor giving relief to people who had problems.'

Not long after she was married her husband was posted to Tehran as India's Director of Foreign Trade for the Middle East. This proved to be a wonderful opportunity as all of the leading beauty schools from Europe had operations there. 'Not long after we arrived in Tehran, I flew to London with my daughter and did a course at Helena Rubenstein. The Indian High Commissioner at that time was a friend of my father's so I was able to stay with them and which made it much easier for me as it was my first time in London.'

Shahnaz and her husband were in Tehran for four-and-a-half years. During that time she completed courses in London and Paris as well as many others, such as with Schwartzkopf in Germany and Lean in Copenhagen.

'During my time in Tehran I made an income from the salon I opened there and from writing in fashion magazines. The salon wasn't actually great because I was only doing a few treatments a day. But I needed all this money to do my studies as the Indian government at that time would only allow you to take out USD 50 for studying abroad. I applied for many jobs in Tehran and all of them turned me down because I was not a graduate, despite the fact I almost certainly had a better education than most of the other candidates. I wrote to my father and told him my problem. He replied, "Baby, I can't help you as I am too far away". But I know it must have increased his guilt in not allowing me to complete my education before marrying me off. Even today I am not a graduate.'

I remarked that this did not seem to have affected her career. She laughed, but one could sense her one major life regret is that she did not go to university as all her father's family had.

'With the small salon and no other job I was getting concerned as the fees for my courses were skyrocketing. Then lady luck played a hand. One night I was at a party and met a British woman and asked her what she did. She said her husband was the editor of the largest Iranian weekly in Tehran, the *Iran Tribune* and that, "In order to entertain myself while I am here I am going to start an English language weekly." She told me she was looking for someone who could write on beauty. As it happened I was already writing articles on beauty for the *Times of India* and sent her some copies. Within half an hour she rang me back to tell me that I had the job.

'Whilst I started out writing on beauty, within a short time I was writing all the stories in the magazine under about twenty different names and my British friend just designed the cover. By the end of my time in Tehran I had taken over the magazine. The magazine proved very profitable. It was very strange as the wheel had turned full circle. When I started in Tehran I had no money at all and wasn't able to pay my fees and when I left Tehran I had a lot.'

After some four years in Tehran her husband was offered one of the top jobs in Iran at that time – to be CEO of Iran Oil. 'We both felt it was an opportunity that he could not turn down. At this time we lived in a large house on top of a hill. It felt like it was our own hill. It felt like we owned a county or something. My business was going fantastically and now my husband was offered a role we could only dream of. Given the importance of the job and the connections we had built up over our time there we were both offered Iranian citizenship.'

Shahnaz had always sought her father's permission for important decisions in her life. Usually Shahnaz says he responded with something like 'go ahead Shahnaz if you think it will make you happy'. So Shahnaz wrote to him asking for his go ahead.

Sometime after writing to her father Shahnaz was having dinner at the Indian ambassador's residence. 'He told me he had received a letter that day from my father and that my father was very disturbed. I told him I had not yet heard from my father to which he replied "you will". Try as I might to find out what my father had written to the Ambassador he would not say. So, two days later I received this letter from Daddy saying, "I have read your letter with great pain and sorrow and I find that the glamour of the West and the gold and the shine and the obvious trimmings of the West have damaged your appreciation of the more important values of life. I understand that you have decided to desert India and settle in Iran. Please remember that, regardless of all the glamour of the West, you were born an Indian, you will die an Indian and you will be buried in the soil of India. If you have any respect and love for your father and your mother you will come straight back."' Shahnaz told me the letter finished even more severely where her father said something along the lines that 'In fact, looking at your letter I am suspicious that my blood doesn't flow in your veins, because if it did you would never desert your country. We are not a family of deserters, but a family of loyalists.' Shahnaz says she cried her heart out after reading the letter and immediately gave marching orders to the entire household and decided to return to India. Her husband went along with her decision.

But to leave Iran was not so simple. There was a twist to having so much money in Iran at that time. The currency was not convertible and was worthless outside the country. But Shahnaz found a solution. 'I bought vast quantities of original French furniture and Iranian rugs. These I could export and sell for cash in India. We tried to buy everything we could before we returned to India. I can remember my husband ringing me and asking if I had spent all the money yet. I told him, "No, but I am trying!"' Shahnaz says with a laugh.

I said I understood on her return to India she had started the business in a large one bedroom home in Greater Kailash, where she converted the verandah into a salon. 'I fitted out the interior with French furniture I brought from Tehran as well as beautiful Persian rugs and furnishings,' said Shahnaz. 'I can remember the press at the time wrote "Shahnaz Husain has opened a store in India that you only read about in books". I must say it was stunning for that time. Like a bit of Paris in India.

'When I came back to India I found I couldn't look my father in the eye. The first time I met him on my return I put in front of him a string of diplomas I had earned during my time away. There were about fifteen of them from the most famous beauty salons in New York, Paris, London and Copenhagen amongst other cities. I said to my father, "Daddy, you were always worried that you didn't make the right decision when you got me married when I was fifteen as I was uneducated. Look at this letter I have just received from the *Guinness Book of World Records* asking whether I am the highest qualified cosmetician in the world at my age."'

Her father told her he was happy for her success and that he had always wanted to ensure she had an education so that she could look after herself and not depend on others for her survival. 'He was very keen on an Urdu saying, which goes something like "*kisi ke saamne haath na phailaana padey*" (you must not beg to live).

'My father was a very highly principled man – very tough to understand – but highly principled. I could tell he was not overly impressed with what I had achieved in Iran and all the diplomas I had earned and asked him why. He asked me if I had planned anything for my spiritual benefit. "Please remember", he told me, "that you can't feed the mind by starving the soul. You will never ever be happy if you only work for your own personal benefit and not give to anybody else. Remember you are sent to this world by God, so apart from the fact that you must justify your existence to him, you have an obligation every day to try and make somebody else's life worthwhile." He went on at some length to give me a lecture as he clearly felt my life was missing the spiritual element. He told me, "We are in this world for a very short while. This is a temporary world. Beyond this world there is a permanent life. Have you made any arrangements for that life? You are making all the arrangements for this world. You have made no plans for the after world." I replied to him that I was very young and had plenty of time to build my spiritual life. This didn't satisfy him and he then did something I will remember to my dying day. He said, "Baby, you look so confident that you have lots of time." He then rang the bell and called the servant and asked him to get a torch. He shone the torch on my face and asked me, "Do you see how bright the light is?" I replied that naturally I did. He then said, "Who knows when there could be a mechanical failure," and with that he switched the light off. He said, "Start now!"

'This shook me and I started thinking about what I could do. I came up with this idea of Shamute for deaf and dumb people. For some reason a lot of deaf and dumb people had been coming to me for a job as in the beauty profession one does not have to talk to the clients. I went to my father and asked him what I should do. He suggested I should open a school to train these people for a career in the profession. He added, "And make sure you do a proper job of it." He was always serious about everything he did.

'So I established Shamute and started taking students. After it had been going successfully for about ten years, I thought it would be good to provide an example to other entrepreneurs of what was possible in terms of helping India's handicapped. I decided to try and get as much publicity as possible and, as my uncle at that time was Chief Justice of the Supreme Court of India, he was able to arrange for me to meet the then President of India, Zail Singh. I asked him if he would be prepared to come to Shamute and inaugurate it officially. His presence raised the profile of the handicapped in India and demonstrated how even a small business like mine could make a difference to their lives. Sadly, my father did not live to see the official opening but I felt he was there in spirit and would have been proud that I had heeded his advice. Shamute has in recent years expanded to provide training to the blind.'

Shahnaz has two children; a daughter, Nelofar born, as mentioned above, a year after she was married and a son, Sameer, born sixteen years later. Her daughter is involved in the business, as is her grandson, Sharik who also joined in the last couple of years. I asked her whether she has tried to bring her children up in a similar fashion to her own childhood and whether she believed in the concept of arranged marriages. 'I am sure I could have been a more attentive mother. When you are skimming on the waves of a certain kind of success you can be so heady that you miss the finer values of life. And you go on missing them, not because you want to, but you get used to missing them. You don't miss what you don't have because you are not having the time for it. As for arranged marriages I don't believe they are the right way to go for modern India and increasingly I believe they will become less popular. It's very simple when you are young, you take what you get. When you are older, you get what you want. If you don't like a man, then that's it. A "no" is a "NO". However, when you are young you are not given an option. I remember the way I was married. I was playing some game outside and my mother called me and said, "This is the picture of the boy you are going to marry". I said "ok" and went back out to play.'

Despite her own marriage being arranged and that she married at such a young age it was my understanding it had been a happy marriage. 'Certainly that is so; he never stopped me from achieving my vision. In fact, he made me what I am today because if he had "put a spoke in the wheel" I would not be where I am. However, I think he learnt early on in our marriage that I was a very strong-willed person and that stopping me from doing something I was determined to would have been difficult for the relationship. In order to be stopped, you must think that you can be stopped. That idea never even entered my mind. Even today if I want to do something, nobody can stop me.

'That should apply to every woman in India. If a woman in achieving her goal and what makes her happy, does not hurt anyone in doing so, then I don't think a husband should have the right to stop her. Then he does not love her. And if they don't love you, they don't deserve your love and you don't need to listen to them. It's as simple as that.'

One can feel the energy emanating from Shahnaz. I wondered if she had any time for hobbies or friends. 'When I'm very stressed I write poetry. That's the only hobby I have and I have had that since my childhood. But I must say I enjoy Indian music and, particularly ghazals, which are romantic soft Urdu songs. My servants are trained to play ghazals on my sound system from the time I walk into the house. I find it very soothing. I guess the only other non-work activity I enjoy, although I would not call it a hobby, is dancing.' 'Dancing,' I said 'that does not sound like you.' She laughed and told me, 'You know after my husband died I remarried Mr Raj Kumar Puri, a lovely Indian gentlemen who was born in England and we both love dancing. But, you may find this strange; I only dance with my husband. That I have done all my life. I have never danced with anybody else. There was this professor from Harvard who I took out to dinner. He asked me whether I would dance with him and I said, "No, I only dance with my husband". He then said to me, "How have you reached where you are with these kind of principles?" I told him,' Shahnaz says with a chuckle, 'I don't need to dance with the world to reach where I am and can do it fine without dancing. Everyone should have certain principles that they stick to.

'As for friends, one has to ration one's time between friends and family. One's family has the right first and only then one's friends. You can't have friends first and then family. The family has a right over you. Friends also have a right, but that's stage two.' I said to Shahnaz with her lifestyle I was surprised she found time for 'stage one' to which she replied, 'No, you have to make the time. You don't have it. You have to make and plan it.'

By now I had taken a large slab of Shahnaz's time and felt we should draw our interview to a close. As a final question I asked Shahnaz what beauty advice she had for young Indian women. Her response was interesting, given she owns and markets India's leading ayuvedic beauty product range. 'I think cosmetics help only 20-30 per cent, 70-80 per cent is internal fitness and body health. I don't think a beautiful woman is only someone who has a beautiful face. A beautiful woman in my definition must have "brain power" which is intelligence combined with "beauty power" which is physical looks and also spiritual power. If a woman is a good human being it will show in her eyes. If she has brain power she can talk to you intelligently and be a pleasure to be with. A woman who has just physical beauty can walk in and walk out and tomorrow she will be forgotten. A woman with all the three qualities I have mentioned will be unforgettable.'

Ever the consummate marketer, Shahnaz noted my Australian accent and said as I was leaving, 'I recently spoke to your Prime Minister John Howard when he was in India and suggested to him that Australia import Shahnaz Husain Ayurvedic sun block as you have a lot of skin cancer in your country.' Just before we got to the front door Shahnaz suggested we have a photo together. One of her assistants took a couple of photos. I thought nothing more about it but next morning when one of my colleagues, Justin Shmith and I had breakfast with her grandson, Sharik, there amongst a goodie bag full of Shahnaz Husain cosmetics, including of course several bottles of sun block, was a lovely framed photo of Shahnaz and me from the day before. I was left in no doubt as to why she has succeeded in her chosen profession!

The **Shahnaz Husain Group** (www.shahnaz.in) is India's leading company in the field of natural beauty and anti-aging treatments. Started in the 1970s by Shahnaz Husain in New Delhi, the group has over time vertically integrated to encompass every aspect of ayurvedic care and cure. The group has activities as diverse as beauty training institutes, growing of its own herbs, to manufacturing of its cosmetics line, to retail, to specialized treatments through its chain of over 400 beauty centres worldwide.

"Then it was a different passion that drove me to work. Today, we look at business in a more holistic fashion where we don't have the time to get into many elaborate details. During those days, I knew each and every employee's name. I used to meet everybody everyday because I was on the floor for most of the time."

BN KALYANI

Chairman & Managing Director
Bharat Forge

I met BN Kalyani at the head office of Bharat Forge in Pune. Kalyani has built Bharat Forge into one of the largest forging business in the world and accordingly, as I expected, the headquarters seemed to run like clockwork. My meeting started on the dot of the appointed time.

Babasaheb Neelkanth Kalyani was born on 7 January 1949 in Kole, a small village near the town of Karad in west Maharashtra, about 150 kilometres south of Pune. His father was a progressive farmer and was involved in establishing the first sugarcane cooperatives in Maharashtra. Kalyani is the eldest in the family and has a younger sister and brother.

'We were the most well-to-do family in Kole which had a population of less than a thousand people. When you go to villages in India you will find many people have farms of about 2 or 5 and at best 10 acres. So if you have a farm of about 50 acres which my family had, then you are reasonably well off. But, of course when you look at it from an industrial activity point of view, then there is no comparison.'

I asked him about his life in the village as a child. 'It was very simple and nice. We were very naive about life in cities. The first time I went to a big city like Pune when I was about seven or eight years old. I thought I was in a different world. I felt the same way when I went to the US for the first time when I was twenty-one. Pune seemed very different for many reasons, including the fact there were many cars which were, at that time, quite rare in the villages.

'When I was about six years old, my father put me into a boarding school because there weren't any good schools in our area. He wanted me to get a good education so he put me into an army school in Belgaum called King George Royal Indian Military College which was later re-named King George's School. It was a tough life. Most of the children were sons of military officers and the remaining few from civilian families like mine.

'The routine was pretty tough – like a typical military school. We woke up to the sound of the bugle every morning at five. We had physical training for an hour from 6 to 7 a.m., followed by a cold shower, breakfast and then classes started at 8.30 a.m. The good thing about boarding schools is there are a lot of extra-curricular activities like sports, drama and elocution contests and public speaking. One gets a fairly well-rounded personality and disciplined upbringing.

'It did, however, take me some years to get used to the life and there were plenty of tears when I had to go back to school at the end of the holidays. I vowed I would never do that to my children. I have one son and I would rather have him with me and teach him whatever we could within the family. There were needless to say some good sides to it as it brought a lot of discipline into my life and gave me a different perspective.

'I was lucky as we had a very good headmaster; one of the best you can find in a boarding school. When I look back today, I realize that it was he and other teachers at that school who moulded my character rather than my parents.

'I was home for two months a year. It was a lot of fun those days because you make up for the lost time and my mother used to spoil me rotten.

'I was an average student in school. I was not brilliant, but I took part in a lot of activities; I played cricket and hockey, acted in plays and participated in elocution competitions.' Kalyani laughed when I told him a lot of young people reading this book would be pleased to hear he was an average student which meant there is hope for them to succeed in business too!

As it happens Kalyani was the only child in the family to go to boarding school; as, by the time came for his brother to go, the family had moved to Pune where there were better schools than in the village.

I asked why the family had moved to Pune. 'My father had decided to go into business at the instigation of some of his friends. At this time, my father was not only very involved in the sugarcane cooperative but also local politics. It's quite normal in this country for a prominent citizen of a village or a little town to get involved with everything that is happening.'

He told me the objective of the sugarcane cooperative was like cooperatives all over the world – to get better prices for their products. 'There was no intermediation in those days, not like today. So all the big traders would come in from all over the country and buy your goods for "peanuts".'

Kalyani graduated from military college in 1964 and then did a five-year engineering degree in Pilani in Rajasthan. 'In fact I did engineering because my father was already in the planning stage of establishing the Bharat Forge business and, in those days, it was expected that the son would go into the father's business. Fortunately, I was extremely excited by the prospect.

'I can also remember as a small boy I had a mindset for mechanical things. I enjoyed doing such things as tightening nuts and bolts. Even when I was around eight or nine years old I could dissemble and reassemble my bicycle and repair it. I did this very often with many things. I also used to build model airplanes and somehow I am sure my parents noticed this because they never forced on me something in which I had no interest or aptitude.'

It seems life in Pilani was better than boarding school but not too much, I observed. 'It was tough being far from home. In Pilani, we were in the middle of the Rajasthan desert. In summer, it was around 45°C and during winter it was around 0°C. Delhi was five hours away by bus and, other than the campus, there was nothing around for a 100 kilometres, not even a movie theatre.'

During his holidays he would come back to Pune and help with the construction of Bharat Forge. 'I was fascinated by the big machines and the workers would let me drive forklift trucks and move things around.'

Kalyani graduated from Pilani in 1970. 'My father asked me if I would like to study further in the US. I didn't want to miss out on that opportunity, as I had heard a lot about higher education in the US. I sat for my exams and was accepted into three or four good schools. In the end I chose MIT where I did a master's in engineering.'

I reminded him of what he had said earlier about going to the US for the first time. 'Yes, the only difference being I went to the US on my own. When my son went to the US to study engineering, we went to drop him there to make sure he was comfortable in school and, after his first year, I bought him a car. When I went to US MIT, nobody came to drop me.'

I commented that surely it was exciting. 'It was exciting, but there was also the fear of the unknown, going into a new country and not knowing what to expect. I was more excited than nervous. I think the excitement was mainly because I was going to MIT which was a very well-known name in India and considered to be one of the best engineering schools in the world. The two years I spent at MIT were fantastic. I did well in my studies and also did some research work. I enjoyed my extra-curricular activities and made lots of friends. I even bought my first car with my own money, with my salary from being a research and teaching assistant.'

I asked how his father got to be involved in the forging business. 'He had two financial partners: the Kirloskars, an industrial family in Pune, who originally came from a village near ours and the Raja of Kolhapur, Chatrapati Shahaji II Bhosle. Kolhapur was the biggest princely state of India during British rule. Apparently, my father met Mr Kirloskar one evening for dinner. Mr Kirloskar asked him if he wanted to do something in the industry as he didn't see much opportunity in being a farmer. The Kirloskar family had at that time just started making agricultural diesel engines but had difficulty in getting a supplier of crank shafts and connecting rods for engines. Mr Kirloskar asked my father if he would be willing to manufacture these components. Whilst my father was not an engineer, he leapt at the opportunity and gathered around him the right people, got the right advice and found a company in Cleveland that could provide technology. That's how he built Bharat Forge.'

As I understood it, even the original factory was large requiring a significant number of foreign experts. I thought doing this in 1965 must have been a huge risk for his father and his investors. Kalyani affirmed that was indeed the case. 'Everything that could go wrong went wrong. For example, when my father first ordered the equipment the exchange rate was Rs 4 to the USD but, before he could pay, the government devalued the Rupee to Rs 8 to the USD. Not only this, but the government increased the import duty from 100 to 150 per cent. You can imagine what that did to the finances! There were also technical problems and issues in integrating the Indian management and foreign experts. But he worked through all these issues. He also had start up problems. It is a technology related business and not having a technical background created many problems. He had problems integrating the Indian management with the American expats, which was an everyday battle; but he saw it all through.'

There were some important developments to offset these increased costs and one of these was that the Indian automotive industry was just emerging. So, in addition to supplying parts to the Kirloskars, the Bharat Forge factory was able to supply the Tatas who had just established an automotive plant in Pune.

'I joined the business in February 1972 and got married to my wife, who was from Bangalore, in the previous month. Our families knew each other well.'

I told him I understood that in his first years he had felt like he had been 'thrown in the deep end of the swimming pool.' 'Indeed, there were a lot of problems and the plant was not making profits but losing money.

'Things were just not coming together. There were a lot of technology and leadership problems as well. I started as an engineer at the lowest level in the sales department. I became increasingly impatient and after a couple of months told my father I was not happy with how sales were being handled. He took me to see SL Kirloskar who at that time was chairman of the Board and a successful industrialist. Mr Kirloskar was very fond of me. Being a close family friend I often used to meet him in his house and have dinner with him. The Kalyani and Kirloskar families have known each other for four generations so there is a close and trusting relationship. He listened to my concerns and turned to my father and said, "I will support him and you too will support him". By the third month, I had become head of sales, which gave me the opportunity to implement my ideas and get business for the company. Within three months, we landed more business than the company could handle. I then turned my mind to the production problems, where the solutions came to me intuitively because of my training and my involvement in the plant since the beginning.

'Once again my father took me to see Mr Kirloskar. Just as you said, he told my father "the only way he's going to learn is put him in the water; he'll learn to swim". By September 1972, I was General Manager of the company and we have never lost money since that year.'

I wondered how this sudden rise was seen by his father and the employees. 'Certainly a lot of the general managers were up in arms against me and left the company. There was a lot of talk about how I was a brat kid just returned from the US with no experience. But I was confident I was right. Many of the employees my father had employed were used to the "licence raj" way of doing things. They did not take their jobs seriously and were incredibly slow at doing any task. I was young and impatient. I could see the potential and wanted results quickly.'

I wondered whether he had a 'thick skin' to guard himself from the negative comments. 'No, I was very sensitive to all of this but I was confident I was doing the right thing and was getting the results to prove it. In the first half of the year I was made General Manager, I was able to double the business. In the second year I doubled it again and in the third year doubled it again. So by the end of the third year people stopped talking and started to follow suit. I was "hands on" and, by the time I went home in the evening, my clothes were black with oil.'

I asked Kalyani what he thought his strengths were. 'I think I provided in the early days two things. First, leadership was missing. In those days, leadership was very important because the whole business model in India and our company at that time depended on using moderate technology and capital with a lot of labour. In 1972, we had about 1800 employees producing a turnover of USD 1 million. In 1975, we had a turnover of USD 8 million with the same number of people. Today, in this plant we have 3500 people and turnover about USD 700 million dollars. Leadership was very important in the early days because we had to gain the support of the workers and, just as important, the trade unions. You had to be a very strong leader to get any organized activity in place. My second strength was implementing new technology into the company and which has come very naturally to me to date. I am confident I can hold my own against any engineer in this business. I kept improving the technology we used and, with the right leadership, a much clearer management processes evolved, which led to success. Success breeds success. I've seen that if you keep doing well, your people are motivated, charged up and are ready to work 24 hours a day with you. It's an engine that just keeps going.'

I wondered if he was a 24/7 owner. 'Yes, I certainly was in those early years. Now I work about 60 or 70 hours a week. Then it was a different passion that drove me to work. Today, we look at business in a more holistic fashion where we don't have the time to get into many elaborate details. During those days, I knew each and every employee's name. I used to meet everybody everyday because I was on the floor for most of the time.

'The typical family manufacturing business in the 1970s days consisted of an office or business headquarters located in some big city like Mumbai or Delhi with the factory located in the interior. The owners rarely visited the plant. It was different for us because our office and plant were located in the same place.

'I now travel twenty days a month because 75 per cent of our business today is outside India. We have three companies in Germany, one each in Sweden and Scotland, two in China, and one in the US.'

I wondered what his strategy is with all of these overseas acquisitions. 'We were indeed the first Indian company in the manufacturing sector to create a global strategy. We went and got businesses outside India, to create a footprint in those markets as a means to acquiring customers, technology and a front end. I started the strategy in 1997 but our first acquisition was when we bought a small business in Leeds in 2000.'

I asked whether the idea is to move the manufacturing plant of the acquisition to India. 'For the first acquisition that was our aim because the company wanted to close down the business and do a residential development with the site. The next businesses we bought we didn't move anything here. I kept everything there and started expanding them. We use the footprint and customer acquisition process to expand our business from here by supplying them. As a result we have got the best of both worlds. I've got a very large presence in Europe. We are the largest forging manufacturer there today.

'You may be interested to know that sometime ago a friend and I attended a seminar on entrepreneurship conducted by a Harvard professor. He emphasized in his talk that one should stick to one's core business and asked each of the participants what their core business was. My answer was obvious but my friend said his core business was creating new businesses. I don't think there is anything wrong with that answer in a country like India is today but, for me, I have decided to stick to my focused area of manufacturing forgings because I am not looking at it just from an Indian perspective but from a global perspective. I had one goal and that was to make Bharat Forge the largest global forging company. It is a dream that we have achieved but there are many more challenges before us to which we have diligently applied ourselves.'

Bharat Forge (www.bharatforge.com), the flagship company of the USD 2.4 billion Kalyani Group, manufactures various forged and machined components for the automotive and non-automotive sector. Since commencement of operations in 1966, BFL has achieved several milestones and is today among the largest and technologically most advanced manufacturer of forged & machined components. As one of India's emerging multinationals, the company has manufacturing operations across twelve locations and six countries – four in India, three in Germany, one each in Sweden, Scotland, US & two in China. Its customers include the top five passenger car & top five commercial vehicle manufacturers in the world. The list includes virtually every automotive OEM and Tier I companies.

"Leadership is like travelling on a road at night with a visibility of 100 metres."

HABIL KHORAKIWALA

Chairman
Wockhardt

Habil Khorakiwala was born in Mumbai on 22 September 1942. He is the eldest of three boys and spent all of his childhood and formative years in Mumbai where he was educated at Bharda New High School, not more than a few minutes walk from home. His family is one of a handful of large Muslim business houses in India today. 'There are hardly three or four Muslim business houses; you can count them on one hand.'

His grandfather's brother, his great uncle, started the famous Akbarally's Department store around 1896 which continues to this day. '"Akbarally" was my great uncle's first name, as our family name through the generations has been Khorakiwala. It is a Bohra name. The Dawoodi Bohra community in Mumbai, of which my family is a member, is a small community of Muslims. Many of us have "wala" as our last name; just like the Parsis.'

In subsequent research I learnt that Dawoodi Bohras are the main branch of the Bohras and most of whom are based in India, although the Dawoodi Bohra school of thought originates from Yemen. The word 'Bohra' is apparently derived from the Gujarati word 'vehwahar', which is interpreted as 'trading'. No wonder that Khorakiwala's forebear opened a department store.

While the majority of Dawoodi Bohras have traditionally been traders, it is becoming increasingly common for them to become professionals. Within South Asia many choose to become doctors, and in the Far East and the West, a sizeable number now work as consultants or analysts as well as a large contingent of medical professionals. Dawoodi Bohras are encouraged to educate themselves in both religious and secular knowledge, and as a result, the number of professionals in the community is rapidly increasing. As I was to learn from my meeting with Khorakiwala all of this is consistent with his life and that of his children.

Importantly, I learnt that Dawoodi Bohras believe that the education of women is equally important to that of men, and many Dawoodi Bohra women choose to enter the workforce.

Today there are approximately one million Dawoodi Bohras. The majority of them reside in India and Pakistan, but there is also a significant diaspora resident in the Middle East, East Africa, Europe, North America and the Far East.

Returning to my meeting with Khorakiwala I learnt that his childhood passed uneventfully, although he can remember, 'As a child, I was full of mischief, a prankster who defied the rules when I could.'

Khorakiwala's interest in pharmacy was sparked in his teens by an eccentric uncle, his father's youngest brother, many years his father's junior. Only a few years older than Khorakiwala, they were more friends than uncle and nephew. 'He was doing a BSc majoring in chemistry. This included a course in zoology and he would bring home the choicest of lab specimens – frogs, cockroaches and such – for dissection. My uncle could see I enjoyed working with him on this and listening to what he was doing in his chemistry course. He suggested to me that I do pharmacy. I said to him, "Ok , I will do pharmacy" and that was it. From that point on all I wanted to do was to study pharmacy.'

He left home 'for the very first time' to join a five-year course at a pharmacy college in Ahmedabad, the premier institution of that time. The first two years he stayed in a hostel weighed heavily on Khorakiwala. 'I was used to non-vegetarian food but the hostel served only pure vegetarian and I found this a difficult adjustment as well as all of the usual things experienced when moving out of home for the first time. My home life in Mumbai was pretty comfortable, I guess you could say I was spoilt, and so it all came as a bit of a shock. For the last three years of my course I moved out of the hostel to stay with relatives who lived in Ahmedabad and my father gave me a moped to get to and from their home to college.

'One particular memory I have of college was an issue surrounding the misbehaviour of a peon with a female student. I had been brought up by my parents with strong ethical beliefs into what was right and wrong. The college authorities did nothing to discipline the peon or apologize to the student so I organized demonstrations and, as these had no effect, arranged a strike by students for a week. The media got hold of the story and my name was plastered all through the local newspapers. The upshot was that the students lost the "battle" but won the "war" because the principal of the college was asked to resign a year later. My parents diplomatically never mentioned this to me although they knew what had happened.'

After graduating, Khorakiwala left for the US to study for a master's in pharmaceutical science at Purdue University. Returning home after receiving his degree, he entered the family business as expected.

This proved more complicated than one might think. 'There were around forty family members involved in the business. There was my father, his four brothers as well as the descendants of my grandfather's brothers. My father, as the eldest in his generation, was the "head of the family" and "managed" the business, but each of the members of the family were allocated different things to do. As it happens Akbarally's had a pharmacy within the store and had also acquired a small pharmaceutical company, Worli Chemicals in a partnership venture and which, amongst other activities, provided product to Akbarally's. This business had annual sales of Rs 400,000 (USD 10,000) in 1966 and about forty employees. It was losing money and, not surprisingly, no one in the family wanted to touch it. Given that and my academic studies, I was appointed to run Worli Chemicals at the ripe old age of twenty-three. And that is how I ended up in the pharmaceutical industry,' he says with a smile.

'I am pleased to say that within two years I had turned the business around and it started to make profits. A few years later I decided to rename the company as Wockhardt.' I wondered why he chose to do that. 'The name has a deliberately European ring, more by design then by inspiration. I reasoned that to stand any chance against the multinationals we needed to play smart. So we coined the name "Wockhardt". We decided a Germanic sounding name would be good. We actually looked at hundreds of different names and permutations. But the name we chose has worked well and some people, even today, think it is a German company,' he chuckles.

In building the business, Khorakiwala was averse to borrowing from family or friends. 'I didn't borrow a single rupee from anybody. Right from the beginning – and it continues to this day – I have been self-reliant.' Procuring loans from banks was near impossible at that time. That left him with no option but to build the company gradually on little or no capital.

After several years he obtained permission from the family to sell the property on which Wockhardt operated. The capital generated from this, plus a little support from the government, enabled him to set up a new manufacturing plant for Wockhardt in Aurangabad. That factory exists to this day.

'Up until the 1990s, Wockhardt grew modestly and had annual sales of around USD 30 million. Then the Indian economy opened up. The growth since then has been exponential with turnover multiplying by more than twenty-five times.'

Whilst Wockhardt continued to belong to the joint family business, over the years Khorakiwala slowly bought more and more of the company for himself and his immediate family. 'It was only in 2002 that I made a move to own the company fully by gradually acquiring the remaining shares owned by other family members.' I asked if there was any confrontation or antagonism with the family? 'No, there wasn't,' says Khorakiwala, 'We always had this mindset of everybody working together for everything; none of us ever thought of owning (any business) on our own. It was only after some of us in Akbarally's started separating in the early 1990s that we actually began to think of this possibility.'

I asked him about his strengths and weaknesses. 'It is difficult to say but I "discovered myself" to some extent from a business point of view when I did a Harvard advanced management programme with some prominent senior businessmen from across the world as my peers.' The three-month programme which he attended in the early 1980s was a season of discovery and rediscovery.' It helped him to assess himself a little better and 'it gave me some clarity on my strengths and weaknesses.' His forte, he discovered, was strategic thinking. On the other hand, he had over-rated his marketing skill. 'I thought I was very good in the Indian context. When I realized what was happening worldwide, I saw I was not as good as I thought,' he says chuckling. Conversely, he was better at business finance than he had credited himself with. 'This whole experience gave me a more realistic perspective of myself and helped me to respond to the demands of modern business.'

Although Wockhardt had started with a single business in pharmaceuticals, Khorakiwala envisioned from the beginning of his involvement that it should move into more complex technologies and businesses. The sabbatical at Harvard also prepared the ground for such a future. On his return, Wockhardt started to move into new areas like backward integration into bulk drug technology. It was among the early movers into the biotechnology space. In the late 1980s Wockhardt started a hospital chain.

Wockhardt raised capital from a public issue to fund acquisitions – first in India in 2002 and then globally – for its growth. 'That is where the quantum jump has taken place. But if you ask me what are the factors behind whatever we have been able to achieve, I would say what I believed early enough – to create ongoing, new values for the organization – were the keys.

'In life you get a lot of transactional opportunities. I didn't want to do anything which was more simple than what I was already doing. Making money was not the agenda. I believed if I was to create a sustainable organization, which would have as one of its main objectives the creation of more value, then I would have to create an organization which was relatively more complex than what we have today – not more simple. If you make it simple then many people can do it. If you move up the chain and do areas which are more complex, either in terms of managing, in terms of technology, in terms of geographies, then you can leverage your strengths to grow. However, as a result, you have to become more complex and complicated. So, the more you go into that kind of space – obviously, not foolishly, but by taking the right call – I think you create a more competitive organization.

'But in growing a more complex business we all make mistakes. In fact we all make mistakes, no matter how big or how complex the business is. I believe making mistakes is important – very important. The company, of course, has made mistakes and I have personally been responsible for some of these blunders. But we learn more from our mistakes than our successes – no question about that. The only lesson we must learn from making a mistake is not to repeat the same mistake. If you start worrying too much about making a mistake what it leads to is all kinds of analysis and frequently leads to inaction. Inaction doesn't produce any results.

'An example of one bad bet that I made was taking on a partner to assist Wockhardt make an early debut in the US markets. After waiting for three-four years, nothing came of the partnership and the effort fizzled out. In retrospect, it appears we lost good time, but you can always catch up. That's the way life moves.'

Khorakiwala sees a world of difference from the time he entered the business at twenty-three and the present. For one thing, the gathering momentum has made speed of action all important. For another, although opportunities have grown, good professional talent – once available readily – is scarce in some areas. The global financial crisis could, of course, change all of that. While he acknowledges that money and status are important in any pursuit, he exhorts youth to balance their personal growth and development on one hand, with their money making opportunities. 'My only message is that, in this "rat race" to make money, the individual should not forget the aspect of building and growing. You should seek work where you get these opportunities – they don't come everywhere. Unless you continue to grow, you will be out of use after some time and you will not have market value. There is no point in working in a company where you're not growing, not learning or not doing well. But, in an organization which provides you with such opportunities, my strong recommendation is that you should think ten times before you change.'

What keeps the spark alive in Khorakiwala is the higher goals that he sets for himself and Wockhardt after every achievement. Never mind Wockhardt's market capitalization of nearly USD 1 billion, far-flung businesses, multiple technology platforms, and hospital chain, his ideal is to continue to grow Wockhardt. 'To be honest, ten years back I thought I would retire by 2010, that 65-68 is a good age to retire. Today, if you ask me, I don't think I'll retire in 2011 – I'm in good health – no health problems, I'm very active and enjoy what I am doing. Why would I retire?'

I then took the opportunity to ask Khorakiwala about leadership. 'To my mind, the true aspect of good leadership is whether you are comfortable with uncertainties? A good leader, a good entrepreneur is comfortable with uncertainties in life and in business because you never have a certain situation or a clear-cut defined situation any time. Leadership is like travelling on a road at night with a visibility of 100 metres. If you say I need to be able to see 200 or 300 metres before I start driving you won't get anywhere. A leader will take the risk that by the time you get to 100 metres you will be able to see another 100 metres and so on.'

At the time of my meeting with Khorakiwala in 2007 he had just been appointed president of the Federation of Indian Chambers of Commerce and Industry (FICCI). 'This year, I'm working harder than ever because I need to keep my eye on the ball at Wockhardt and, at the same time, try and make a significant contribution to FICCI; partly fulfilling an obligation to put something back into society but also because I feel FICCI can make a difference to the future of Indian society in general and business in particular. For example, I came to the conclusion a few years back that unless the private sector takes some of the burden in important areas like education and health, India may find it difficult to sustain a high growth rate over a long period of time. FICCI is working towards bringing inclusive growth and the privatization of education.'

On the family front he has been married to Nafisa since May 1969. 'It was, as you might anticipate coming from my community, an arranged marriage. However, what is unusual, is that we were engaged for about three and half years before we married so we knew each other well enough to be confident it would work.' The Khorakiwalas have three children – daughter Zahabia, and sons Huzaifa and Murtaza. Their sons are working in Wockhardt, one trained as a doctor and the other is a management graduate, whereas their daughter, much younger and a graduate in liberal arts, with their encouragement has started her own business in an entirely different field. However, Khorakiwala is quick to add, 'Wockhardt is a listed company run professionally and it will continue to be run professionally. The family ownership remains, but if I have to protect the family's wealth, I would rather Wockhardt be run by people who know how to run it best. You can't run a business like ours with family members. You need professionals all around.' I told Khorakiwala that this was a sentiment expressed by almost every person in this book.

In drawing our meeting to a close, we then spent a few minutes chatting about how important family is to the overall emotional health of most entrepreneurs in keeping them grounded. In this regard we noted that we were extremely fortunate that our parents, both in their late 80s, were still alive and well and contributing to the well being of our families.

Wockhardt (www.wockhardt.com) is a global pharmaceutical and biotechnology company that has grown by leveraging two powerful trends impacting the world of medicine – globalization and biotechnology. The company has a market capitalization of over USD 1 billion and an annual turnover of USD 650 million. Wockhardt is distinguished by a strong and growing presence in the world's leading markets, with more than 65 per cent of its revenue coming from Europe and the US. Wockhardt's market presence covers formulations, biopharmaceuticals, nutrition products, vaccines and active pharmaceutical ingredients (APIs). The company has its headquarters in India, and has fourteen manufacturing plants in India, UK, Ireland, France and US; subsidiaries in US, UK, Ireland and France; and marketing offices in Africa, Russia, Central and South-East Asia.

'If you want to go down the entrepreneurial path, go with a passion and enjoy what you're doing. It's important through the entire journey to enjoy what you do.'

UDAY KOTAK

Founder & Executive Vice Chairman
Kotak Mahindra

Uday Kotak was born in March 1959 into a joint family where sixty members stayed in Mumbai together. The joint family was comprised of the families of his grandfather and his grandfather's five brothers.

The brothers jointly managed a business of trading in agricultural commodities and raw cotton from Shanghai, Karachi and Mumbai. Family members lived in each of those cities but, on partition, the Karachi family which included Uday's grandfather and father moved to the joint family home in Mumbai. Uday Kotak spent the first four years of his childhood in this house. 'There were a number of cousins and a great excitement at being a part of a large family.' Being the first grandson and son of the eldest of his grandfather's four children – two were daughters who married and left home – entitled young Uday Kotak to the privilege of sleeping in his grandparents' room with them.

'Being in a joint family was a great experience, a lot of learning. You got to see both facets: in business the joint family was capitalistic; as a family, it was run like a socialistic outfit. The challenge of dealing with your cousins, who become great friends and, at the same time, there's some element of sibling rivalry, was great learning for me in human nature and very valuable when you run businesses.'

For young Uday, the most interesting aspect of growing up was to see his father and grandfather wake up at 5.30 in the morning everyday to call other places in India, small agricultural towns, and order raw cotton which was the key commodity for their business. In the days of the early 1960s, calls were at half-rate before 6 a.m. Kotak observed the ritual every day, perched on his grandfather's lap, sipping milk.

'Even as a child of nine or ten I saw very different styles of my grandfather and father. My grandfather was very precise and calculative about cost. My father was big picture. He said even if we make less profit, we must build the business. They were a great team; the two of them together would come to a fair conclusion because they were so very different in their styles.' Kotak, fascinated by their work as a child, absorbed both philosophies. There was no formal training for Uday. What also impressed him about his elders was their passion about running the business, caring little for the time of day. 'It was a very important phase of my life which gave me great insights and I learnt how to get comfortable with the whole process of commerce, and more importantly, with different styles and how to take decisions.'

Mealtimes at the Kotak household were deeply orthodox. The Kotaks had two cooks who fed the entire family of around sixty people out of one single, large kitchen. The men ate first, then the children, and lastly, the women.

When he was around five, his grandparents and Uday's family moved to a separate home and the family was then reduced to a satellite of seven-eight members who included – apart from his grandparents – young Uday, his parents and one uncle. This uncle became an engineer and set up a manufacturing business. The other uncles and their families remained in the previous house and handled different parts of the commodity business. The profits from the family businesses were split amongst the different members.

'My mother played a big role in my growth as well as, of course, my grandparents. They were a very strong influence on me because I stayed a lot with them.' For eight years, Kotak remained an only child. Then, he had a sister, who is now settled in Singapore. He was a good student, always ranking in the top three at Hindi Vidya Bhavan, then a new private school that his family had selected for the importance it gave to Indian culture. It became something of a tradition for Kotak boys to study there. Some of his cousins, three-four years apart, also attended the school along with Uday. The school was co-educational up to Standard 4 and became a boy's school from then.

Kotak had a well-rounded school life; he enjoyed academics and sports equally. 'It was a great school and I had a lot of fun.' He had no inkling at that time as to whether he would be in his father's business or not. 'There was no pressure on me to do so. I kept my options open.' If he was a good student at school, Kotak fared even better in college. He topped Mumbai in junior and senior college at Sydenham from where he completed his bachelor's degree in commerce in 1979.

His father and grandfather were very liberal but drew the line at sending him overseas for further study. Their main concern was that he would not return once he left. 'This was the time when most people who went to the US never came back.' Not that he was enamoured with a foreign education; his heart told him to make his career in India and that meant he had get to know India well. Overseas study ruled out, Kotak weighed his options: chartered accountancy or business management – which was it to be? He settled for the second and joined Mumbai University's Jamnalal Bajaj Institute of Management Studies in June 1979. 'It was the best school in Mumbai then.'

In September 1979, Kotak suffered a major injury at play. A cricket ball thrown by a fielder knocked him down when he was taking a run during a club game at Azad Maidan, a cricket pitch in South Mumbai. 'The ball hit me in the head and apparently I fell like a stone,' he says. He had to be rushed to hospital for an emergency surgery that just barely saved his life. He had to spend the next two-three months recovering in bed. The accident cost him a year at management school.

'After I came home from hospital, that's the time I decided to spend some time at the family business'. He delved deeply into it, touring godowns and studying the movement of cotton. The period of recovery marked a very important change in his life. 'It was like a shock. The way family and friends would look at me "Is this guy ok, is his head ok, is everything fine with him?"' Uday laughs. It didn't change his attitude to life, except that he had the opportunity to learn the family business – with every intention of returning to business school – six months after he became well.

The family business operated out of a 6000 sq ft office shared by fourteen family members. 'I found it very tough at that point of time to deal with some of the family members because it was always a balance between what was commercially right versus what individual family members wanted to do. That was my big learning of dealing with family at work.' That work experience also exposed Kotak to other elements of business. 'I dealt with blue collar workers in the godowns ... with clearing and forwarding agents ... with overseas buyers ... with family issues. That six month period was a very significant point of my career.' While he learnt a lot, and especially how to deal with inter-personal relations, it also became clear to him that he was 'not necessarily very excited about joining the family business. I just felt that I was not cut out to be one of the sixteen family members in the same business.'

After this stint, Kotak returned to business school to complete his MBA. At the end of his two years of study there, he had the opportunity to join Hindustan Lever, one of the most prestigious companies in India. It was time to have a heart-to-heart discussion with his father. Kotak told him, 'Dad, I don't want to join the complicated family business. I love commerce, I love trading, I love everything which is being done, but I find it difficult to manage the complexity of family relations. I would rather take professional employment at Hindustan Lever. To which his father said, "Uday, what if I gave you an opportunity – on the family platform – for an independent business? What is interesting to you?" So I said "financial consultancy". Actually I didn't know anything about it but he said, "I will try and convince the family to give you 300 sq ft of office space in Fountain and you can do what you want." That was 1982.

'I was tempted by my father's offer, so I took it up.' Kotak began a business in financial consultancy services. One of the first opportunities was from a friend at business school who had joined Nelco, a Tata Group company. In those days, under Reserve Bank of India regulations, banks offered 6 per cent per annum on term deposits and lent them out at 16.5 per cent – a huge margin. Furthermore, there was a ceiling on borrowings. His friend proposed that Nelco would be ready to pay 16.5 per cent interest for whatever additional finance that Kotak's firm could raise for them, that is, over and above what Nelco was able to raise from banks. Kotak approached family friends individually with the offer to pay 12 per cent on their money on a Tata risk, against the 6 per cent offered by banks on fixed deposits. The skeptics among them said, 'He's a young fellow; he doesn't know what he's talking about, but certainly if we got 12 per cent on a Tata risk, we're ready to put in the money.' That marked the birth of Kotak's bill discounting business.

Kotak would discount bills at 16-17 per cent and get them cheap finance at 12 per cent to make a spread of about 4-5 per cent in intermediating between the regulated markets. Business boomed and soon 'we started getting refinance lines from banks. They would give me money at 14.5-15 per cent and then we started doing it under letters of credit, so it became inter-bank exposures.' Once that happened, the requirement of 16.5 per cent did not remain. So, the business started as a huge arbitrage in a regulated system.' He adds, 'There was no law to say you could not do it. Hence no approval was necessary.' The business, Kotak Consultancy, was an independent division of the family company.

Then, at a common friend's home, Kotak met Sidney Pinto, who ran merchant banking in India in Grindlay's Bank. Mr Pinto suggested that Kotak create a separate company so that he could really grow the business. Around this time Uday got married and, as it happens at the wedding, Mr Pinto talked to Anand Mahindra of Mahindra & Mahindra about taking a stake in the business. Mahindra indicated he would be happy to do so with the proviso that Uday would have control. 'We were delighted to give him that equity.' Anand Mahindra obtained his family's permission to attach their name to the new venture. The Mahindra's were an established business house so that the brand equity of the name would mean a lot to the fledgling investment bank. 'That's why it became Kotak Mahindra.'

Kotak set the company with a start-up capital of USD 80,000. In addition to Anand Mahindra, Kotak and some of his close friends, Kotak joint family members also participated individually as well as the joint family company. 'So, here we were – in 1986 – off to the races.' The company's main activity was bill discounting. Then, he added equipment leasing. At the age of twenty-six, Kotak was young to be running the business 'which is probably good because you took risks which today, you would think ten times about.'

Earlier, in 1985, Kotak had bought a stock broking licence at the cost of USD 6000 to get into the stock broking. The law did not allow this business to be part of Kotak Mahindra. When equipment leasing started in 1989 in India, Citibank started giving loans against cars. 'This was unheard of. You could actually borrow money for buying a car!' Kotak decided that this was a good business 'so we quickly got into it in 1990. In those days, the cost of funds from banks was 17 per cent and car loans were going at 30 per cent per year. This sounded like a good spread business to me, except for one problem, cars were in short supply. So, how did we compete with a Citibank? Well, we just started ordering cars in advance. Almost like car dealers, the company booked hundreds of cars at a time. This ensured that a car was available "off the shelf" to customers – the normal waiting period was six months – on condition that they take Kotak Mahindra finance. That's how the car loan business started.'

In 1992, Kotak bought a fixed deposit retail brokerage business from a friend and thus the investment banking service was born and later that year Kotak Mahindra became a public limited company.

Kotak sensed a wind of change in the business environment. After the then Finance Minister Manmohan Singh announced his 1992 budget, he knew that the time had come to look for opportunity outside of India. A meeting with a Goldman Sachs executive at a Euromoney Conference in Delhi in 1992 was the spark for Kotak to visit US firms. Among these were Goldman and Oppenheimer. Kotak made a small start in alliance with Goldman for GDR transactions from India. 'The relationship went well.' Then, he met some partners of Goldman in Hong Kong; among them was Mark Evans. Evans invited Kotak to dinner to meet Goldman's New York partners, John Corzine and Hank Paulson. 'I understand from Mark that the first question they asked Mark after the dinner was, "Why don't we hire this guy?" to which Mark said, "No, he's building a business back in India".'

A year later, Kotak prevailed on Mark Evans to get Hank Paulson to India, which he did in 1994. The relationship with Goldman was getting better. Between late 1995 and early 1996, Kotak entered into a joint venture with Goldman in the brokerage firm and in the investment banking business. Goldman took a 25 per cent stake in these firms – both subsidiaries of Kotak Mahindra. In 1996, Anand Mahindra made a deal with Ford Motor Company. In the auto finance business, Ford Credit did a joint venture with Kotak Mahindra.

'With both these joint ventures in place, we reached a very important turning point. We had really learnt some of the global processes, the way these global firms thought, it was like an opening for us in terms of how the world worked. The formation of these joint ventures was a very critical juncture in the life of our company.'

In 1998, Kotak started an asset management business with its own mutual fund and, in 2001, when India opened up the life insurance field to the private sector, Kotak got into the business with Old Mutual of the UK as its business partner.

In 2003, the Reserve Bank of India issued a commercial banking licence to Kotak Mahindra Finance Ltd which became Kotak Mahindra Bank, a full service commercial bank.

Kotak Mahindra's metamorphosis into a bank transformed the Kotak group. In 2005 and early 2006, the company restructured its joint ventures. It bought out the Ford Credit stake in the auto finance business and it bought out Goldman Sachs' stake in investment banking and securities. Both became wholly owned subsidiaries of Kotak Mahindra Bank. 'These changes were a very good thing from our point of view but beyond that, the relationship, both with Goldman and with Ford, continues to be good. There is no acrimony, no bad blood today. That was very important. We were in the financial sector; we just wanted to do it right.

'My mind state is one of enjoyment. There is a deep sense of enjoyment in building. There are two important elements to the building of Kotak Mahindra. The first came out of my first trip to the US where I met global institutions such as Goldman Sachs and JP Morgan. These were started by individuals but, over time, have become great global financial institutions. I suppose putting your name on the block was saying that you'd be putting your reputation at risk.

'That's how you build trust. For me, it was a great "eye opener" because I said to myself "why can't Indians aspire to building such institutions over time?" Sure, in the beginning it might be a family business. So that we are potentially building a global business is a big driving force. The second important point for me is that if what you have created, does not outlive you, then you've failed. This point is deeply connected to joint family businesses because in these and more generally, it's all about preparing for succession.

'In many ways, our growth is a reflection of the evolution of the Indian financial sector. A completely regimented and closed sector – which is what it was in 1984-85 when we were just building the early stages of our business – is now about timing and thinking in a very commonsensical way.'

I asked Kotak about his management style, 'Yes, I'm a delegator but, having said that, there are times in business when you have to delegate and times when you have to be prepared to go into detail. You have to be able to be detached and a surgeon at the same time. People very often try to take simple solutions such as "either/or". I'm a believer in what I call the "and" principle.

'My children have grown up now; one is nineteen and the other, sixteen. The older is in New York – with my approval which is, of course, the opposite of what my father thought!' he says laughing. 'However, I think my father was correct at that time. It's quite possible if I had gone to the US I would still be working for a Goldman, Morgan or a Merrill, rather than having this opportunity to build something in India. Actually at that time the logical and obvious thing for me to do would have been to go to the US. For the next generation, India itself has a lot of opportunities and young Indians can learn from what is happening in business all over the world. It is their time in the sun and it's up to them. I think they will be drawn back to India, not because I want them to come back, but because the opportunity in our country today is significantly large.'

I wondered what had happened to the joint family business. 'The family separated smoothly in 2000 and a few of them – five-six family members including uncles and cousins – completed the separation of all the family businesses over a weekend. As long as one or two family members say we're ready to go the extra mile for everybody, it seems to work.'

His father, aged seventy-five, still keeps some part of the old business separately with a couple of his nephews. His passion is cotton and agricultural commodities. 'He's doing it because he enjoys it. It's not a very big business; it's a business he's done all his life. I always say "Dad you work harder than me". He has never ever interfered in my business life.'

Kotak brought our interview to a close with some advice for young Indian entrepreneurs. 'If you want to go down the entrepreneurial path, go with a passion and enjoy what you're doing. It's very important through the entire journey to enjoy what you do. I'm a believer that your goal cannot be money or wealth. Your goal is to be what you're really passionate about. Wealth is a consequence of that ... not the cause of it. I also believe that Indian entrepreneurs need over time to involve professionals in their business. Entrepreneurs need professionals and professionals need entrepreneurs. It's the combination of these two forces which, in today's world, is the key.'

Kotak Mahindra (www.kotak.com) is one of India's leading financial conglomerates, offering complete financial solutions that encompass every sphere of life. From commercial banking, to stock broking, to mutual funds, to life insurance and to investment banking, the group caters to the financial needs of individuals and the corporate sector. The group employs around 20,000 people in its various businesses and has a distribution network of branches, franchisees, representative offices and satellite offices across cities and towns in India and offices in New York, London, San Francisco, Dubai, Mauritius and Singapore. The group services around 5.6 million customer accounts.

"Every person is born with certain strengths. I recommend that a young person determines what his or her strengths are and then leverage those strengths rather than merely aspire to be "something"."

HARSH MARIWALA

Chairman & Managing Director
Marico

All of the interviewees for this book were, without fail, generous with their time and, given the busy lives they lead, often met at what I would think were most inconvenient times. My meeting with Harsh Mariwala in Mumbai is a case in point. We had made several attempts to meet during one of my trips to Mumbai; in the end we settled on the evening of a public holiday at the Otter's Club in Bandra. It was teeming with members and their families enjoying the facilities, such as the large swimming pool where Harsh's son, Rishabh, was exercising and later joined us. The club was buzzing with the chatter and laughter of those relaxing on a holiday evening; it took some time for Harsh and I to find a quiet spot to talk.

The business history of the Mariwala family is quite well documented from the time Harsh's grand-uncle, Kanji Morarji, moved from Saurashtra to Mumbai in 1862 and started trading in spices from Kerala. In the early twentieth century he inducted his cousin, Vallabhdas Vasanji, Harsh's grandfather, into the business. Together they built up the business and expanded it to export of pepper and ginger to Europe. His expertise in pepper trade led to Vallabhdas being nicknamed 'Mariwala' as 'mari' means 'pepper' in Gujarati and in most Sanskrit based Indian languages. Vallabhdas eventually adopted the name Mariwala as the family name. The business expanded beyond pepper and ginger into other agricultural commodities such as copra and coconut oil.

Vallabhdas had four sons – of whom Charandas, the eldest, was Harsh's father; and six daughters. All four sons were involved to varying degrees in the family business of which Bombay Oil Industries was the 'mother ship' and of which eldest son, Charandas, was the chairman and managing director. Harsh related the story from the time of his arrival on the scene in 1951.

'I was born on 14 May at the family home in South Bombay rather than at a hospital. I was the first grandson in my generation and my grandfather and father were ecstatic to have me. I am told my grandfather held huge celebrations to celebrate my arrival.

'I grew up in a large family home with my grandparents, my parents and my three sisters on one floor. My three uncles and their families also each had a floor to themselves. There was a common kitchen and everybody had dinner together, so it wasn't unusual to have more than twenty people at the dinner table. To me, of course it seemed a normal experience. Looking back, perhaps partly because of the powerful personalities of my grandfather and father, I believe I was a shy and, to some extent, an introvert child. I was average in terms of studies – nothing very bright but not bad, somewhere in the middle – and I was also average at sports. I think these complexes led me to work harder. Once I started working, I wanted recognition. Despite talking myself down in terms of my scholastic and sporting prowess, I knew I had a flair for numbers and not surprisingly, in the environment in which I grew up, I felt naturally drawn to business. I still remember in my college days, I used to organize home-sales of things I had collected. I would call my uncles and aunts and cousins to come for the sale. There could easily be over 100 family members there. I got a lot of pleasure at making small money from whatever I could sell at these family gatherings.'

I had read that Harsh wanted to go overseas to business school but his father had not agreed. 'Yes, this puzzles me to this day. After I finished school I did a bachelor's degree in commerce at Sydenham College in Bombay. I felt it would have been logical for me to study overseas as one of my uncles had done and as the family could easily have afforded it. Anyway, my father believed that the biggest and best learning one could have was "hands on" experience and not theory from some "fancy business school". I guess he was largely right.'

I asked Harsh whether he really had any option but to go into the family business. 'Not really. The only alternatives would have been either to start my own business or get a job somewhere. In those days jobs didn't pay much and hence, that wasn't really an option. Venturing into my own business was also a non-starter as I had no idea of any business I wanted to get into.

'During college vacations, I spent time in the family business writing up ledgers in the accounts department. I didn't have any clue what I was going to do in life. Just that I was going to join the family business. I really didn't know what I was going to do and how big I was going to make it and I think it is probably fair to say my career has just evolved over the years. And of course, it is still evolving. In a way I'm quite independent as a person. I have learnt a lot of things over the years, more so from people below me and from consultants. I am still learning every day. Again in that quest for knowledge I have been exposed to some fantastic professionals from whom I've learnt a lot. Another source of learning has been reading books. All of the books I read are in the area of management and personal development. Incidentally, you may be surprised, but I never read fiction. Currently, one of my areas of interest is the future of retail trade, which could either be a threat or an opportunity for us.'

Harsh began with Bombay Oil in 1971 without a formal portfolio. He had spent his early days travelling around the various businesses and asking questions. One area which fascinated him was the distribution and retailing of vegetable oils. 'It did not take me long in the business to come to a view that it could be managed better. Like most family businesses of that time various parts of the businesses were managed by different members of the family and like many, the company needed better organization of roles and responsibility and a clearer linkage between profits and business decisions.

'I look up to my father for being a great visionary, in the sense that he was the one who transformed the family trading business into a manufacturing one. He was responsible for the setting up of four different manufacturing factories: a plant at Sewree, Mumbai, to extract coconut oil from copra; a refinery at Mazgaon, Mumbai, to refine vegetable oils; a chemical plant at Bhandup, Mumbai; and a plant near Cochin in Kerala for spice extraction. The plants at Sewree and Mazgaon produced bulk coconut oil and refined vegetable oils from groundnut, coconut, and safflower. The chemical plant at Bhandup manufactured fatty acids from vegetable oils and the plant near Cochin manufactured extracts from spices and exported its entire produce to Europe and North America.

'As I observed how the businesses were being run I saw a great scope for improvement in many areas. For example, we were selling most of our oil in bulk. We sold unbranded coconut oil in bulk to someone who then rebranded it and sold it in the retail market. I felt this was a huge opportunity for us. Retailing our own brand seemed obvious to me since those who re-branded the oil were buying it wholesale from us in the first place.

'Fortunately for me no one from the family was actively pursuing what eventually became our consumer products division. I could pretty much do what I wanted to as long as it did not involve spending large sums of money.

In those days each decision had to be taken carefully. I had to take it incrementally, which I have to admit was a good thing, because I was experimenting and learning too. With every step I would take, I would test out certain hypotheses and then take one more step. Like moving from one region to another in India. In fact my growth strategy even to this day has always been a prototype approach rather than a "big bang" approach.'

I asked Harsh what were some of the initiatives he introduced in those years. 'Probably the most significant were the development of the markets for our Parachute coconut oil brand and Saffola safflower edible oil brand. I appointed an advertising agency to help me position and market the Parachute brand and hired a seasoned front-line field supervisor from Hindustan Lever to join me. Some of our most significant innovations were in the packaging arena. We were the first to introduce Parachute in plastic bottles – a major shift from the then prevalent tin packaging. The move was so successful that a blue plastic bottle is today synonymous with Parachute coconut oil. We were also the first to market edible oils on a health platform. Saffola was carefully positioned as a healthy alternative to coconut oil for cooking. We promoted it aggressively through doctors and in the media. Another key aspect of business was an aggressive focus on building a strong supply chain model and a large retail distribution network comprising of depots, distributors, retailers and salesmen. These initiatives were greatly successful in expanding the presence of our brands from the small pockets of Maharashtra and Gujarat to the rest of India.'

By the late '70s or early '80s the consumer products division had outgrown the other businesses within Bombay Oil; principally with the success of the Parachute and Saffola brands. There were also some failures. 'I was keen to make sure not all our success rested with those two brands and sought to introduce a number of other products. Some failed. For example, we launched a tooth powder, "Whistle", to compete with Colgate and a number of smaller regional brands. Within a year or so, we withdrew it from the market. We had not reckoned on the strength of Colgate. Similarly, we developed a groundnut oil in 1984 but had to call it quits in 1986. We can always attribute these product failures to some phenomena outside of ourselves. But I think the truth of the matter is the poor quality of thinking we managers did back then. There was little attention to product development and quality.'

Harsh had dreams of expanding the FMCG business in India but to do that he needed the family business to change drastically. 'I believed that each family member should have autonomy to run his business so long as there was accountability for results. Unfortunately, there were no defined methods in which funds and other resources were allocated to the various family businesses. One of the key things I needed to grow my business was the right professionals. But, to attract the right people, I needed a positive corporate image and the ability to pay competitive salaries. The location of the head office of Bombay Oil for a start, put people off. We were located in an area of Bombay which was in the heart of commodity markets. While the office was good, the locality was undesirable and this posed a hindrance to recruiting the right talent. I remember I would not call candidates to the office and would suggest we meet in a club instead. Leaving aside the issue of competitive salaries, the prospect of not just working with one Mariwala but many Mariwalas, intimidated good candidates.'

Harsh says he read widely about management and the development of organizations and tried to work out how that could be applied to his family business. He says he thought about how many joint family businesses eventually disintegrate over time. He did not want that to happen to his family business. 'I was keen to find a way of creating autonomy for me and the other family members within an overall joint family business structure. The first step to achieve this was the splitting of the business into three divisions in 1980. I became head of the Consumer Products Division and other family members became heads of the Fatty Acids Chemical Division and the Spice Extracts Division.'

The reorganization of the family business did not end with divisionalization. 'Whilst it was certainly better in providing autonomy to my cousins and I in our different businesses, it was not enough. I still had seven cousins of my generation in the business. The businesses developed differently and, as time went on, there were fewer and fewer synergies between them. I needed focus for my consumer products business and this was dissipated by the other non-synergetic businesses.'

After a few years of deliberation, five separate companies were eventually formed as wholly- or partly-owned subsidiaries of Bombay Oil in April 1990. The consumer products division was hived off as a separate company and the newborn entity was named Marico Industries Limited (Marico). Harsh took over as the Managing Director of Marico in 1990. There were four other companies: Kancor, which was a joint venture with McCormack involved in the spice extracts business, Hindustan Polyamides involved in specialty chemicals, Kanmoor Foods, involved in processed foods and Epro Bio Technologies which produced and marketed hybrid seeds.'

It was decided that Bombay Oil would be equally owned by the four branches of the family and each of the above subsidiaries would be run by one member of the family. Bombay Oil as the holding company gave each subsidiary broad guidelines on how to operate.

I asked Harsh what he got a buzz from, the vision like his father, or from running businesses. 'No, I like running things, but my style is very different. I am not a control freak, on the contrary, I don't control at all. If I'm out of office for ten-fifteen days I will not get a single phone call because I'm not running day-to-day things. But, I have to say that I'm very deeply involved in the business. I know exactly what is happening. I have monthly review meetings with each of my businesses. The whole objective is to add value rather than control it. So, I see myself adding value to business by guidance on broad business direction rather than saying reports need to come to me for decisions. I don't know about my management style but basically it's grounded in common sense. Get the best people on board, trust them and once you trust them, give them a lot of independence. Give them a broad business direction in terms of where the business should be and go on adding value on a regular basis.

I commented to Harsh that many of the traditional family-owned businesses seemed to particularly control the expenditure of money. Harsh responded, 'This is an area where we are very different from family businesses. The time I am closely involved in expenditure is at the time of the annual budgets. At that point I will go into each item but once approved that is it. You may be interested to know we have a unique practice in Marico on authorization for expense accounts.' Harsh laughs and says 'we don't have one. It is based on self authorization. If an executive goes on trip, for instance, he or she can approve their own expenditure. All our executives know we will do some selective random audits. If someone is found to be misusing authority they will be dismissed. We have no signing muster, no leave records and many other examples of self regulation. Basically, there is a high degree of trust and openness.'

'And what about recruitment?' I asked Harsh. 'That is an area where I spend a lot of my time. At a senior level if I need to recruit someone I will spend some time with the person so I can gain an understanding of how he or she thinks. For me the gist of business is people and innovation so it is crucial I put a lot of time into this area.'

Having come such a long way since he joined the family business in 1971, I wondered what drove Harsh now. 'Earlier, there is no doubt it was recognition I was seeking; I must admit I still get a kick out of reading positive press about Marico. But I hope my journey is far from over and I now seek new drivers to those that satisfied me earlier. For example, having made a success of Marico in the domestic market, I would like to replicate this success on the international stage. At the same time, scaling up domestically through sustainable and profitable growth, remains an important goal for the near future. Another area I want to focus on is "solutions". Marico started out as a products company but, now I see it as a beauty and wellness solutions player. We began this with Kaya Skin solutions that encompassed products and services along with diagnostic and advisory services. I hope to further this approach both domestically and overseas and expand the solutions franchise through Kaya. A lot of my drivers now come from within the company, such as wanting to satisfy our employees and shareholders. We need to attract top people to work for us and to do that we have to ensure that the company is both respected and successful.' I asked him whether money is a driver for him. 'Not at all, beyond a certain point what will I do with money. My lifestyle is simple. It's basic. Thank God, my children seem to have the same philosophy and I have never seen them splurge on something which is wasteful. Maybe it is in my family's "blood".'

I then asked Harsh one of the questions I have asked most of the interviewees; namely his advice for young Indians wanting to make a go of their lives. Harsh responded immediately and with clarity, 'Every person is born with certain strengths. I recommend that a young person determines what his or her strengths are and then leverage those strengths rather than merely aspire to be "something". So it could be a hobby which is turned into a business or, it could be someone who is good at sports and goes into a sporting related industry.'

This led to the obvious question of asking Harsh what he thought his own strengths were. 'My main strengths have been an enquiring mind and common sense. I'm not technologically strong so it would not have been a wise move for me to go into a business based on technology. I believe I have built a business using both my strengths as one needs both common sense and an enquiring mind to identify what consumers want now and in the future.'

The evening was getting late and having finished our dinner, we wandered down to the entrance to the Otter's Club where we parted ways. It had been a fascinating day of contrasts for me having interviewed Captain Krishnan Nair of the Leela Hotel Group early in the afternoon followed by Harsh Mariwala in the evening. Both were clearly men with a large amount of common sense and a flair for identifying what their customers wanted.

Marico (www.marico.com) holds a leadership position in the Indian FMCG space. Marico's products and services in hair care, skin care and healthy foods are sold in more than twenty countries in the Middle East, Asian subcontinent, Australia and the US. The company generated a turnover of about Rs 19.1 billion (about USD 455 million) during 2007-08. Marico markets well-known brands such as Parachute, Saffola, Kaya, Sundari and Fiancee. Marico is present in the skin care solutions segment through Kaya Skin Clinics (77 clinics in India and the Middle East) and weight management segment through Kaya Life (three clinics in India). Marico was ranked in 2007 amongst one of eight Indian companies in Standard & Poor's list of Global Challenger Companies. One out of every eight Indian is a Marico customer.

"When I am asked to speak to students about success, I tell them that in order to be successful one has to have strongly held convictions. I tell them what my convictions are, and they are not rocket science:

- Whatever happens, happens for good;
- There are two sides to every coin; and
- All crises pass."

SUBASH MENON

Founder Chairman, Managing Director & CEO
Subex

I met Subash Menon in the coffee shop of the Oberoi Hotel in Bangalore, at the same table where a few days earlier I had interviewed Dr Anji Reddy. The first thing one notices is Subash's calm and smooth voice and his clear diction. It was not surprising to learn during our meeting that he has always loved oratory and became a wizard at sales. Subash was born on 28 May 1965 into a middle-class family in a small village about fifteen kilometres from Palakkad which is a district capital in Kerala. His father was a lawyer and his mother a homemaker. Two younger brothers followed a short time after Subash.

'My life as a child was full of fun. It was a very easy time with studies coming a distant second in terms of my priorities at that time. It was a small village of a couple of ten thousand people and remains a small village even to this day. First and foremost, everyone knew everyone and was somehow related to each other.

'The fact my father became a lawyer demonstrates that his father, my grandfather, believed education was important. I think my father was probably the most educated of our joint family, but everyone in the family received some sort of education. But at the same time it was not what you see today. You were expected to just make sure you had the basics.'

I asked Subash whether there was pressure to study or do this or that course. 'No, hardly any pressure. It was quite limited and the decision was left to me. This is one thing about me that I continue to see today, I don't think I bother about peer pressure. I think that peer pressure is a very bad phenomenon that we should all stay clear of. I used to set my own absolutes.

'When I got to standard 12, I thought I should pursue engineering. Once I had made the decision to do engineering I checked out what marks I needed to get. I found out with "x" percentage I would get into engineering. So that became my target and whether I came first or last in class was unimportant. I did the same when I was studying engineering as well but I will get to that later. That is how my life was, relatively easy, hardly any pressure, one could do whatever one felt like doing. I know and appreciate I was very lucky.'

On finishing school in 1982, Subash travelled to Durgapur about 160 kilometres to the west of Calcutta in West Bengal to do his engineering studies at a Regional Engineering College (REC). 'There were about fourteen RECs all over India which had a partial objective of achieving national integration. So in each REC half the students would come from the state where the REC was located and the other half would come from all over the country. And you have a quota system for each state. In that year for Kerala, 64 seats were available in the other thirteen RECs. I ended up being one of the 64. I got around 90 per cent in the exams which was well above my cut off. I was fine, I made it.

'My father took me to be admitted as I was only seventeen and I needed a parent or guardian to sign me up. It took us two days on the train to get there. But I was so excited that I was leaving home and seeing the world. And I always dreamed of travelling, even as a small child. I can remember telling my parents that I would do three things when I grew up – reading, travelling and eating.' Subash laughs and says that whilst he still does a lot of the first two he has cut down on the 'eating'.

Durgapur REC was actually located within the steel township of Durgapur. Subash told me that, in addition to the Durgapur Steel Plant, there were many downstream steel industries located in the town but most of them were running at a loss. 'This was the era of socialism in India and the worst examples of union excesses were to be found in West Bengal.'

I asked Subash whether it was a pressure-cooker existence like the IITs of today. He replied, 'No, see again, I did not let peer pressure be a factor and was not concerned about the other students. One experience I had demonstrates my attitude. Every department of the college had a "blue board" up on the wall and on which would be put the name of the topper of that department for each year – be it electrical, mechanical or civil and so on. On the day we arrived my father saw these boards and asked me if I planned to get my name up there. I told him, "No way, that is just not going to happen." He then asked me then what were my objectives. I had already determined that one needed 60 per cent to receive a first class degree and 75 per cent for a degree with distinction so I told him I planned to achieve the latter. I am pleased to say I did achieve what I promised my father as I scored 77.2 per cent. That was my plan, I was very clear.'

I was interested to know whether it was an expensive exercise for Subash's parents to send him to college. He told me, 'To answer that question you need to understand my financial background. As you know my father was a lawyer, and a reasonably successful one at that, but his true passion was politics and unfortunately he did not pay enough attention to his profession. And at some point in time he became involved in film business with the aim to make a lot of money. Unfortunately, the result was the opposite and he lost a lot of money. The film business is a "dog eat dog" world which he was not cut out for. So right from when I was twelve years old we had severe financial difficulties.' I wondered if he noticed this as a child. 'Oh, you cannot but notice it. You don't have money at all, you ask for things and there is no money. You see loans being taken and then you see the hassles that flow from that. But one good thing was that my father never sacrificed our education. He was very particular about that. Things were tight – you may have two shirts to wear instead of four, but that's ok if you still have your education.

'The REC was a very inexpensive college as it was run by the government. You know my annual tuition fee was Rs 200, that's like USD 5. Almost anybody could afford that. In fact I could not afford to go to any other college and when I told my father I wanted to study engineering he told me I had to get a "merit" seat. There was no way that they could afford a paid seat at a non-government college. And I knew that.

'Food cost me another Rs 250 a month which was, of course, much more expensive as compared to my concessional tuition fee. For my four years of study, including my travel, as I travelled twice a year to my home town during holidays, it cost me Rs 30,000. In terms of dollars it would be around USD 750. It was definitely an inexpensive proposition, but even that was not easy. I was on a "shoe-string" budget which I augmented by tutoring. This earned me Rs 300 a month which would take care of my food costs and some other expenses.'

I asked Subash what, if anything, he learned from his father's financial difficulties. 'First and foremost I learnt that one should never lose focus. You should only do what you know, not what you think you know. I learnt things like that. Today I'm a very focused person. I go after one thing. If I have some extra money, then sure I can spend it, but not when you are on a "shoe-string" budget borrowing money.

'During my engineering I decided to become an entrepreneur. There were two reasons why I wanted to do this. Firstly, I just knew I wanted to have my own business. I was not sure what that business was, but I knew that is what I wanted. Secondly, my family had some fairly substantial loans that needed to be repaid and, as I knew my father was not capable of doing this, becoming an entrepreneur was likely the only way I would be able to generate the money to do this.'

I told him that sounded like a heavy burden for a twenty year old. 'Yes, looking back it was, but I did not feel like I had an option. I felt that if I worked out my career as an employee it would take me the rest of my life to repay the debts. I figured as an entrepreneur I had the potential to make money much more quickly. However, I knew I needed some experience before becoming an entrepreneur. I decided that I should get experience in small companies as there was no point getting experience in large companies because I would not be starting something big. So I steered completely clear of the campus recruiters as they are usually looking for people for the large companies. For the same reason I did not go to any interviews or take any exams to get into the large government corporations.

'I went to Calcutta for two days and walked unannounced into a few companies and handed over my resume. Believe it or not but this tactic worked and I got a job in Delhi with a company called Subash Projects and Marketing Ltd. It was an electrical engineering firm manufacturing and supplying motor control centers, switches and circuit breakers. It was the Calcutta branch of a Delhi company. The owner had three sons and each of them managed an office – one in Calcutta, Delhi and Guwahati. The son running Delhi happened to be in Calcutta and met me and was able to make a decision on the spot.

'I made it very clear that I wanted a sales job and nothing else. I had figured out that sales are the most important thing when you start a business. You don't have to manufacture something; you can always buy and resell. You have to bring the contracts in. I had always felt that I was a good speaker. This was one of the things I inherited from my father who also had the "gift of the gab".

'I moved to Delhi and shared a room with one of my cousins. My job was extremely poorly paid as I only received Rs 750 a month whereas, at that time, a secure government job would have paid Rs 3500. I have never told anyone this part of the story but I only remained with Subash Projects for one month. You see, they put me in production when they had agreed to put me in sales. I hated it and felt like it was a breach of contract. Not that I could do anything about it. So I gave it a try, but after about a week I went and asked my bosses to transfer me to sales as agreed. Another week went by and there was no transfer. So I did what I did best and went to another company, Controls and Switch Gear and "sold" myself. They liked me and gave me a job as a sales trainee, effective immediately. The next morning I went to my bosses at Subash Projects and told them I was leaving. They promised to transfer me to sales the very next day but I told them it was too late. The salary at my new job was perfect as well as it was Rs 1250 per month. But I made the move for the sales role and not for the salary.

'Then I had a very lucky break, it seems surreal, but it happened to me, so I have to believe it. When I reported to work on the first day at Controls and Switch Gear, they told me the salesman in their Eastern Regional office in Kolkata had just left the company and they wanted to promote me and put me in the job. I would be reporting to the regional sales manager. I was shocked. This was my first day in the job and I had a total of one month's experience of working in a company and none in sales!

'This was probably the only time I have consulted my father on my career as I thought there must have been a catch. I asked the company if I could have a few days to consider the promotion which must have seemed very strange to them but they agreed. I wrote to my father for his advice. In those days calling on a phone was too expensive. I know it sounds silly now but I was so inexperienced I asked my father if he could see any ulterior motive in what they were offering. Of course he wrote back saying it was a good offer and I should take it. I did. They then put me in sales training for the next three months and I had a further month's briefing on the company. At the completion of the training, I received a further shock as I was transferred to the regional office in Calcutta handling West Bengal, Assam, Bihar, Orissa, and the whole of Northeast of India. I was not to report to the head of the regional office but I was to be the head of the regional office! It was unbelievable as I was only twenty-one and had two engineers reporting in to me even though they were more experienced seniors. My regional office also had a secretary and a receptionist all reporting to me. It was exhilarating and I just could not believe it.'

I said that I imagined his meteoric rise must have put a lot of noses out of joint. 'Yes, I experienced this even before I got to Calcutta. My boss, who was the all India sales manager, flew with me to Calcutta to settle me into the job. It was my first flight but it nearly did not happen. The finance manager initially refused to pay for my air ticket saying I was new to the company and did not qualify for a ticket. My boss put his foot down and so I had my first flight. In India in 1986 flying was not a daily activity.'

I asked Subash if he ever found out why he had this meteoric rise. 'Yes, I asked the All-India sales manager after I left the company. He told me that when he met me at my interview he thought I had promise and had thus introduced me that day to two of the directors who were the owners of the company. They apparently agreed with his assessment that I had promise and they decided to take a risk on me.

'After about fifteen months with Controls and Switch Gear I started thinking about starting my own business. As the business conditions in Calcutta were not very positive I thought Bangalore would be a good place to start a business and that it would be good if Controls and Switch Gear could transfer me there. They actually agreed to do so, but said I would have to report to the existing regional head there. As I had been working as a regional head for over twelve months and doing a good job, I was not very keen on moving backwards in my role and responsibilities. I decided to resign. I wrote to the managing director and told him my reasons for quitting and about my plans for starting my own company. I also told him that I hoped that some day my company would be as big as his company. I know he had a lot of hope for me and I felt like I was letting him down. It is one of the regrets in my life that I did not keep in touch with him as I owe him so much for the faith he put in me.'

I wondered why he had chosen Bangalore. 'My main reason was that I had relatives here and it was much closer to home than Calcutta or Delhi. Chennai was another option but my impressions of Chennai on my way to and from my college were negative. I felt it was a much more crowded and dirty city. I had also heard a lot of positive comments about the then quality of life in Bangalore. As you know Bangalore is now over-crowded and getting dirtier.'

I asked him whether he immediately set up his own business in Bangalore. 'No, I got a sales manager's job with a very small electrical engineering company called Eltel Industries. Shortly after I joined, I was promoted to head of sales for India. I worked for Eltel for a few years but in 1992 at twenty-seven I decided to quit and told my boss who was the owner of the company. I was still not sure exactly what I wanted to do other than build my own business. My boss surprised me because he put an unusual proposition to me. He had decided to move the sales process to a commission based one rather than the sales team being employees. I told him I had no money and provided he could advance me Rs 20,000 I would be prepared to set up a company and take a chance on the states of Maharashtra and Karnataka as my region. He agreed and I signed a promissory note for the loan. I did that job for exactly one year and, by that time, I had already figured out what other things that I wanted to do.

'First of all I paid back the Rs 20,000 in full as I had done really well in my first year selling his equipment. I decided I wanted to be involved in a business that was more global or national in nature and wrote to a whole bunch of companies to advise them that my business, which I called Subex, wanted to sell their products and represent them in India. I got a few responses, including one from Australia and one from Canada. The Australian company, Fibernet produced fiber optic equipment and, acting as their agent, we participated in the first fiber optic tender released by the Department of Telecom in 1992. We won the tender. Sometimes when you think back and wonder what happened, sometimes you just can't say why it happened; it just happens.

'At this time the telecom contracts were awarded purely on merit and it was a very straight forward tender. The responsible official was a gentleman called KC Raghavan who was the deputy director general or some such position. There were 32 companies which had participated. We were one of the three companies which were awarded the contract. Several years later I got a chance to ask Mr Raghavan why he had chosen us, although he knew that we were a very small and new company. I have always remembered his reply which was, "I liked you and I thought you were a very reasonable and trustworthy guy so I gave you the contract". It was a fantastic break as the profit on this contract was around USD 145,000 which was huge for someone who had started the business with a capital of USD 400 not long ago.'

I asked Subash was there anything behind the name, Subex. 'It's funny but I had selected this name years before when I was in college. One of my best friends was a chap called Alex. I always wanted to go into business with him and the name Subex has the first letter of our first names as its first and last letters. Alex was not in too much of a pressure to start his own business as he was quite secure financially. He is quite a character. I remember when we were living together in Bangalore he bought a car but was not very fussed about using it to get to and from work. More often than not he went by bus and I used his car. After we won the fiber optic contract I went to him and asked him to join me in Subex. He agreed and became a silent partner in 1993 and an active partner in 1994. He quit in 2004.'

Subex grew rapidly and represented a number of companies from around the world. By 1998 Subash told me that the revenue had grown to around USD 2 million and that he started thinking of expanding into software. 'We identified one particular product which was a telecom fraud management system as a product that we could develop. So we went out looking for software developers as none of us came from the programming background. This was completely against any rational chain of thought as none of us had any experience with software development and we just decided to develop a product when the whole industry was getting into the services side of the business. I had never sold a software product in my life; we only had one or two computers in the company. That was the closest relationship I had with software – using a computer.'

I asked Subash how they came up with this product given their lack of knowledge of the industry. 'Well, we came up with three parameters to choose the product. One parameter was that it should be a product with an opportunity in India. The second was that it should be a product that would have to have a developing country twist to it because we were sure that we were not going to come up with anything new. Rather we would adapt from an existing Western software product. The third thing was that it should have a reasonable market opportunity but it should not be something that the existing software guys looked on as their "bread and butter". If they saw it as their "bread and butter" then they would have killed us in no time at all. We would not have been able to fly under the radar or sneak in. Using these three parameters we decided on telecoms fraud management as our model.

'Once we had chosen and started developing the product we started our search for funding. All the venture capitalists in India turned us down because they said we had no experience in software which was of course correct and wondered why we did not focus on services as most of the other companies were. We only needed USD 1 million and I am sure in the US we could have raised USD 10 million at that time. But not in India. So we did the only alternative.'

I asked what that was. Subash replied, 'We went public in 1999. We raised USD 1.5 million on a valuation of USD 5 million. We launched the product in February 2000 and shortly thereafter secured our first major customer. By June of that year we were confident we were going to succeed and exited the sale of hardware. Since then our market capitalization has grown to today being around USD 750 million [August, 2007]. It would be remiss if I did not mention about what Alex has done. Alex was always more interested in hardware than software products and not long after we exited the hardware business, he became inactive in Subex until he sold all of his stake except 10 per cent in 2004. Needless to say he did very well on his investment in Subex and is currently working on a number of hardware products and the steel industry.'

Subash and I decide to spend the remaining time of our interview on his family related issues. I asked him whether the family was able to sort out its financial situation and whether he ever had time to get married.

'As to the first question, yes we were able to pay off the family's loans within a couple of years after establishing Subex.' I remarked that his father must be a very proud and happy man now. 'Certainly,' Subash said, 'he is now retired from his work as a lawyer and is full time involved in social activities. But my success in business has not changed their lives in many ways and they insist on living in the same home they have always occupied.

'As to the second question regarding my marital status I am pleased to say that yes, I did find time to get married. In fact I got married in 1992 not long after I started Subex. It was an arranged marriage, although I had known her all my life but never with the intention of marrying her. My wife's family approached my parents with the idea of us getting married. That's how the system works in India and it is not good for the honour of the male family if they go seeking a bride,' Subash says laughing. 'We have two sons.'

I asked him whether he felt he was a different sort of parent to how he was brought up. 'Naturally, I am trying to inculcate the same value systems as my father inculcated in me. As I mentioned at the beginning of our meeting I believe the ability to speak in public is an important skill. It has always helped me in life. If they want to become leaders in their careers it is essential that they learn how to communicate well. I am also pushing hard for my sons to avoid peer pressure. I honestly don't care if my kids are not first in class, that's all right with me. I have to say there is one difference between the way I was brought up and how I want to bring up my sons. Like many men of his generation, my father was not very involved in my brothers' and my lives as children. He had so many financial worries that it made him very impatient and it was extremely difficult to talk to him and get guidance. I am trying to spend as much time as I can with my sons and hope they will always be able to approach me.'

As we wandered towards the lobby at the end of our meeting I asked him if he had any final thoughts about what life has taught him this far and which might be of value to young Indians. 'I think in today's world, in today's India, there are tremendous opportunities, and these opportunities are all taking India to the forefront of economic superiority and prosperity. We have the assets to do that and I think the youth of today has to decide what they want to do and then go for it "hammer and tong". When I am asked to speak to students about success I tell them that in order to be successful one has to have strongly held convictions. I tell them what my convictions are, and they are not rocket science:

- Whatever happens, happens for good;
- There are two sides to every coin; and
- All crises pass.

'So I tell the students that when they find themselves in a tough situation they should use these three convictions or that they should develop their own set of convictions. I use my three convictions every time I am in a corner and I use these beliefs to motivate and keep myself going.' With these words of advice, as we had reached the lobby entrance, I wished Subash well and he headed off to another meeting.

Subex (www.subexazure.com) is a leading global provider of OSS solutions with a mission to empower communication service providers to achieve competitive advantage and deliver new service experiences to subscribers. In only ten years, Subex has won a client list that includes thirty-two of the world's fifty largest telecommunications service providers. The company has more than 150 installations in over 60 countries. Subex is organized into three distinct business units:

- Revenue Maximization Solutions
- Fulfillment & Assurance Solutions
- BT Business

The company pioneered the strategic concept of the Revenue Operations Center (ROC) – a centralized and integrated infrastructure for end-to-end monitoring, measurement and control of an operator's revenue chain – to foster operational dexterity and hence sustained profitability.

"I strongly believe that people get into trouble when they become victims of money. As long as you are the master of your money, as long as you can live without a luxury there should not be a problem. Many of those who violate laws and behave unethically do so because they are victims."

NR NARAYANA MURTHY

Founder, Chairman & Chief Mentor
Infosys

I met Narayana Murthy some ten years ago and will always remember the first time when we were staying at the Hyatt in Canberra. He asked me to come by his room to pick him up for a meeting we were attending. I knocked on his door and he invited me in for a moment while he finished ironing his shirt. This is not what I expected of one of India's most successful businessmen. As I got to know and read more about him, I gathered that little was predictable about Murthy – other than his integrity and modesty, which are now a legend.

And so when I met him in his office at the Infosys campus in Bangalore I was not surprised to find him in a small interior office with no windows, with western classical music filling the room. He was hunched over a desktop computer finishing off an email. He turned to me with a welcoming smile that lights up his whole face. I remark on this and he nods, 'Yes, my father used to say "success is when your eyes light up when you meet other people, and when others' eyes light up when you walk into a room". I believe he was right. The beauty of this philosophy is that it encompasses all people – rich or poor.'

We then get back to when the smile started. He was born in 1946 in Sidlaghatta, his mother's town, seventy kilometres northeast of Bangalore, the capital of Karnataka. There were eight children – three brothers and five sisters. Murthy (as he is widely known) was the fifth child. His father, Rama Rao, was a high-school teacher who taught physics, mathematics and English and, as was the custom those days, was transferred within Karnataka every three or four years. When Murthy entered 10th grade, the family moved to Mysore and remained there until he completed his bachelor's degree in electrical engineering.

I asked him what it was like growing up in a house with eight children. 'There were eleven people in the house, eight children, my parents and my paternal grandmother. In those days we did not have modern conveniences which meant my mother had to cook using wood, not even charcoal. I think she must have spent almost fourteen hours a day in the kitchen from breakfast at 6 a.m. Parallel with that she also had to make sure that water got heated because we had to take baths in the morning. Then there was lunch, afternoon tea and big dinners as my father would often bring guests home unannounced. It was not an easy life but it was a lot of fun because we were so many kids. My father insisted that everybody eat together so we would all have dinner together at around 8.30 p.m. We would sit on the floor and mother would serve all of us, my father, his mother and the eight children. He would talk about the news of the day and give us his views on what was happening in the country and the world. Once in a while, he would ask us questions to check if we were reading newspapers or not. He was very keen that we do so. While my father was flexible on many things, one thing was non-negotiable. We had to study for a certain number of hours everyday; on this he would not tolerate any slip-up.'

I asked Murthy about the living conditions of his family and he chuckles at the memory, 'In most of the houses where we lived we had two bedrooms and most of us slept in the drawing room. It was fun. Frankly, I tell you, today we have a reasonably big house, and only my wife and I live here because both our children are studying in the US, and you know, I don't have the same level of pleasure that we had when we were all together.'

He explained that his father was quite a disciplinarian. 'He would tell us once. The second time he would warn us. And if we made the mistake a third time he would beat the hell out of us,' Murthy says with a laugh. 'But he was always affectionate. I can see now how all the things that he insisted on helped quite a lot in life. He was very particular about honesty, integrity and about discipline. He was also particular about respecting elders and teachers. It was the typical old fashioned value system which is in Australia, India, China, everywhere you know.'

Being a teacher I wondered if his father had any vision of the careers his children should follow. His father had hoped Murthy to become a civil servant which, at that time, was considered the top job. His father had also wanted to become a civil servant. The only hitch was that, during the pre-independence days, he would have to travel to England for the exam. Murthy laughs remembering that his grandmother did not want her son to go because of the then Hindu belief that one became impure if one crossed the seas. Murthy believes his father hoped for at least a couple of civil servants and, maybe, a lawyer. 'Having one son in law was a big thing as it was a well-respected profession with good earning potential. Other than that, I don't think he had any other dreams for us.'

Murthy then recounts another instance of his father's disciplinarian streak when he came fourth in the state out of 300,000 students for his 11th standard exams (like senior Cambridge). He rushed to tell his father the good news only to hear 'and what happened to the other three positions?' 'I was so upset. My mother passed it off as an expression of affection and encouragement. I saw it as an expression of disappointment.'

Murthy went on to study electrical engineering at the National Institute of Engineering, Mysore because he was reasonably good in mathematics. He found the course fascinating; made even more fascinating because he had a wonderful professor, Professor Rao, who taught them, in particular, about electromagnetism, circuits, television, motors and generators.

I enquired as to how he made ends meet while he was a student. He explained that there was no concept of pocket money and few opportunities for students to work. In any event his father's salary was only around Rs 150 per month so there was no spare money to give out as pocket money. But Murthy went on to explain how from his high-school days the government had initiated a scholarship scheme for the first ten students in the state and he received Rs 50 a month, being one-third of his father's salary as a headmaster! Needless to say Murthy contributed almost all of this back into the family kitty but kept a little for treats such as going to the movies.

'In the fourth year of my five-year degree, I decided I wanted to become an engineer in a hydroelectric power plant because hydroelectric power plants are clean, located in valleys where it is green and fertile and I figured life would be wonderful. However, when I came to my final year, as I had stood number one in my class all along, my professors urged me to consider studying for a master's degree. After considerable thought, in 1967, I agreed and moved to IIT Kanpur. Like most Indians of that time, I had never seen a computer until I got there. I decided to take control theory as my subject for my graduate studies as it involved a lot of maths, which was one of my strengths.'

IIT Kanpur was supported by eight American universities (including MIT, Caltech, Princeton, Michigan and Berkeley) and was set up under a programme called the Kanpur Indo American Programme (KIAP) resulting from an agreement between President Kennedy and Prime Minister Nehru.

'I loved my time at Kanpur. It was a wonderful place. It was like a typical American university in the sense that the rules of the game were as flexible as an American university. One could take courses from humanities or courses from electrical engineering or mathematics, as long as you completed your mandatory courses.

'One semester into my control theory course, I went to my hostel cafeteria one Sunday morning for my breakfast. At one table I saw an American professor with half a dozen students sitting around him. On an impulse, I went over and joined them. He was talking about this new thing called computers and told us how they would change our lives, what role they would play in the future, and so on. He suggested four or five papers for us to read. I went straight to the library after breakfast and read those papers. By the evening I had decided to change my field of study to computer science.'

I remarked that it is amazing how often it seems there is a single event that changes the course of a person's life! It seemed to me that had he not gone to the cafeteria for breakfast that day and decided to join the professor's table, Infosys, more than likely, would never have been founded. Murthy agreed.

Murthy finished his master's degree in 1969 and as IIT Kanpur was in those days the only place in India where one could do a master's in computer science, he had several job offers. Murthy adds, 'Can you believe it? At that time there were only fifteen people in India who had a master's degree in computer science?'

But then fate played another hand in Murthy's life as he met, by chance, Professor Krishnayya from the Indian Institute of Management (IIM) of Ahmedabad, who talked about his plan to bring a time-sharing computer system to the institute. 'He wove a wonderful story of the power of the time sharing computer system. I knew about the technical part of it but he talked about how it could be used by managers to do a lot of simulation, to play a lot of management games and to do a lot of "what if analysis".

'At IIT Kanpur we had to share computers, whereas Professor Krishnayya told me that I could have my own terminal and that I would be one of two or three people who would actually run the centre. This all sounded wonderful and I decided on the spot to take his job offer even though it meant a salary 30 per cent lower than the other offers I had received.'

Murthy believes this was one of the most important decisions he made in his life as it took him immediately to the cutting edge of what was happening globally in the field of computer science. 'This was because time-sharing systems were coming into their own at that time. I also had access to the source code of the operating system which meant I could get into the details about how these programmes are written. I had done all of this in theory but to actually see them in action and have an opportunity to improve them – that was a wonderful experience.'

Murthy worked at the IIM Ahmedabad for a couple of years and then in 1971 was awarded a scholarship from Technon in Israel to do his PhD in computer science. 'I am a great fan of Israel and its people.

'There are lots of brilliant people with excellent professors. In most fields, I believe you will find a large number of people from Israel doing really well in whatever they have chosen to do. Anyway, there was a professor in Israel who was doing work at the leading edge in an area that was called deadlock resolution. That is, let's say there is a task A which has seized a certain resource X and is waiting for resource Y. There is also another task B that has seized resource Y but is waiting for resource X. Unless task A releases resource X task B cannot release resource Y and vice-versa. This is called a "deadly embrace". The kind of work that was being done was which tasks should be aborted to minimize wastage of resources and ensure minimal work for the operating system to roll back all the updates and so on.'

But fate again plays a hand in Murthy's life. At the same time as he made his decision, Professor Krishnayya was in Italy to present a paper which he and Murthy had written. The paper was voted the best paper of the seminar. The chairman of the seminar was a senior management executive in a French company. 'He approached Professor Krishnayya to see if I might be interested in coming to work in France to be part of the team that would design the cargo handling system at the new Charles de Gaulle airport.' Murthy received the job offer by telex and, at the urging of his friends and the lure of an opportunity to live in Paris and doing interesting work with a good salary, he opted for France over a PhD in Israel.

I again remarked on the spontaneity of many of the decisions he made in his life. He replied, 'You know, in my opinion, most important decisions in life are seemingly made on the spur of the moment. However, the decision may well have been preceded by a long period of analysis and reflection.'

After some four years in Paris, Murthy decided it was time to return to India. Rather than fly back, he chose in 1974 to wander the 'hippie trail' back to India and spent almost a year doing so for the princely sum of USD 450, being almost all of the money he had saved. I wondered why he did not have more, given he was earning a good salary in Paris. He explained, 'Oh, the reason I had no more money is because I gave the rest away to a charity called "Brothers of the Third World". Looking back, I am glad that I made this contribution.

'That trip was so wonderful and carefree. I slept on railway platforms, hitchhiked, was briefly incarcerated for talking to Bulgarians in Bulgaria, met interesting people from all over the world and visited fascinating places. With no timetable, I could spend a couple of weeks wherever I wished to stop. This was long before everyone started to worry about terrorists and security became a big issue. The only criterion was to generally head East towards India.'

On arriving back in India Murthy immediately took the train to Pune where Professor Krishnayya had opened the Systems Research Institute. He offered Murthy a job. In Pune, Murthy met his wife-to-be, Sudha Kulkarni, an electrical engineer, working in Tata Motors. Around the time they married in 1978, Murthy felt it was time for a change. He was frustrated that much of the good work the institute did for the government ended up gathering dust and not being used.

'During my time in France I met a lot of people from the left, from the right and from the middle of the road. Before I left for France I was a leftist in India because we were all brought up in Nehru's vision. Leftism was the fashion of the day. However, while in France I came to the conclusion that leftism was not for India. It took me time to work out what system I thought would work here. In fact, it was during my time in Pune that my view on India crystallized. For me, the solution for India had three elements. Firstly, the only way a country like India can solve the problem of poverty is through entrepreneurs and the creation of jobs. Secondly, these entrepreneurs are human beings and need incentives to perform. Thirdly, it is not the task of the government to create jobs but it is the responsibility of the government to create an environment where these entrepreneurs have incentives to create more and more jobs.'

This realization made him aware that, whilst the Research Institute satisfied his intellectual curiosity, it was of limited value to the Indian society. Murthy decided to once again join the corporate world. He joined Patni Computer Systems (PCS) in Bombay in 1978 and his wife conveniently got a transfer to the Bombay House, the headquarters of Tatas in Bombay. This was where their daughter, Akshata, was born in 1980. He stayed with PCS until March 1982 when he decided to strike out on his own with six colleagues from PCS – NS Raghavan, Kris Gopalakrishnan, Nandan Nilekani, K Dinesh, Ashok Arora and SD Shibulal. On 7 July 1981, Infosys was launched.

I asked Murthy how he selected his fellow founders of Infosys. 'First of all, I looked at their value systems. This was crucial because any enterprise demands a lot of sacrifices in the beginning. We had to make sure that our families would not be unhappy with whatever little money we had and the time and effort we had spend outside home to make the company a success. Secondly, I wanted to partner with "high learnability". What I mean by this are people who could not only adapt quickly to new ideas but also could unlearn old ideas. Thirdly, I wanted complimentarity of strengths. All of us knew software but I have also always been comfortable with finance. For example, Nandan was comfortable with sales and marketing, Kris with technology, and Raghavan with human resources. So, in other words, I wanted to bring in people who had mutually exclusive but collectively exhaustive set of skills, expertise and experience.'

Before leaving Murthy to his music and emails I wanted to spend a little time asking Murthy about the way he has handled his success and its impact on the family. I told him I understood he still lived in the same house in Bangalore he has had for many years and that there may be a tinge of the leftist still in him. He laughs, 'Oh yes. I think some of these beliefs don't change, which is good, I guess. I say I am a compassionate capitalist. That is someone who is a capitalist in mind but a socialist at heart.

'And you are right, our Bangalore home is our first house. We moved into it in 1987 and have been there ever since. We have in fact purchased the plot of land next door and built an annex with modern amenities for friends and family who visit us frequently.'

But I wondered how he has managed to inculcate in his children the basic values of integrity and honesty which he had mentioned had been passed to him from his father. He replied, 'I don't know how we did it but both our children are adults now and I can feel the value system is there. I strongly believe that people get into trouble when they become victims of money. As long as you are the master of your money, as long as you can live without a luxury there should not be a problem. Many of those who violate laws and behave unethically do so because they are victims.'

Murthy finished our interview with a chuckle in telling the supposed story of where first Ford rebukes his son for spending too much money. The son is reported to have looked up and said, 'My father is a rich man; yours was not, so stop comparing.'

Infosys Technologies Limited (www.infosys.com) is a multinational information technology services company headquartered in Bengaluru, India. It is one of India's largest IT companies with over 100,000 professionals. It has nine development centres in India and over seventy offices worldwide. Infosys was founded on 2 July 1981 in Pune by Narayana Murthy and six others – Nandan Nilekani, NS Raghavan, Kris Gopalakrishnan, SD Shibulal, K Dinesh and Ashok Arora. Infosys went public in 1993. In 2001 it was rated Best Employer in India by *Business Today*. Infosys won the Global MAKE (Most Admired Knowledge Enterprises) award, for the years 2003, 2004 and 2005, being the only Indian company to win this award and is inducted into the Global Hall of Fame for the same.

> I do not believe in luck. If there is such a thing, then it comes to those who dare and act.

CAPTAIN CP KRISHNAN NAIR

Chairman
The Leela Palaces, Hotels & Resorts

I usually stay at The Leela when I visit Mumbai for my regular work as an investment banker cum lawyer and, of late, as the author of this book but had never met its chairman. Working in its favour, for someone who logs in as many frequent flier miles as I do, is the hotel's proximity to the Sahar international airport which, in the light of Mumbai's chronic traffic problems is a big plus!

On the 8th floor of the hotel is the office of the man behind the premium luxury group named Captain Krishnan Nair. With much expectation, but not sure what to expect, I entered his office. Captain Nair was seated behind a large conference table, clad in a beige suit, suspenders over an orange shirt. As I introduced myself, his eyes sparkled. He exuded an energy that belied his eighty-seven years.

Normally, I spend a couple of hours with an interviewee; with Captain Nair, in the same time, we had barely covered the first quarter of his life. I had to return the following day for another long sitting with him.

As the interview progressed, Captain Nair struck me as a self-assertive leader who follows his own mind to the last detail. I did note, however, that there was one person who could demand his attention at will. That was his wife, Leela, after whom the hotel group is named. She rang frequently on the first day regarding plans for dinner as it was their 58th wedding anniversary.

Captain Nair was born in 1923 in a small village some distance from Kannur in North Kerala. The siblings totaled ten, but only eight survived childhood. Captain Nair was the fifth oldest of the surviving siblings.

The family was poor, but, 'I had a very happy childhood. Appa [father] was a bill collector. One of those humblest government positions from which he earned about Rs 9 a month.' It was his mother Madhavi Amma who really kept the family afloat. 'She owned about 2 acres of land on which she produced four crops of coconuts and two crops of rice paddy each year. She would sell the shells and produce oil from the nuts.'

His earliest education was the small elementary school close to home. When the young Nair reached 4th standard, an uncle took him to stay with him in Edakkad, eight miles away from Kannur where he went to the local higher elementary school for three years. Nair was the only one to do so in the family as his two older brothers, Kunhiraman and Nanu left school and joined the army after 7th standard. 'I think because I was my mother's favourite and appeared to be bright, I was encouraged to continue at school.'

Then, upon reaching the 7th standard, he was brought back to Kannur by his mother to join the Rajas High School, Chirakkal which was about two miles from home. 'I had to walk all the way and back. For breakfast, I would eat rice from the previous night to which my mother would add fresh buttermilk made from yoghurt (curd rice).'

The higher elementary school at Edakkad was riddled with casteism. As was the custom, boys from the lower castes were expected to make way for men of the upper caste, even for the mundane crossing of the rice fields to his school. Captain Nair recalls getting into many a fight for standing his ground when he did not make way for the upper-class people to pass by. 'This made me popular with the girls,' he chuckles.

From where did he get this rebellious streak? 'Maybe, I have taken after my mother. She was upright, bold, could not stand any injustice.'

Young Nair would return home every weekend to help his mother with her household chores by sweeping and cleaning the courtyard where coconuts were dried. 'This was a tedious job which I did so that my mother would not have to do it. I guess I was a "mamma's boy", but it is my proudest memory that I helped my mother. She, like many mothers of that time and even today in India, have extremely tough lives making ends meet.'

During his first year at high school, an event changed his life. One day, the local Maharaja, Valia Raja of Chirakkal who owned the school came to preside over a school day celebration and spoke to all 700 students. 'I vividly remember sitting there and listening to him speak. I had never seen a man of such great stature and aura beaming with nobility, who was dressed so finely and who spoke so eloquently. After his speech I could not resist making a poem on this august personality comparing the Maharaja to the brilliance of the sun and the cool radiance of the moon.'

When the Maharaja finished speaking, without any invitation or permission, the young Nair spontaneously jumped up from his seat and ran up to the stage. He stood before the Maharaja and poured forth his poem to the entire assembly. 'I can still remember some of the words to this day, "If a thousand suns and moons joined together, what will be the impact on the universe? That is the impact you have on us. We worship you." Then I said, "You give us the gift of education or vidya, the highest form of wealth or dhana. He who imparts vidyadhana is the highest being in the world, not a king or businessman."'

But that wasn't all. 'When I completed my poem I told the Maharaja that if we school children became educated, we would fight for India's freedom from Britain. The audience was stunned into a hushed silence. The Maharaja, too, was speechless for some time.

'Our headmaster Ryru Nair was livid but he waited to see how the Maharaja would respond. After he recovered from the shock, the Maharaja held me to his breast and said, "What is your name, boy?" "Krishnan, sir", I replied. He then told the headmaster this boy will be given a scholarship for life by me. He then looked at me and whispered that I should come and see him as often as I could in his palace. I was thrilled to the core. The headmaster was so proud of me he made me the school monitor that afternoon. The Maharaja then contacted my father to say they did not have to pay for the rest of my studies at his school.'

Several months later, the local Congress leader, AK Gopalan, who later became a leader of the Opposition in the communist party of free India's Parliament, visited the school to start a students' union against British rule. The young Nair took the opportunity to lead the initiative. Gopalan would drop in to teach them the fundamentals of the freedom movement, how to organize protests and meetings against the British Raj.

Was this student movement widespread in India at the time? 'No, we were the first student union in Malabar. My parents were opposed to my getting involved in the movement but they knew once I had set my mind there was little they could do to dissuade me.

'AK Gopalan asked me to attend many meetings which he organized to fight the British. I would take contingent of over 100 students to these meetings which became the bulwark of the freedom struggle. These students became the shield when the police tried to disperse the crowd. I was arrested and put into lock-up, kicked and beaten. When we students were in the lock up, we would all recite the words of the poet Rabindranath Tagore from his work *Gitanjali*. I remember them to this day:

Where the mind is without fear and the head is held high
Where knowledge is free
Where the world has not been broken up
Into fragments by narrow domestic walls
Where words come out from the depth of truth
Where tireless striving stretches its arms towards perfection
Where the clear stream of reason
Has not lost its way into the dreary desert sand of dead habit
Where the mind is led forward by thee into ever-widening thought and action
Into that heaven of freedom, my Father, let my country awake.'

Upon finishing high school, Nair had little idea of what he wanted to do. 'I knew I should go to college for further education but had no wherewithal.'

He remembered the generous offer that the Maharaja had made him four years ago. 'I went to see him. We had a long chat. "I will gladly sponsor your college education," he said and then told me, "Krishnan, I am having a rather bad financial time at the moment and have no cash to give, all the same I want to keep my promise," saying that, he pulled off from one of his fingers this great big diamond ring ... "if you take this ring to the jeweller in Madras where I bought it, you will find it is enough for two years of your education at college and if you have any surplus give the amount to another dependent of mine." It was incredible.'

When he went to sell the diamond the jeweller named Bappalal of Madras could not believe that such a diamond ring could be sold, but Maharaja's name meant everything and he readily bought the ring back for Rs 4500 which was enough money for Nair's two years of education and a surplus of 500 which he gave to another dependent. He was thrilled.

With the proceeds of the diamond ring, Nair attended Madras Arts College for two years of undergraduate studies. By the time he under graduated in 1942, WW II was in full swing. AK Gopalan, who by then had joined the underground patriotic force for causing rebellion and disruption of the British Raj, sought refuge in Madras at Nair's home during the day to hide and sleep and by night he carried out his underground activities with fellow freedom fighters. However, with both his parents being old, Nair felt he was in no position to support the movement. Rather than add to their problems, he was compelled to earn some money to contribute to the family. These were fearful times as a German submarine *Emden* had bombed the High Court building in Madras.

Nair approached the army recruiting office to apply for a suitable job. It would seem the colonel who interviewed him found him to be smart and offered to hire him immediately at a senior post with a salary of Rs 120. They paid him a month's salary in advance. From that, he bought two pairs of trousers and shirts for Rs 20 and sent Rs 100 to his parents. The army sent him from Madras to Delhi and then on to the North West Frontier Province, to a place called Abbottabad.

He was delayed two days in Madras and two days in Delhi due to the war. 'I could not get rail reservation and by the time I boarded the train, I had spent virtually all my money on accommodation and food. I had just enough left for the bus trip I needed to take from Takshila to my final destination in Abbottabad close to the military academy of Kabul.'

With no money, he decided he would not eat on the train. 'As I was an officer, I had a first-class railway warrant. The gentleman in my compartment, who was heading to Peshawar and whose name I later learnt was Karunakaran, noticed I had not eaten for the whole day and night. He kindly offered me food which I refused saying, "I am not feeling well." It was only a pretext not to accept any help from a stranger. He insisted and bought me dinner and lunch the next day. When the Frontier Express stopped at Takshila and I was stepping down from the train and bidding goodbye to this samaritan, he stopped me and thrust a Rs 10 note in my pocket and said, "Don't worry, you use it, I know you are broke." I had tears in my eyes and said, "Sir, please give me your address and I shall return your money when I get my first salary." He patted me on my back saying, "I don't want this returned, please give it to someone whoever you may encounter facing such a situation in life." I clearly remember his advice and to this day have re-paid this many times over by helping the needy in life.'

Captain Nair spent two years in Abbottabad with some spells in Delhi doing his work monitoring radio transmission. He enjoyed it greatly and regularly sent home half his monthly salary to his family. 'While I was there, we worked long hours but it was a time when I started to understand the spiritual side of life. In the evenings, I would listen to news on Netaji Subhash Chandra Bose's speeches which were beamed from Shonan radio in Singapore to freedom fighters of India and this would thrill me. In fact, the first speech by Netaji addressed Gandhiji for the first time ever as the "Father of the Nation". His resounding words still ring in my ears. My nights would be spent reading books on palmistry and astrology.'

During his time in Abbottabad, Captain Nair met Khan Abdul Ghaffar Khan, also known as Frontier Gandhi. Ghaffar Khan was close to Mahatma Gandhi and was in the working committee of the Indian National Congress. At the same ashram of Ghaffar Khan in Murrie in the North West Frontier Province, Captain Nair met two other great leaders – the future prime minister of J&K, Sheikh Abdullah, and the chief minister of North West Frontier Province, Dr Khan Sahib, who was Ghaffar Khan's brother. Khan Saheb invited Captain Nair to visit him in his home at 7 Commissariat Road in Peshawar. As a result of that chance meeting, he became a great friend of Sheikh Abdullah's son Faroukh Abdullah. 'Later in life I became the friend of his son, Omar Abdullah, now chief minister of J&K.

'Years later I met Khan Abdul Ghaffar Khan again in Sewagram and he took me to meet Mahatma Gandhi. I stayed at Gandhi's ashram in Wardha for ten days. It was a wonderful experience as Gandhi encouraged everyone to implement constructive programmes in life to help the people and which I was later able to put into practice in Kannur.'

Wasn't it unusual for a young man without contacts to meet all these famous people? Krishnan responds, 'You must have great aspirations in life or you will get nowhere.'

Captain Nair speaks of one particular event that occurred in that period which benefited him throughout his life. 'My mother knew Pankajam Menon, the wife of VP Menon. At the time, VP Menon held the important role of the Reforms' Commissioner based in Delhi and worked closely with Lord Wavell, India's Viceroy. Mrs Menon on her visit to her home in Kannur used to get rice from my mother in those days of rationing. My mother requested her to carry some prawn pickle back to me as I was living in Ananda Parbat in the Wireless Experimental Centre in Karol Bagh in Delhi at that time. Unfortunately, the address got smudged and all Mrs Menon could read on her return to Delhi was "Krishnan Nair, c/o Wireless Centre". She gave it to her husband, the famed VP Menon, who forwarded the inquiry to the Defence Secretary and bid him to track me down. You can imagine my amazement, and that of my superior officers, when an instruction came down the line from the Defence Secretary that I was to report at the residence of the Reforms' Commissioner.'

Captain Nair remembers travelling by rickshaw until he stood in front of Akbar Road, VP Menon's home which was later Mrs Indira Gandhi's residence. 'I had never seen a home like this. It had a huge semi-circular driveway, up which I trudged after passing through the security check at the gate. I knocked on the door to be met by Mrs Menon, or "Mummy", as we used to call her. She told me she had a parcel from my mother and invited me to stay for lunch. I did not think that was proper and, so, took my leave after thanking her. Now, it turned out, that VP Menon was returning after a meeting with Lord Wavell. As I was reaching the end of the driveway, in swept a Rolls Royce flying the crest of Viceroy. The car suddenly stopped, VP Menon opened the door and said, "Aren't you Krishnan?" I replied that I was and he insisted I get in the car and join him and his wife for lunch. After lunch, VP Menon asked Lord Wavell's driver to take me back to my quarters. To this day, I remember the driver was an Englishman named John. Can you imagine the looks I got as John dropped me off at my Wireless Experiment Centre where many people stood agape at the Rolls Royce car. I will never forget that day.'

While in Abbottabad he visited Haridwar and Rishikesh in search of spiritual men who could change people's lives in the hope that he might become a disciple. There he observed Dr Kuppu Swamy, who later became Swami Shivananda, a spiritual aspirant who had been an eminent doctor in

Malaysia. 'He was wandering around the countryside and my friend and I created a "parnashala" (a thatched hut) for him to stay in. He initially hesitated but eventually agreed. He would go every morning at 3 a.m. to the river Ganges. I used to join him and stayed by his side for two days at which point I asked him to take me into his Order. He refused. He told me that I was a man of the world and that my job was to achieve other things and to help humanity in other ways. I was bitterly disappointed. However, I stayed on for another week while he taught me concentration and to meditate on the sound of "Aum" the Ganges makes.'

After the war ended, and before India won its independence, Captain Nair wanted to join the Free India Army but chose to return to Kannur to help his villagers. India was at that time in the grip of an artificial famine created by black marketeers who controlled grain distribution. He met the Collector of Malabar, RP Kapoor, who was a British civil servant and volunteered to shake up the grain distribution in his area without pay. 'He took me up on the offer. First, I mobilized several volunteers to unload a supply of grain into a warehouse I had leased for the purpose. Next, we distributed the grain promptly through rations' shops without corruption or black marketeering. The district administrator and civil supplies commissioner, Mr Jacques was so pleased with the job that he moved to appoint me as chief executive of the Producer cum Consumer Cooperative Federation in north Kerala.'

Not everyone was happy with his effort to stamp out corruption. 'I was to be appointed chief executive at a board meeting. As I wanted to start with a clean slate, I arranged for a sudden and surprise inspection of stocks in the warehouse to be carried out before the meeting. While I was counting the gunny sacks of rice, the incumbent chief executive, whom I was replacing, ordered his men to push sacks of rice on me so that I would be crushed, but I had a narrow escape. I immediately suspended the four supervisors in charge and they were arrested. Over time, we recovered the losses. In two years I could submit a very handsome profit. With this job done I applied in 1947 for the selection as an army officer in the Maratha Light Infantry of the Free India Army.'

After completing training in Pune, he was commissioned as a First Officer. Three years later in 1950 he married Leela, the daughter of AK Nair, a successful handloom owner from Kannur. 'Leela was from my place and I wanted to marry her.' Fortunately it seems Leela's father was impressed by Captain Nair who he knew to be rebellious but was impressed with the job he had done as chief executive of the cooperative.

Captain Nair regaled me with many more anecdotes from his time in the army. Regrettably, I can only fit in a couple of them in this book. In one story, he accompanied General KM Cariappa, then Commander in Chief of the Indian Army, as his ADC on an incognito visit to Goa while it was still under

Portuguese rule. Together, in a boat named Sabarmati, they did a clandestine reconnoiter of how to take Goa militarily. In another, he told me that when he was Staff Officer to General Brar, he would accompany him on inspections. 'Once, when we were in Pune, where the General was on an inspection, he asked me to take notes, as the Colonel who was assigned this responsibility was preoccupied with a problem on the base. General Brar was very pleased with my report because it not only detailed the problems on the base but also gave recommendations on how to fix them. As a result of this and other work I did for him, he promoted me.' I remarked that he must surely have set a record by becoming a Captain in four years. 'Yes,' he said, 'I was lucky because I happened to be in the right place to impress a few important generals at the right time.'

After four years in the army on the instance of his wife, Captain Nair resigned and joined his father-in-law's business around 1952. 'The state of the handloom industry at that time was terrible; the workers were very poor and the whole industry was stagnant and disorganized. I wanted the handloom and textile industry to prosper and add to the growth of the country's economy. I thought the first thing we needed to do was to organize the industry. Fortunately for me, one of my friends, Captain V Nanjappa was the textile commissioner and I pitched to him the idea of setting up an All India Handloom Board. He told me that in order to get this idea through we would need to convince Prime Minister, Jawaharlal Nehru. First of all, I went to Lal Bahadur Shastri who was a close associate of Nehru, and later succeeded him. He did not think Jawaharlal Nehru would see my handloom delegation because Nehru was in favour of a mechanized industry. Next, I went to VP Menon and asked him to introduce me to the Deputy Prime Minister, Vallabhbhai Patel. I saw him, he liked the idea and arranged a meeting with the prime minister instantly. We succeeded in persuading him to support the establishment of the Board and to introduce a levy on textile mill producers of 1 paise (one hundredth of a Rupee) for every yard of textile sold from their mills. The levy was collected by the government and applied in developing the handloom industry. By the end of the first year, we had Rs 300 crore available which was at that time a huge sum of money. The moneys were used to modernize the handlooms by converting pit looms to frame looms and setting up dye houses for the industry. This brought about a major revolution in the handloom industry in just three years.'

Captain Nair then told me a story which changed his life and of many people in India who now work and stay at Leela hotels. 'In 1958, William Jacobson, a leading US textile importer, visited Bombay to see Mr Swaminathan, the Commissioner of textiles, as he was in pursuit of exotic fabric from India. The Commissioner directed him to me and I showed him my collection which included a fabric he liked and wanted. It was a Madras plaid (checked pattern) fabric with a musty, pungent smell of vegetable dyes and gingelly oils and was available in brilliant colours. I agreed to supply this fabric to him but warned him that the colour would run and that the fabric must thus be washed with extreme care with cold water. I was selling it to him at USD 1 per yard and he was making it into jackets selling at USD 50 at Brooks Brothers. The jackets were a big hit but he failed to pass on the washing instructions. Customers were furious when the colours ran and ruined their other garments. William Jacobson was livid and summoned me to the US to meet with him and his lawyers. I managed to dissuade the lawyers from suing me. Instead, we designed a mutually agreeable solution. Do you know what this solution was? Well, the lawyer arranged an interview for me with the editor of *Seventeen* magazine in which I pitched a story about this miracle fabric made exclusively for the US and only available at Brooks Brothers store in New York. The editor ran a seven-page spread on the fabric under the sobriquet "Bleeding Madras – the miracle handwoven fabric from India". The article carried beautiful pictures of the fabric with the caption "guaranteed to bleed". It was a huge hit. Within a week of the magazine hitting the stands Brooks Brothers had received thousands of inquiries for the item. I became an overnight celebrity in the US textile sector. William and I both made our fortune from the sale. "Bleeding Madras" opened a door for future fabric import and created thumping exports for India.

'A couple of months after this, I displayed a number of fabrics, including "Bleeding Madras", at a large International Trade Fair in Chicago. An American gentleman named Bill Axelrod telephoned me from New York and indicated he was interested in buying my whole production. He was willing to pay my price and asked me to come to New York to sign the deal. This was a huge contract for me and I readily agreed. I asked him, "Where shall we meet in New York?" He replied, "I am staying at the Waldorf so I suggest we meet there." This was to be my first trip to New York and I was not very familiar at that time with hotels so I asked, "What do you mean, 'Waldorf'?" "Waldorf what?" Axelrod was exasperated. "The Waldorf Astoria of course. Surely, you know the Waldorf Astoria Hotel?" "Of course," I replied pretending to know. On getting off the phone I checked with people in Chicago and found it was one of the most famous and expensive hotels in all of America.

'After my faux pas with Mr Axelrod, I thought I had better stay at the Waldorf to impress him. I had no idea whether I could really afford it but I had to take a chance; after all, it was a huge potential contract. So, on arriving in New York, I took a cab to the Waldorf. The doorman opened the cab door as the cab driver said, "$3.50, Sir." I handed over a $5 note and told him to keep the change. As I got out, the doorman said, "Sir, in New York $4 would have been fine for the cab."' I thanked him and tipped him the rest. A bellboy then arrived to carry my battered suitcase to the reception desk. I said to the reception clerk, "I understand my friend Mr Axelrod is staying here." He replied, "Yes, Sir. He is on the 22nd floor." I asked if they had a room on a higher floor. "Not in Waldorf Sir, but in Waldorf Towers we have a suite available on the 29th floor." On arrival in my suite I tipped the bellboy another $5. I knew these were large tips but I had to give the impression in the hotel that I was a successful Indian businessman which, at that time, of course, I certainly was not. I immediately rang Mr Axelrod from my room and delighted in telling him I was staying in Room 2908 of the Waldorf Towers. He could not believe that I had such an exquisite suite; this was enough to impress him that I was a bona fide businessman capable of doing this large deal with him. The next day I bagged a million yard order from him for "Bleeding Madras" which literally turned the tide for textile exports from India to the US. I was a very happy man and Mr Axelrod and I became good friends.

'As it was my first trip to New York and I had fallen in love with the Waldorf, I extended my stay by several weeks. During those days several US textile luminaries would come to interview me wanting to know the secret of "Bleeding Madras". One morning as I was having breakfast by myself in the Peacock Alley restaurant in the lobby, I felt someone standing beside me and thought it must be another textile manufacturer. This well-dressed man asked if I was Captain Nair? He said he was Conrad Hilton and owned the hotel and that his friend Bill Axelrod had told him about me. He asked me to lunch the following day. Instinctively, I did not want to give the impression to Mr Hilton that I was overawed with his invitation (which I was) and told him that I would love to have lunch with him but was booked solid for the week (which I was not) and would let him know when I was available. He was clearly rather stunned but we did have lunch the following week and thus started a long friendship with the illustrious Mr Hilton and my love affair with beautiful hotels. On that stay at the Waldorf, I became inspired to build similar hotels in India.'

The Leela Hotel in Mumbai where I was meeting Captain Nair was his first venture into the world of 5-star deluxe hotels and the first hotel to be built in North Mumbai. He has now added a number of others throughout India in cities like Bangalore, Goa, Kovalam (Kerala), Gurgaon (Delhi NCR), Udaipur and will soon open in New Delhi and Chennai.

Captain Nair raised much of the money for his hotel enterprise by collecting USD 5,000 from about 200 friends in the US. Many of these people remain shareholders of the Leela Group today. Building the hotel was not without difficulties. 'This area was, until the mid 1980s when they decided to build the international airport, just a place with swamps, shanties and barren land. This hotel is located on what was once in the backyard of my Leela lace factory. Other hotels tried to stop me. For example they caused one of the newspapers to publish an article claiming the hotel was a hazard to the airport and should be reduced to four storeys. The then Chief Minister Vasant Dada Patil who laid the foundation stone told me, "Don't worry, you must see Prime Minister Rajiv Gandhi." So I went to meet Rajiv Gandhi who, as you may know, was formerly a pilot in Indian Airlines. Rajiv Gandhi told me, "Your hotel is not on the flight path. What's the problem, then? You should get approval from my minister." It was as simple as that. After six months of blockage, the project was cleared on the Prime Minister's instructions and there has been no looking back.'

It did not take Captain Nair long to realize that he would profit more if he exported finished products rather than just raw textiles. Leela, his wife, loved cotton lace and believed they should produce it in India. This was a complicated process. Captain Nair knew he needed an expert partner from Britain. In Nottingham he met Swift and Wass Ltd, the leading manufacturer of lace machines. 'Charles Goodley from that company told me ,"I cannot sell these machines to you as I manufacture them exclusively for Johnston Shields and Co in Scotland." He suggested I approach that company so I met Lawrence Mitchell, its Managing Director. I told him I wanted to enter into a joint venture with his company to produce lace in India. Not surprisingly, Mr Mitchell told me he needed a reference as he did not know me or my company. I wondered who I could give as a reference but it came to me in a flash, who better than Lord Mountbatten who I had known when he was Viceroy in India. I rang him in the presence of Mr Mitchell and chatted to Lord Mountbatten for several minutes as we had not spoken for many years. He told me he was happy to speak on my behalf and I handed the phone to Mr Mitchell.' Captain Nair laughs as he tells me he remembers how Mr Mitchell sat upright and sweated as he spoke to Lord Mountbatten. Needless to say the joint venture was entered into. 'Leela Scottish Lace was the first lace manufacturer in India. We exported lace all over the world and people in the industry still talk about it.'

As our meeting drew to a close, I asked Captain Nair what advice he had for young entrepreneurs. 'You must have a vision, and in order to implement this vision you must plan and work hard with perseverance and persistence until you have achieved that vision. Just as our first Prime Minister Nehru said, "Success comes to those who dare and act." I do not believe in luck. If there is such a thing then it comes to those who dare and act.' In the way Captain Nair has lived and continues to live his life, there is a message for us all.

Captain CP Krishnan Nair is the chairman of **The Leela Group** (www.theleela.com) of premium 5-star deluxe palaces, hotels and resorts. A first-generation entrepreneur since 1957, when he began manufacturing niche fabrics for the international markets, the former army captain is also founder of Leela Scottish Lace, India's first and only manufacturers of premium lace.

‘Banking was definitely in my blood.’

DEEPAK PAREKH

Chairman
HDFC

I met Deepak Parekh late on a weekday afternoon – having driven back from Pune in the early afternoon at HDFC's headquarters in Ramon House, Churchgate, one of Mumbai's busiest commercial spots. His office, which is on the 5th floor, is modest and has a comfortable feel to it. He was seated at his desk and behind him I could see several piles of crisp new books stacked up on a long thin table. I wondered about the number of books.

Deepak was born in Bombay on 18 October 1944 but was almost immediately taken to Burma, soon after the war ended in early 1947. 'That is where my father had been working before the war and after it ended. In India, and I assume for most Asian cultures as well, tradition dictates that the wife should go to her parent's home to have their baby.'

I asked what his father was doing in Burma. 'He was working for the Central Bank of India, a large Indian commercial bank with presence in Burma. My father was the branch manager at Rangoon. The bank was subsequently nationalized, but you should know it is not the Reserve Bank of India as it is not the regulator.

'The story of my father's time around the war years is interesting. He was the last person to leave the bank before the Japanese arrived in Rangoon in 1942. Everyone else in the bank had left and taken a boat back to India. My father locked the bank, put the key in his pocket and then travelled out of Burma. He used various modes of transports including a bullock cart, and walked through the mountain ranges all the way to Assam in India. There were no telephones at that time so he sent my mother a telegram when he got to Assam some six weeks later. Until then my mother did not know if he was dead or alive. I remember seeing a photo of him with a long beard.'

Deepak laughs when telling me that, 'Following the end of the war, the bank asked him to return to Rangoon with the key he had kept and to re-open the branch.

'We lived in Rangoon until 1955 when my mother, sister and myself returned to Bombay, while my father stayed back. By that time, I was well into high school attending what was known as Methodist English High School, as was my elder sister. My parents wanted to stay but the government introduced a rule that the language of instruction for education must be Burmese. We knew a little bit of Burmese but we didn't know how to read and write. So, at this stage, we were getting zero marks in our exams. Even my father, who had lived there many years, found it difficult to speak Burmese. In fact, the business language was English. Anyway, as a result of these changes, my parents correctly decided there was no alternative for my sister and me but to return to India for our schooling and that my mother would come with us. I guess they knew it was just a matter of time until my father got transferred back too. I can remember the excitement of the trip home as we flew on an airline called UBA – Union of Burma Airways. Can you believe the flight on a Dakota aircraft from Rangoon to Calcutta took almost four hours; a flight which would be less than an hour today?'

I asked Deepak what, in particular, he could remember about those childhood years in Rangoon. 'Well, it was a very peaceful life. Politically, though, it was always unstable. I can remember the Prime Minister being killed and the army junta coming into power. The parliament was about five to ten minutes walk away from the house and I remember someone was shot there. Despite the peaceful life my family led, for rich Indian trading families it was quite different; many were kidnapped for ransom.

'I returned to Rangoon to celebrate my 25th wedding anniversary. We stayed at the Strand Hotel, which was at one time one of the most famous hotels in all of Asia, just like the Raffles in Singapore and the Oriental in Bangkok. It was a fascinating journey back in time. I went to see my old school. I also spent several hours finding our old home. I knew the street name when we lived there was "Judah Ezekiel" but the name had been changed. However, I eventually found our home and went up and rang the bell and met the people who now lived there. Sadly, as exciting as it was for me to return "home", it was obvious for all to see that whereas Rangoon was a thriving city for most of the time our family lived there, it is now a shadow of that and life is now hard for most Burmese.

'The writing was on the wall even when we were living there so many years ago. I remember my parents trying to help their Burmese friends get permission to settle elsewhere. Some of the Burmese women fictitiously married Indian men because, without a husband, they could not get permission to leave Burma.

'But Burma is certainly an important part of my childhood and, as I rang a gong at the Shwedagon Pagoda on my recent visit with my wife, the monks shared a superstition that says I will return! We shall see,' Deepak says, laughing.

Unfortunately, Deepak's father was not immediately posted back to Mumbai where his mother, sister and he were living, so it was some years until they were able to all live permanently together. 'I was attending St Xavier High School and my sister was going to a Parsi school called JB Petit High School for Girls. My parents decided not to interrupt our schooling yet again. During these years, we lived with my mother and sometimes with my maternal grandmother, and visited my father on holidays at his bank posting. Needless to say, this made me much closer to my mother in terms of guidance.'

I asked whether he had any particular memories of his school days in Mumbai. 'I can remember it was a large school with each class having about fifty-five children. It was a missionary school and had the lowest fees going at the time – Rs 10 per month. Even so, there were a number of families who could not afford this but the school nevertheless accepted them and did not chase them for payment. I have to say, we all got a wonderful education there. The school exists to this day and I really wanted my children to go there too. Sadly, they did not want to.

'By the time I was in the 7th standard, I could see that the science stream was not my cup of tea. I was pretty poor at physics and chemistry,' he laughs. 'Most children in my school went on to St Xavier's College which was affiliated. This was – and remains – a very reputable college. However, it did not offer commerce which I saw as my only option, given a science-based degree was out of the question.'

I asked him whether a humanities degree would not have been possible. He chuckles, 'Oh no, we always had the impression that only girls did arts and then got married.'

So, Deepak attended a government college, the Sydenham College of Commerce and Economics. I wondered what sort of student he was as I told him many of the people interviewed for this book were consistently ranked in the top of their classes. He laughed and replied, 'In school I was an indifferent student. I had to take help from my classmates, and my mother had to teach me.' I told him that would be wonderful encouragement for many young people reading this book.

Upon graduation with a Bachelor of Commerce, Deepak decided he needed an additional qualification. He had quite enjoyed accountancy during his undergraduate degree, so he moved to England to be trained as an accountant.

'I did four years of articleship with Whinney Smith & Whinney, which morphed into Whinney, Murray & Co, then Ernst and Whinney, then Ernst & Ernst, to finally become Ernst & Young. I was very lucky to get these Articles and the reason I got them was because Whinney Smith & Whinney were associated with the Indian auditors of Central Bank where my father worked and was, by that time, a senior manager. He made the introduction for me. In fact, at this time it was not easy to study abroad; the government only allowed about fifteen students to go abroad for accounting studies. My father encouraged me to avoid a third-class degree from college. He told me that with a third-class degree even he would not be able to help me get my Articleship abroad. Fortunately, I managed to scrape through to a second class,' he laughs.

I asked Deepak if he stayed in England for that entire time before coming home. 'No, I came home at the end of the first year. I found it terrible. I had never lived away from home and was living a frugal existence, with no money in my pocket and a dark, gloomy weather. The salary was not enough to survive and I had to depend on remittances from home to supplement my tiny wages as an articled clerk.

'However, I began to adapt to life in London. Once I had my chartered accountancy qualification, I loved my time there. I still did not have much money. I had my 21st birthday in London and took three of my friends to dinner to celebrate. I told them I had 2 shillings and 6 pence for each of them. We ate and drank and had a great time. Unfortunately, the bill came to 13 shillings, so my friends had to shell out the rest.

'There is another event which I cannot forget about that period. Only about 50 per cent passed the finals to become chartered accountants. The Association of Chartered Accountants sent you the results by mail. If you received a heavy envelope from them you knew you had passed. At that time, I was staying in a guesthouse in Harrow and, on the evening before I knew the mail would arrive, I went out and bought a small bottle of whiskey to calm my nerves. I dropped the wretched bottle and broke it so I had neither drink nor sleep that night,' he chuckles.

'Fortunately, it was the heavy envelope and, as a result, my salary doubled overnight. I don't think I was any wiser but my qualification led to this doubling.'

After a few more months of working in London, Deepak asked his firm for a transfer to the New York office, which they did. He worked in New York as a consultant to the US firm but decided not to get a Green Card. 'It was time to go home.' It was 1972.

'That was a fun trip. I took two months to get home. I travelled from New York to California, hitchhiked and stayed at a friend's house in Berkeley, and then to Honolulu, Tokyo and Bangkok before taking a flight to Bombay. As I did not exactly know when I would arrive home, I decided to surprise my parents. The joke was on me because the flight arrived in the middle of the night and the first thing I had to ask my mother on waking her up was money for the taxi!

'Next morning, after she had a good look at me, she declared that she would not feed me unless I had a hair cut.' I told Deepak his mother was not alone. It was common for parents in Australia to bemoan the length of their son's hair in those years.

I wondered why he decided to come back to India at that time. 'As the only son with one sister, I felt it was my duty to come back and provide for them after all they had done for me.

'Having cut my hair, I went to meet a friend who was in college with me. We met near the Oberoi Hotel as she was working at the National Grindlay's Merchant Banking division. She then took me to meet her boss who told me there was a vacancy available in four months. I accepted the offer and, in the meantime, worked with a friend in his company.

'I spent three years at Grindlay's and then joined Chase Manhattan. As they did not have a Bombay branch, they immediately posted me to Hong Kong and then to Singapore. I was away for about a year. Not only did I get some excellent banking training but I also played mahjong and learnt some Mandarin and Cantonese,' he laughs.

I observed that he was by now around thirty and not married. 'Yes, that was quite late to marry at that time but, even though I was certainly under pressure to marry, my parents were broad-minded and were not forcing me into an arranged marriage. But by the time I was thirty-one, I was married.'

I asked how that came about. 'Well, I had some very good Indian friends who lived in Canada. We had met during our studies in London. They too were chartered accountants. We were such good friends that they wanted me to attend their wedding in Canada and even offered me a ticket to fly there provided I paid for the return. I was unable to do that and so missed their wedding. Anyway, they visited Bombay and suggested I should meet this friend of theirs who was living in the same building as them. I agreed and that's how I met my wife, Smita.

'Shortly after I married, I was offered a job in the Gulf with Chase. It was by then 1978. I took the job but, not long after I started, my uncle asked me to come back and join him in HDFC which he had just founded. The salary was half what I was getting in Saudi and, as by that time we had one small child, my wife was not too happy when she learnt I wanted to take the job.

'To be fair, my uncle did not pressurize me; he persuaded me. He had this vision to start a mortgage company. It was something unknown and untested but I was reasonably confident – having worked for three years with Grindlay's, and for Chase in Hong Kong, Singapore as well as in Saudi – that if it didn't work, I would do something else. I was not worried.'

I said that I imagined banking must have been in his blood, given his father's career with Central Bank. 'Not only did my father spend his career in the Central Bank but his father – my grandfather – did too. My grandfather was the first employee of the Central Bank which had been founded by a Parsi family. I would have loved to also carry on the family tradition at the Central Bank but, by the time I was ready to join, all banks had been nationalized and were not hiring. My uncle, prior to founding HDFC, had worked with ICICI. So yes, banking was definitely in my blood.'

Deepak started with HDFC as a Deputy General Manager and worked his way up to Executive Director and then Managing Director to eventually becoming Chairman in February 1993. These years saw HDFC's transformation from a modest mortgage provider for middle income groups into the by-word for housing finance in India. Deepak became India's 'homemaker' for making affordable home finance available to millions of Indians. I asked him what he felt his main contribution had been. 'I think it is that I am a practical man.' There's more to it, of course. Mahindra and Mahindra Chairman, Keshub Mahindra, is reported to have said, 'His ability to see the big picture before anyone else is unique.' His friend and member of Parliament, Murli Deora would say, '... his knowledge of economic and financial matters is unsurpassed.' Contemporaries see him as being a street-smart man, equipped with the instinct and resourcefulness for survival. They respect his intellect and his shrewd head for business.

Deepak is a prominent voice on issues relating to governance and corporate citizenship. He serves on various governmental and industry committees on financial services, capital markets and infrastructure reforms. He is known in political and business leadership circles as the man for a crisis, as he demonstrated by playing the pivotal role in saving scandal-ridden Satyam Computer Services from the brink.

Even on a first meeting, Deepak comes across to me as a 'people person.' The common refrain about Deepak among his colleagues and friends is his genuine interest in the lives of people he meets. The way he bonds with people both within and outside HDFC is evidence of his accessibility and availability. To any old-time customers of the bank, he is simply '*aapro* Deepak' which is Gujarati for 'our Deepak' and they want to meet him personally to handle even small deposits. Deepak has no fashion statements or management mantras; his style is all his own. According to wife Smita, he does what he thinks is in the best interest of the company and family. 'He's always been thoroughly grounded in reality', she says. Other close family members talk of him as a person who lives by the tenet 'to thyself be true' and leads a simple life.

Given the family connection, some people have the impression that HDFC is a family business. 'Far from the truth. I started as a salaried employee and I will retire as one. I don't own a single private company. Even when I retire I have no plans to start one. As it happens, until we introduced stock options for employees, I only owned a few shares in HDFC that my uncle HT Parekh willed to me on his death.'

Towards the end of our meeting, I inquired about the mountain of print behind him. 'These are all books that people have written or highly recommended and given to me. I plan to donate them some day to a library. I have to admit I have not read all of them. Perhaps, one day,' he chuckles, 'when I am retired I will have time to do this.'

Incorporated in 1977, **HDFC** (Housing Development Finance Corporation) Ltd (www.hdfc.com) is India's largest housing finance company with interests in banking, life insurance, general insurance, asset management, credit information and real estate venture capital.

"The government at that time wanted the Indian entrepreneur to go and box in a boxing ring with his arms tied behind his back and win the bout. An Indian businessman in those times had to find a way to win a boxing bout without using his arms."

DEEPAK PURI

Founder, Chairman & Managing Director
Moser Baer India

Deepak Puri was brought up in Delhi in a joint family. His father and his three brothers were government servants. 'I had a very happy childhood. We were three siblings: two brothers and a sister. I am the oldest and was born on 28 July 1941, my brother is younger to me and our sister is the youngest. I would not hazard to expound that mine was a "rags to riches" story for I was born in one relatively well-to-do family.

'My paternal grandfather, Captain Jamunadas Puri was a very well-to-do person with large landed property. He used to go to the homes of each of his three sons who lived in Delhi every morning. He would have breakfast with one and then go to the other two just to check on how the families were. I can vividly remember, he used to have the most peculiar breakfast every morning: a glass of hot milk with a raw egg thrown in. I used to feel terrible just looking at that raw egg.

'When independence came in 1947, there was not enough housing for mid-level government officials and so the government initially provided tents; actually the site was where the Supreme Court is located today. I can recall sleeping in those tents until we moved to the former British Army barracks on Secundra Road. This is close to where the Federation of Indian Chamber of Commerce has its offices today and even closer to Bengali Market, nearby where my grandfather lived. Our home was essentially five rooms in a straight line to make what they called a "house". Despite the fact that it was very small, we knew we were very lucky to have a roof over our heads.'

When Deepak was born, his father, Krishan Lal Puri was director of Civil Aviation. He went on to become director general of Civil Aviation. He graduated from Imperial College, London, with which there are close family ties. Not only did Deepak's father study there, but one of his uncles did as well and, in due course, so did Deepak.

Deepak remembers that their joint family was close-knit and that when his father was offered a job at the Civil Aviation Authorities Headquarters in Quebec in Canada in the early 1950s, he turned it down. 'My father told everyone who asked why he turned it down, when most people would have leapt at the opportunity. He said that his father was in Delhi and so were the rest of his family. He said he was very happy here with his family. It was very close-knit, and I am happy to say it remains so until today.'

Deepak was educated at Modern School, no more than a five-minute walk from home. 'It was a wonderful, care-free life. Perhaps my entrepreneurial spirit was stoked when I was about ten years old. My school wanted us to bring our photographs. My father rang up a friend (who owned a photography shop at Connaught Place) who told him that this could be done for Rs 16 at his shop. My father gave me the money and told me to cycle to the shop – it was safe in those days to cycle anywhere in Delhi. When I got out of our house I met a friend of mine. He was a Sindhi boy – I don't know where he is now – I've lost track of him. He asked me where I was going and I told him. He said, "16 rupees! You've got 16 rupees?" I said that I did. He said, "Look, at Red Fort you can get a photograph taken for only 4 rupees. So sixteen minus four, that's a surplus of Rs 12, my dear chap. We can go to that new restaurant in Connaught Place and have lunch and then to Red Fort." That was the day I ate my first hamburger and spent the Rs 12. We then cycled off to Red Fort and had the photos taken. Even in those days they did instant photos. The photographers had what were called pinhole cameras. It was quite funny because, after the chap took the photograph, I looked at it and said, "Hey, this looks like a monkey". Now, the photographer was quick-witted. He responded, "Sir, I beg your pardon, the camera does not lie. If you look like a monkey, so be it."'

Deepak passed out from Modern School in 1957 and proceeded to St Stephen's College from where he graduated in 1960. He maintains he was lucky to graduate from St Stephen's as he spent a lot of his time partying and having fun with his many friends and, as he says, 'particularly those from

Miranda House, the women's college which was right next door to St Stephen's.'

Deepak is tall and lanky and I thought he looked like a sportsman. 'I may look like it but, frankly, I was not very good at sports although I love all forms. By way of example there is one embarrassing story of my sports career. When I was at college, I was the goalkeeper in the finals of the water polo competition. I let in 14 goals in 14 minutes,' he laughs.

If he wasn't a sportsman I asked Deepak if he was a good or keen student. 'No, not really. The other day the Modernites' class of '57 met after fifty years. I met guys who were with me, who had passed through and gone into the Indian Administrative Services, the IAS. I told them there was no way in the world I could have passed that entrance exam. I'm a disciplined individual and I work hard but I don't know if I could ever have worked under someone, particularly within the confines of government service.

'India in the 1960s was stifling for people like me, even more so after I had spent three years in London attending Imperial College. The country which produced the Kama Sutra became absolutely rigid and prudish. Delhi was particularly snooty at that time. Old British Clubs like the Delhi Gymkhana Club would never have given membership to a businessman. The only reason I managed to become a member was because my father was a member and he therefore got automatic membership for his children. By the time I left St Stephen's I knew that a career in the government was not my "cup of tea", it was too conservative and restrictive which would have stifled all my initiatives and ideas.'

Believe it or not, Deepak has only been an employee for nine months in his entire career. Initially, this was with ESSO Standard Eastern, immediately after he returned from Imperial College as a mechanical engineer. 'I was based in Bombay and worked in their marketing department for a short period before they transferred me to Calcutta. I quit not long after and joined Shalimar Paints, which was then part of the British Courtaulds' group, for the balance of my nine month career as an employee.'

Not long before he was transferred to Calcutta, Deepak had met Nita, his wife-to-be in Delhi. They were married in 1964 and spent the following eighteen years in Calcutta.

'I had little money. My salary at Shalimar Paints was about Rs 1020 per month and after paying my landlady who charged me Rs 400 per month for accommodation, including breakfast and dinner there was not much left. Maybe, I had Rs 400 to my name.'

I asked Deepak what he did to survive. 'Trading,' said Deepak. 'See, when you don't have capital, and you don't want to take money from your father, what do you do? You buy on credit and sell in cash. Now how do you do that? How do you sell in cash? Before you can sell in cash you first have to establish your credibility. I had no assets other than the shirt on my back. The only way for me to establish credibility was to go to people who knew my family. I went to an architect who knew my family and said, 'Look you are designing buildings – can I please provide you with aluminium doors and windows?' He agreed. Building contractors, who traditionally did this job, were notoriously slow in paying. I had to convince the suppliers to give to me extended credit and then get the money out of the contractors before my credit line expired.'

Deepak established a few companies in Calcutta to carry on his business. There was Metal Industries, Metal Shop Products and Met Industries. 'I gave the best years of my life, from 1964 to 1983 to Calcutta. My Calcutta businesses did not take off like Moser Baer but we struggled and incrementally grew from trading to manufacturing metal products such as wire and pipes and overhead transmission lines. At the time I left Calcutta, we were probably turning over Rs 30 million with a profit of about Rs 3 million.

'My philosophy has been – stand by yourself, always. That's how people have faith in you. Also, be fair to every human being. Let's say, today you desperately need a job with me ... your children are hungry, and I give you a job for peanuts. You'll join because you have to feed your children but within a month, you'll start looking elsewhere.

'Up until his death in 1970, my father thought I was insane as with education from Imperial College I could easily have got a good job in the government or the private sector. He could see that I was struggling and could not understand why I would not give up my attempts at becoming an entrepreneur. I always teased my mother and father that I knew why they called my younger brother "Sooraj" and me "Deepak". The first son was named "Deepak" but do you know what that means?' Naturally I replied that I did not. 'It means the same as "diya" in Hindi which is a small earthen lamp which gives off a small amount of light. Do you know what "Sooraj" means? Again I replied I did not. 'It means the "sun" which, of course, gives off a huge amount of light. So I used to tease my parents that they knew from the time I was born that I was average and would not give off too much light in my achievements. It was, of course, light hearted and just fun with my parents. However, I knew I felt unconsciously drawn to business as the pursuit where I would make my mark – as small as that may be.

'Look, life is a struggle, but in Hindu philosophy every struggle teaches you to do something better in future. You have to be like those nine bowling pins – you get hit, you fall down and then get up again. And I've done that all my life.'

In 1983, Deepak decided to return to Delhi and I wondered why he would do this after twenty years in Calcutta. 'Even in the early 1970s, I could feel the business environment in Calcutta getting worse. Why, you ask? Well, the communists came to power in Calcutta but the problems were not so much caused by the communists as by extremist union groups such as those supporting the violent Marxist-Maoist movement – the Naxalites. This led to severe power shortages, strikes and damage to much of the city's infrastructure. This eventually led to complete economic stagnation. Large British companies such as Braithwaite, Burn and Company, Guest Keen Williams and Dunlop were powerhouses in the days before this all came to pass. Metal Box shut down and Lipton and other tea companies moved out of Calcutta. The unions in Calcutta at that time had the bizarre doctrine 'our employees do not have to work but you, Mr Employer, still have to pay their salary'. It was the most stupid doctrine you could come across. At the drop of a hat they would insist on a 20 per cent bonus for their members, whether or not there was the money to pay it.

'So, life was getting increasingly tough and consequently the quality of life was deteriorating. Sometimes, workers would have a "gherao" at the owner's home. "Gherao" means circle in Hindi. They would encircle the house and "gherao" the owner so that he could not leave home. A more severe form of gherao or encirclement was, if they do it at your office room and not allow you to do anything. The owner would remain there until he agreed to the workers' demands or help came to get him out. I knew this was likely to happen to me some day so I decided I needed to have an escape route from our apartment. Fortunately, we lived on the top floor and I could access the roof of my landlord's house through one of the windows. Unfortunately, all the windows had metal grills. So I had one of the window frames with the grill hinged so that it could swing open like a window, for safety sake it was padlocked. The day the workers turned up I was ready. There were about 300. What provoked them to come was that I had decided the only path was to largely ignore their ridiculous claims. I just stopped going to the factory and told them to do what they wanted. I think this surprised them. So when I heard they were gathering outside the house, I unlocked and opened the window and jumped down to my landlord's roof deck. He got the shock of his life. I said to him, "Quickly, tell me how to get to the back of your home." He pointed the way to go and I ran to the end of his garden and climbed over the wall to the adjoining home which, as luck would have it, was the home of the Russian consul. His security guards quickly grabbed me, wondering who was the crazy Indian climbing into their mission, when most people would have been trying to get out,' Deepak says with a laugh.

'This experience taught me that one needs to always have sufficient escape routes from every situation. Like many other employers in Calcutta, I began to adopt the path of least resistance. I would agree to the union demands and then not implement them on the basis they were agreed to under duress. In most cases, the threats were verbal and psychological rather than physical but there were nevertheless murders carried out by the Naxalites. One, I can remember, involved the shooting to death of the owner of a motor agency in Calcutta's famous Chowringhee Street; at that time just like Pall Mall in London. In another, the manager of a Ludlow jute mill who did not agree with what his workers demanded was thrown into the mill's furnace. Almost every business which could get out of Calcutta did so. I decided there was no alternative but to do the same. I started moving my businesses in about 1983 and by 1986 the whole family moved to Delhi.

'It really was a terrible time. Another example springs to mind. I would be sitting in my office when the union representative would walk in without any appointment. He would sit down in the chair on other side of my desk and put his feet up on it and start smoking a cigarette. Then he would begin trying to negotiate with me. When he felt like a cup of coffee or tea he would not ask me but would ring the bell I had on the desk and ask for one for himself but not for me. Bizarre. The current government of West Bengal is trying to turn this around but I have always said that "a dog's tail cannot be straightened".

'There is one more story I would like to tell you of this time in India. It is not about the unions and Calcutta but the ridiculous "licence raj" under which all Indians lived at that time. In those days, there were no cars available in the showrooms and you had to place an order some years in advance. There were only two or three sorts of car available; one was Ambassador, a Bengal built car and the other a FIAT built in Pune. I booked the Ambassador paying a 30 per cent advance. After two or three years, I received an invitation to come and collect the car after paying the balance. As you can imagine this was a big day so my wife and I turned up at the showroom where an agent pointed to a car and told us that was ours. I said, "I don't think so, Sir, I booked a black car and that one is white." He asked me my name and went to look up the records. He came back and told me that it was my car even if it was white. We had waited two years and therefore reconciled to white and went and sat in the car. As soon as we got in, we noticed many deficiencies such as the ash trays were rusted and the ones in the rear would not even stay in their slots. I then tried the headlights and saw on the showroom wall only one lighted up. I called the agent over and said, "What's going on? We ordered and paid for a new car. Please get me the manager." Shortly after the agent came back with a short, plump fellow. I told him I had waited two years for a black car and had been given a white one full of defects.' Deepak then stops talking for a second and looks at me, 'Peter, you are recording this, aren't you because I would like you to put this down in the book. That company was Hindustan Motors, which is owned by a good friend of mine and, of course, a completely different organization these days. Back then, the manager, having listened to me very patiently, said to me, "Mr Puri, this is the car for you; take it or leave it. There are hundreds of people waiting, and there is also a black market on this car." It only took my wife and me a few minutes to decide we had no option. We took the car and then paid a garage to remedy the defects.'

I asked Deepak whether he had a clearly thought-out business plan when he moved back to Delhi. He explained that through his work in Calcutta he had come to know of Moser Baer from Switzerland and after discussions with Urs Moser, the owner they decided to go into the manufacture and sale of master and slave clocks. These are the clocks one sees in Swiss train stations. The master clock ensures all the clocks – that is, slaves – on all the stations show the correct time. Although the parties agreed on everything, after two years of frustrating discussions, the Indian government rejected the venture's right to import some of the components. 'Urs Moser and I agreed the venture was doomed so I returned his 49 per cent interest in the Indian company and asked him if he would object if I used the name for another business. He told me I was welcome to keep it.

'So, I moved from master and slave clocks to time recording systems. At that time, the only time-keeping system available in India was the good old 1920 one from Britain using a pendulum system produced by the Anglo-Swiss Watch Company of Calcutta. I went to Japan to meet a few companies and picked up an agency under which I imported their systems in a knock-down condition. That is the strange thing about that era in India. Whereas, I was turned down in the case of the master and slave clocks – we got approval for Japanese time recording systems.'

I remarked that I was amazed at how any small- or mid-sized entrepreneur managed to survive during the 'licence raj' era. Deepak responded, 'In fact, what I say is, it is not so amazing they survived but it is an absolute miracle that some actually did well. I have been quoted on this very often. The government at that time wanted the Indian entrepreneur to go and box in a boxing ring with his arms tied behind his back and win the bout. An Indian businessman in those times had to find a way to win a boxing bout without using his arms.'

On his return from Calcutta, Deepak was fortunate to be able to move into the family home on Ring Road, where his mother had been living alone since his father's death in 1970. Not only did the family reside there, but Moser Baer had its first office there; an office on the top floor and an assembly workshop in the garage where three workers assembled time recording systems.

What happened next was unpredictable, as it was for so many of the other entrepreneurs in this book. Call it luck, call it foresight; I still don't know which even after talking to so many entrepreneurs in Asia. The story goes that Deepak went to Bombay one day in 1985 on some business and caught up with a friend.

'At that time India was for some crazy reason throwing out American businesses such as Coca Cola and IBM. This friend was working for International Data Management which was originally IBM, of course, wholly Indian-owned. I told him, "Look I am sick and tired of all these time keeping systems. Indian factories don't require them very often. What do you think I do now?" So he went around the office ... and this is a well-known fact ... and he came back to me with an eight-inch square black plastic object. It was flopping around. He told me, "This is called a floppy disk. It records data. Why don't you make these in India." I said, "This is something new to me. I'm a mechanical engineer. I understand engines. I don't understand this, what the hell is it?" He was very patient and explained how it worked. I asked him if I could have one. Unfortunately, he said I could not as he had very few and that was why he was desperate to have some made in India. But he did have one damaged one which he could give me. After I flew back to Delhi I immediately contacted my brother who was living in California and said I understood there was a company in California called Xidex making floppy discs. He discovered that not only did Xidex make floppy discs but that they owned Dyson which was the "grand daddy" of the electronics and data storage sector. Even more of a fluke, he told me that we had a common Indian friend who worked for Xidex. As they say, the rest is history.

'They gave Moser Baer the licence to make the floppy discs in India. We went public in 1986 as we needed funds to build a plant. The first plant was in Noida in Delhi. I was really getting fed up with the "licence raj" and went to the government in about 1989 and asked them if I wanted to export whether I needed approval to increase my production capacity. I knew India was going through a foreign exchange shortage at the time and they responded no approval was needed. So, I went out looking for export offers because I couldn't sell more than the licensed capacity in India. But another technological development was taking place at the same time and that was the advent of optical media. I was in two minds. I was not sure what to do. In three-and-a-half years demand for the floppy disc had taken off vertically. By the way, my first export order – remember the first order is the most difficult one to get – was to BASF in Germany. The Germans told me they did not mind where it is made provided it met their specifications. In fact, I would say BASF has taught us a lot. When we started regularly supplying to them they indicated they were not happy with the quality and sent engineers to us for six weeks free of cost.

'Despite the success of our floppy discs, which we still make, we invested in optical media and I think it would be fair to say that after a decade of learning, we now make optical discs of cutting-edge quality which are accepted all over the world. But to go into optical disc production required money that we did not have. I can remember I held a road show in Bombay to raise capital. After the presentation we were all having tea at the hotel in Bombay and I overheard two executives of a venture capital fund talking; one Indian and one foreign. The Indian executive asked his colleague, "Sir, do you think we should invest in this company? It sounds very impressive, based upon what Mr Puri and his colleagues presented at the roadshow." The other man replied, "Fools walk in where angels fear to tread." Two months later, their fund was the "fool" who "walked in". They were wonderful and I am sure they have not regretted being "fools" as we are now the second largest producer in the world,' Deepak laughs.

To supplement Deepak's ever increasing burden of the expanding company, Nita joined him on the board of Moser Baer in 1987 as Director, Administration & HR, and she has continued in the same ever since.

This success has not been without challenges. 'Certainly, I believe the key to success in dealing with people is to be very open and honest. If you have a problem in your business or life, or if you have a problem anywhere, what is there to hide? Go and tell your investors, "Hey, we're having a problem. Do you know how to improve it?" Don't hide anything. In my opinion, failure is not to be hidden. In fact, if you talk about it, then in my experience, you are likely to solve the problem and eventually turn into a success.'

I asked him how as an Indian company he managed to compete successfully with Chinese companies. 'I have been waiting for that question,' he said. 'We have been documented by the International Finance Corporation, part of the World Bank, as having the lowest cost optical discs in the world. Not because of the labour; our labour is indeed more expensive than the Chinese as we are in the organized labour sector in India. In China, employees may work twelve hours a day without overtime. In India if you ask an Indian to work overtime without overtime payment, there would be a riot. So on that calculation, India is more expensive but when you add other factors such as quality and productivity we come out tops. Still, we have more than two hundred projects on ways and means to reduce costs. One cannot rest on past laurels.'

Ratul, Deepak's son having graduated fron the Carnegie Mellon University in the US returned to India and joined the company in 1995 as an apprentice and has gradually made his way up.

Having achieved such success with his optical discs I sensed an entrepreneur like Deepak would already be thinking of the next opportunity. I asked him if that was the case or was he satisfied with what he already had on the plate. The game plan for Moser Baer is photovoltaics – conversion of the sun's energies into electrical power. 'Believe me, when we succeed with our photovoltaics, it will have greater valuations than Moser Baer's optical media.'

As our meeting drew to a close Deepak mentioned one last business activity that he thought might be of interest. 'You've no doubt heard Indians love their movies?' I replied that indeed I had. 'Did you know,' he continued, 'India is the world's largest producer of movies; its total usable movie library strength today is 24,000 movies. I don't think Hollywood would have that many. Today, Moser Baer is the largest content owner; we own the rights to more than 11,000 movies in Tamil, Telugu, Bengali, Hindi, and a few in English. In India, DVDs of movies usually sell for Rs 400 whereas we are selling them for Rs 40. What's the reason? Using optical discs, I make cheaper movie DVDs than the pirates. He has to buy my discs for around Rs 20 to make his pirated copies. I've broken the back of the pirates in India,' he said with obvious pleasure.

As I left his office, I noticed in the reception room a plaque which cites Deepak as DataQuest IT 'Man of the Year in 2003'. The citation reads: 'He chose to defy all traditional business conventions and while doing so, scripted a new chapter in the Indian IT industry's success story. Even when the world around him sought its fortunes in the services business, he challenged the norm and invested in manufacturing, matching international quality benchmarks and setting new standards all the way. He and his team have put India on the global map of manufacturing, driving his company to the number three position in its field and becoming an original equipment supplier to many of the world's biggest brands. An alumnus of St Stephen's College in Delhi and an engineering degree holder from the Imperial College of Science and Technology in London, he's been associated with the high-tech engineering industry for over thirty-five years now. He demonstrated his visionary leadership when he chose to invest close to Rs 300 crore in world-class manufacturing facilities in India at a time when the plummeting product prices threatened to push the sales revenues below the manufacturing cost. But proving analysts and their conventional business wisdom wrong, his company went on to achieve astonishing success. It increased capacities by more than thirty times to reach the current capacity of over a billion units. In a short span between 1997 and 2002, his company has registered revenues at a CAGR of a whopping 170 per cent. In the last two years, when hardware companies across the world have seen their revenues drop, he has led an unrelenting upward march with his company posting a staggering 102 per cent and 53 per cent revenue growth, respectively, and while doing so he has unearthed a new paradigm for the Indian IT community that after all, manufacturing is a good and profitable business to be in. For blazing a trail through unchartered waters, creating a new industry and helping position India on the global manufacturing map, DataQuest is proud to present the

IT Man of the Year 2003 to Deepak Puri, Managing Director, Moser Baer India.'

Deepak, however, is far from finished with his life's endeavours. I wonder whether in a few years' time I will meet him again and at the end of the meeting see another plaque with another citation, this one for his pioneering effort in the area of solar photovoltaic energy.

Moser Baer (www.moserbaer.com), headquartered in New Delhi, is a leading global technology company. Established in 1983, the company successfully developed cutting-edge technologies to become the world's second largest manufacturer of Optical Storage media like CDs and DVDs. The company has also emerged as the first to market the next-generation of storage formats like blu-ray discs. Recently, the company has transformed itself from a single business into a multi-technology organization, diversifying into exciting areas of solar energy, home entertainment and IT peripherals & consumer electronics. Moser Baer has over 8,500 full-time employees and multiple manufacturing facilities in the suburbs of New Delhi.

"You may have all the education in the world but what's more important is common sense which, in the real world, is not at all common. Recently I was invited as the chief guest to a meeting of auditors. I think they must have regretted inviting me because I told them that, although I did not know much about the auditing profession, in my experience all one needs is common sense to understand how a company is faring."

AVS RAJU

Founder & Chairman
Nagarjuna Construction Company

One of the joys of writing this book is the pleasure of meeting extraordinary people with extraordinary lives. Even so, every now and then, one person would spring something totally unexpected.

I must admit that I had not heard of AVS Raju or his company, Nagarjuna Construction. A number of my friends, however, insisted that I must include AVS in my book.

After the usual hectic to-and-fro's in arranging one of these interviews, a meeting was lined up for the morning after I arrived in Hyderabad. An hour or so before the meeting, we received a call from AVS's team to check if we would be on time. My hotel was only 10 minutes away; we assured the caller we would be on time. As we left the hotel 30 minutes before the appointed time we received another call to check on our whereabouts. We got into the car, and we got another call, followed by another as we waited at the traffic signal near Nagarjuna Circle a few hundred metres away from his office, and yet another as we went past the gate of his office building at Nagarjuna Hills.

Waiting for us, as we were shepherded into the boardroom, was AVS with a number of his senior colleagues in tow. 'Welcome to Hyderabad!' he greeted us expansively. Two women stepped up to offer us flower bouquets as a video camera went into action, lights and all. Immediately in front of AVS, on the boardroom table, was the largest book I had ever seen in my life, about a metre high. 'A book of poems I have written,' AVS explained.

AVS was born on 18 April 1937 in the village of Antervedipalem between Vijayawada and Visakhapatnam in the East Godavari district of Andhra Pradesh. He was one among eight children. Two children passed away young and, by the time AVS was born, he had four elder sisters and one brother. AVS was the youngest.

'My father combined the professions of being a farmer and a contractor. He had about 20 acres of agricultural land. The profit from the land was marginal, probably only a couple of hundred rupees. My father's real profit came from contracting but he gave almost all of it away. If he earned Rs 100, he probably gave away Rs 80. When he went to a restaurant, he sometimes took 100 people with him, known and unknown, and paid their bill. He was known for his charity and large heart. One of his pet projects was the coconut palms he grew on the banks of the river so that the poor could take the fruit for free.

'I suppose you could say it was a typical middle-class home. My life continued in an uneventful way until I was a teenager.' When AVS was sixteen, his father, who was ill, took a turn for the worse. His sisters had all married and moved away. This left AVS, his mother and brother to look after him. It was obvious to the family that AVS's father did not have long to live. The situation prompted AVS to make two important and eventful decisions.

First, was the subject of marriage – the customary arranged match – so that 'my father was satisfied in the knowledge he had managed to have all his children married. That is a big thing in our culture.'

Second, he discontinued school and tended full time to his father. 'He suffered from a severe nervous disability. He needed to be bathed, dressed, and fed. I did this for two-and-a-half years until he eventually passed away.'

A third major event in his life occurred when AVS turned eighteen. 'I became a father for the first time. Do you know I now have ten children – seven sons and three daughters?' So not only had AVS not finished school but he was a father and had to earn a living.

For several years, after his father died, he and his brother, Suriname Raju continued tilling the land but with little profit. Then, for about fifteen years between 1960 and 1975, they split their time between agriculture and contracting.

From those years AVS considers the vineyard he established in Hyderabad as one his most successful projects. 'It consistently achieved the highest yields seen in India at that time. We still own the vineyard. Even now, every day when I wake up, the first question I ask of my manager is how much it rained the day before.'

On the construction front, the Raju brothers took on a few small construction projects in Andhra Pradesh's coastal areas. However, by the mid '70s they decided to focus on construction and founded Nagarjuna Steel. Nagarjuna Construction, the current flagship, was founded in 1978. 'We decided it was no good being small; so we set our sights on being the top two construction companies in India.'

I wondered what sort of struggle it was for him in those early days. 'Actually it was a lot better for me than it was for my father trying to get contracts during the time of the British raj. At that time if you did not have a father or close relation working for the government, it was almost impossible to get a government contract.

'Early on in my career we had two small projects up in the mountains near Machilipatnam, Andhra Pradesh. These projects were ten kilometres apart. I used to walk to visit both sites twice a day. This meant a forty kilometre walk each day. To do this meant starting before dawn and coming back home late at night and you can imagine how hot it was doing this in summer! But by doing this I could make sure that my workers completed my projects on time and on budget. There was another difficult project we did in those years in the mountains and which involved me walking 30 kilometres each day over difficult terrain. I cannot remember how many pairs of shoes I used up in that project.'

I had heard from my friends of AVS's penchant for hard work, particularly in his early years, but there's another obsession of his that borders on the fanatical – punctuality. 'In India if you have to meet someone at 11 a.m., the general rule is to leave their home at 11 a.m. Up until today, I have never been late for an appointment. I am always 10 minutes early. My belief in punctuality goes back to my childhood. In my early working years as a farmer, I had to be at the fields by 7 a.m. If my breakfast was not ready, I used to eat half-cooked food and go.'

This explained why his assistants were chasing my colleague Chandra and me all morning – to make sure we were on time. 'I apply this rule to myself and everyone I come into contact with. When I invited the then chief minister of Andhra Pradesh, N Chandrababu Naidu, to my sixtieth birthday, I requested him to please be on time. He knew that tardiness irks me and was kind enough to come 5 minutes early.'

But surely this must be an extremely difficult rule to enforce in India? 'Yes it is, but I am a tough man. An appointment is like a contract: once we agree to the terms – in this case, the time of the meeting – come what may I will never be late. I see things through my client's perspective. In return, I get the client's respect. We are currently building a Singaporean style housing estate in Hyderabad. To get this contract I met with this lady who is the vice-president of the company. She asked me to lower my rates but I would not. She tried to persuade me to do so for 30 minutes. In the end I just said, "In this world there is no such thing as the cheapest and best. I asked her where for the price of silver can one expect to buy gold?" The best quality goods are never available at the cheapest rates. Finally, it was Nagarjuna which won the contract. There can be no compromise on quality and on the timeline.'

AVS passed me a small cardboard note pad that is used by his employees – a sort of daily planner. Blazoned across the top of each page is the word 'Think'. In the section dealing with appointments is the motto 'do one thing at a time and first things first' and at the bottom of the page are the words 'plan for results, not for activities'.

I noticed AVS was in a wheelchair. 'It was only a few years ago that I developed a bad streptococcus infection in my leg. Up until then I was very active physically. My leg was amputated above the knee two years ago and when I use my artificial leg, I feel as though I did not lose any part of that leg. I am also, of course, extremely grateful that I did not lose both legs,' he smiles.

We then turned to talk about his passion for writing poems. 'Actually my passion for poetry is driven by a life changing experience in 1996 when I met His Holiness Bhagawan Sri Sathya Sai Baba of Puttaparthi. I met him when Nagarjuna won a contract to construct buildings in his ashram.' I learnt from AVS that even as a child, Sri Sathya Sai Baba's spiritual inclination and contemplative nature had set him apart from other children of his age, and he became known as 'Guru' and 'Brahmagnani' (knower of Brahman or Godhead) in his village. However, it was not until 1940 when he was fourteen he made the historic declaration of his Avatarhood. Today, millions of devotees from all over the world follow his teachings and many gather at his ashram, Prasanthi Nilayam beside the village where he was born. I learnt that among his teachings was the one that 'I have come not to disturb or destroy any faith, but to confirm each in his own faith, so that the Christian becomes a better Christian, the Muslim a better Muslim and the Hindu a better Hindu'. AVS told us, 'Sri Sathya Sai Baba's most famous poem-like pronouncement was:

There is only one religion, the religion of Love
There is only one caste, the caste of Humanity
There is only one language; the language of the Heart;
There is only one God, he is Omnipresent

'He changed my life and I started writing poems, including many about Sri Sathya Sai Baba himself. I write an average of five poems a day. Some days I write up to twenty poems and the last one I wrote just before meeting you at

9.50 a.m. this morning (10 August 2007). I keep a running total and can see it is number 18,304. In just over ten years I have written more than 18,000 poems. They are all contained in this book,' he says pointing to the enormous book in front of him on the conference table.

AVS shows us a certificate from the *Limca Book of Records* for 2007 which states that AVS holds the Indian national record for the most poems written on one subject or theme – that of Sri Sathya Sai Baba. It records that, as of 30 June 2006, AVS had written 16,740 poems on him and that these were released at Sri Sathya Sai Baba's 81st birthday celebrations on 23 November 2006. To date AVS has found mention five times in the *Limca Book of Records* continuously from 2005-09 and will also feature for the sixth time in the book's 2010 edition.

'I only write in Telugu. When we tried to have this feat recognized by the *Guinness Book of World Records* they rejected it because they did not have anyone who could check the language,' he laughs. An update: in 2008, AVS found mention in the *Guinness Book of World Records* for writing the single largest volume biography for this book, written between 1997 and 2007. As of now, the single bound book consists of 32 separate volumes.

Some of AVS's other books are *Sri Rama Rasamruthan*, *Sri Sai Sudha Madhuri*, *Pothana* (108 poems), *Ganga Himalayam* (108 poems) and *Tulasi dalalu* (558 poems). He has also composed a song. 'I wrote *Andhra Vaibhavam* for the 1995 World Telugu Conference hosted in Hyderabad.' This is no mean achievement for a man who claims to have read very few books ('only the newspapers') and has never been to college. For his skills in prose, rhyme, and verse, he was awarded a Doctor of Letters by Acharya Nagarjuna University in 2008.

I tell AVS it is surprising to find a businessman like him so involved in the creative and spiritual side of life. He said that he believes spirituality and business can co-exist. I told him that Narayana Murthy would agree with him as he calls himself a 'compassionate capitalist'. AVS responded with a smile, 'Then I hope people will see me as a "compassionate contractor".'

AVS then tells me a story demonstrating his deep belief in spirituality. 'Right now I have a guest at home. His name is Ramanuja Jeer. He was a bank manager and secured a gold medal for his studies in atomic energy. Many years ago Ramanuja Jeer quit his career with the bank and became a holy man. Every four years he meditates and fasts for fourteen months straight. During that time he renounces clothing and lives in a small brick hut. The only thing he drinks during the first five months is a small cup of milk. During the next five months he sustains himself on a small glass of water. For the final four months he neither eats nor drinks anything at all. He says he survives on air. He started doing this in his late forties; he's now almost sixty.'

I wonder why Ramanuja Jeer is staying with AVS. 'As he is a yogi he is teaching me more about spirituality. He has been staying with us for over four months now. I support him financially so he can go out each day and visit Hindu homes in our city and perform vatika (holy fire) ceremonies for those who want it.'

Having convinced me of his spiritual qualities there was one question which interested me. That was his beliefs on the importance of education and family involvement in business. 'What I have learnt is that you may have all the education in the world but what is more important is "common sense" which, despite its name, is not that common. Recently I was invited as the chief guest to a meeting of auditors. I think they must have regretted inviting me as I told them that although I was not well versed about the auditing profession, in my experience all one needs is common sense to understand how a company is faring.

'Sadly, my first two sons only studied up to the 10th standard like me as I had no money at that time. In fact Rangaraju, my eldest son had sat four of his five exams for 10th standard when I asked him to leave school and join me immediately.' I said this seemed to be a bit harsh. AVS replied, 'I owed someone some money that I said I would repay by a certain date. With Rangaraju working with me we could make the payment. Without his help I would not have been in a position to do so. As you know from our discussion this morning I will do anything not to break a promise. I told Rangaraju that "your exams can be re-taken next year, but a broken promise can never be redeemed." Rangaraju is now CEO of the company and, as you would have seen from the annual report, a number of my other sons and grandsons are now working for the company.

'The heart can only be operated upon by a doctor; the depth of a river can only be gauged by a sound engineer and a civil engineer knows how to build a road. In our company we have experts in all relevant areas and Rangaraju's job is to interpret their advice and put on the finishing touches. His most important strength is "common sense".

'I feel that if your only strength is that you are highly educated then you may not be fit for the rough and tumble of business in India. When Nagarjuna is seeking to employ senior executives for the company I get involved only at the end after they have been fully scrutinized. I look for only that one single trait: which class is the person – 1st, 2nd or 3rd? In Telugu we call them "Uttamuddu", "Madhyamuddu" and "Adhamuddu". The class 1 person shows drive and self-initiative and doesn't need to be prodded or cajoled – he can be trusted to be decisive and, thus, independently represent the company; the class 2 person will have to be told what to do; the class 3 person will not act even when told what to do. I look for first-class people. I am not saying that education is not important; all I'm saying is that, to succeed in business, classroom education is not the most important ingredient.'

As you have probably gathered by now, the multi-faceted AVS has clear views on life and business. In many ways he seems a paradox in so far as he is clearly also a deeply spiritual being, caring of those less fortunate than him. The many charities he supports include his own orphanage, Sirisha Trust, which provides a home, education, clothing and food as well as helps the orphans find employment on completion of their studies. AVS ended our meeting by reciting a quote from the famous author, Ralph Waldo Emerson: 'What lies behind us and lies before us are small matters compared to what lies within us.'

Nagarjuna (www.ncclimited.com) is one of India's leading construction groups based in Hyderabad. Its range of business verticals comprises construction (including real estate projects), transportation, water and environment, irrigation and power generation. Nagarjuna was the only construction company in India to achieve the recognition as one of the 250 'best under a billion' listed companies in Asia Pacific in 2005 by Forbes Asia.

"The important lesson all this taught me was that, whilst it is important to resolve business issues, in a family business it is just as important to work to resolve family issues. If you cannot manage your family ... it is very difficult to work together."

ARUN BHARAT RAM

Chairman
SRF

My meeting with Arun Bharat Ram took place on a beautiful Saturday morning in May at the family's country home outside Delhi. The roads around the country home were wide and tree-lined and I could see beautiful gardens and large homes peeking out from behind the greenery. It was very hard to imagine I was only half an hour from the centre of one of the largest cities in the world.

To understand his family, Arun Bharat Ram told me one has to start with his forefathers who they have been able to trace back for over 300 years to a village about thirty kilometres from Delhi and now situated in Haryana. Most of his immediate ancestors were government employees up until his great-grandfather Girdhari Lal who, together with a number of friends and colleagues, invested small amounts of money to build a textile mill near Delhi and which commenced operating in 1889. What was particularly significant about this mill, 'Delhi Cloth Mills', Arun told me, was that it was the first textile mill outside the eastern region of India, which was British controlled, and the western region, where the Parsis and Gujaratis controlled most of the textile industry from the mid-nineteenth century following the Indian mutiny. The mill owned by this company represented in many ways the first industrialization of the north of India.

'The mill employed many of the investors, including my great-grandfather. By the early 1900s, the mill was struggling and somehow they called on my grandfather Shriram to come in and take over to turn it around. At that time my great-grandfather and his family owned a very small part of the shareholding. As the company started to succeed under my grandfather's management he received big bonuses and all of which he invested in buying more shares in the company. At the peak, I understand my grandfather owned 40 per cent of the company. It is thus primarily my grandfather who was responsible for the initial business success of my family. He had only been educated up to the matriculation level but had a charisma and people could feel his acumen and vision.

'By the time I was born in 1940, our family had become the leading business family in Delhi, if not all of North India. In the intervening years since taking over the original textile mill, my grandfather had expanded the family's business to include four more textile mills, sugar mills located in the fertile Ganges plains and light engineering firms as well as a pottery business in Calcutta. The ceramic business known as Bengal Potteries became the largest of its kind in India.'

Arun then told me a story that illustrates the raw energy of his grandfather. Back in the 1930s, his grandfather decided to erect a new sugar mill in May in time to catch the processing season in October. Everyone told him he could not do it but his grandfather was not prepared to wait for the next harvest season. So he went to the local commissioner, an Englishman, and asked him if he could rent him twenty cars each night for the following six months. His grandfather parked these cars around the site and had the car engines and lights running all night so work could continue 24 hours a day. To make sure the schedules were met, his grandfather moved into a tent on the site.

'The India into which I was born was an India in the midst of change. Although, of course we did not know it at the time, but it was only seven years from independence and partition but Indians could feel change was on the way. My grandfather was a nationalist and, on the strength of his business standing, was invited by the prime minister to lead and chair many important government commissions and public sector companies and interacted with personalities from the business community, union leaders, politicians, scientists and academicians. He had a deep desire to learn, perhaps as he himself had not had the privilege of having a formal education. Many of these meetings with people who became household names in post-independent India took place in our family home and, so, it was an amazing environment in which to grow up.

'I should explain that there were around twenty-five family members living at the home of my grandfather. It was a typical Indian joint family where my grandparents with three sons and families lived together. When I say "home" we, in fact, lived in two large houses built on six acres of land owned by my grandfather. It was on the main arterial road from Connaught Place to India Gate, where the Hindustan Times is located today.

'My grandfather insisted that everyone who was at home had to join him for dinner at 8 p.m. sharp. He was particularly insistent that the male grandchildren be present at the dinner because he believed by sitting and listening they would absorb what was happening in the real world. And so a lot of the values that we have inculcated came from conversations that took place at the dining table. At those dinners there might be Pandit Nehru one night and, the next, the leader of the Opposition or they might even be there on the same evening and we would hear robust debates and discussions. When we were young, of course, we did not understand a lot of what was said but, even as a small child, I can remember feeling the electricity in the air. These were incredibly important times for the country and people were passionate about their beliefs.'

Arun then told me a couple of stories which demonstrate that living in the house was more than a little eccentric. 'As I mentioned earlier, my grandfather had this enormous energy and supported everything he felt needed support. For example, he decided to become a patron of the arts. Back in the '30s, the leading Indian dancer was Uday Shankar. Believe it or not my grandfather used to invite Uday Shankar, and his whole troupe of thirty or forty dancers and musicians to come and stay at his big house. And they used to stay, not just for a night or two, but for many months in a year. Uday Shankar was not just an Indian icon but had made a name for himself in the world and had danced with Pavlova. Despite his support of Uday Shankar,' Arun says with a chuckle, 'my grandfather never really understood art or music.

'And so, it was fairly much "open house" all year round at my grandfather's home. Part of the reason was that there were few hotels so visitors had to stay with friends and sometimes through introductions by friends. In the '30s and '40s I am told, people used to ring my grandfather and say, "I'm sending so and so to Delhi. Is it all right if he comes and stays with you?" I can remember one occasion at dinner when a friend's friend staying with us was sitting at the table next to my grandfather and introduced himself to him, "I am so and so and who exactly are you?" My grandfather replied with a laugh, "I'm Shriram and, incidentally, I live here." It was just so strange and yet wonderful.

'One of the great things about this "open house" was the people I met and one in particular. One of the leading musicians of India, Allaudin Khan was a part of Uday Shankar's troupe. He was the teacher of Ali Akbar Khan, his son, who also became a famous musician as well as Ravi Shankar of whom I am sure you have heard. Ravi Shankar also stayed with us and taught my mother and me how to play the sitar.' Arun then points to a painting on the wall and tells me this is Ravi Shankar painted by the famous artist Anjoli Menon. 'From the time I was a baby, I heard music and so it just became a part of my life. In actual fact, until last year, I used to play the sitar regularly and even gave a few concerts.'

Arun's opportunity to participate in these dinners dropped from the time he went away to boarding school. I was surprised to learn that his elder brother stayed at a school in Delhi. Arun laughs and explains, 'My elder brother did not like boarding school and somehow managed to persuade my parents his health was better if he stayed in Delhi. As a matter of fact this did not worry me as I enjoyed boarding school. I was a normal child, sometimes lazy, but easy going and I used to be a voracious reader. Reading was one thing both my parents and grandfather insisted on. Academically, I was probably just above average and certainly not in the top 10 per cent.'

Arun returned to explain the family tree and that his grandfather had three sons. The eldest, who died in an air crash in 1949, appears not to have been involved very much in the family business. He loved the finer things in life, such as art, which no doubt his father could well afford for him. Upon the death of Arun's grandfather in 1963, it was Arun's father and his younger brother who took over the business.

'My father's elder brother left behind two sons and two daughters. The daughters duly married and were not involved in the family business but his two sons joined the business. The eldest did get involved in the business but his true interest and passion lay in gardening and horticulture. But in my family it was expected as a male you would go straight into business. Sadly, for my cousin it was only much later in life that he realized his calling was quite different. Peter, do you know what that was? He is one of India's leading botanists and growers of exotic plants and, today, he is in his late seventies. It is so sad it took him so long to find his calling and a large part of the responsibility for that lies with the family.'

But it appears the younger cousin of his deceased uncle had the family business genes and was a hardcore businessman and contributed positively to the growth of the family business. Arun then moved to his immediate family. 'As you have heard I have an elder brother ... yes ... the one who did not go to boarding school. At one level he was a connoisseur of "the finer things of life". In his heart he was an artist, and he actually became a very good musician and I am sure if he had put all his efforts into that he could have become a professional. But, as with my older cousin, he split his life between the family obligation to go into business and his true love which was music. It would be wrong of me to say he was not interested in business because he was, but that was not his passion. Indeed, he became an economist earning a genuine doctorate.' Arun says with a laugh, 'Not one of those that are handed out.'

Arun's younger brother, while intelligent and sharp did not really have his heart in business. He was an individualist who would like to do things by himself.

As was traditional in India, when Arun, after having finished school, his grandfather and parents debated as to what he should study. His elder brother, Vinay had done economics and it seems the family decided they needed an engineer. The debate then turned to where the best engineering school was. They settled on Germany. So in 1958 Arun went to the university in Darmstadt, which lies between Frankfurt and Heidelberg, to study engineering.

I wondered what it was like to be a young Indian in Germany in those post-war days and whether there was any racism he experienced. 'Surprisingly, there were a hundred Indians there at the time. Although it was not an economic factor for me, one of the reasons was that universities in Germany were free for foreigners as well as Germans. This led to a lot of Indians from middle-class families studying there. As to racism, I experienced none. Indians were, in fact, very welcome. There was this old Indo-Aryan connection and, so, we were treated much better than the Arabs and other foreigners because we were considered to be an old civilization with an Aryan link. We were welcomed into our classmates' homes and I must say it was an enjoyable experience other than the fact I found I really did not like studying engineering at all. Due to this, I never really took much interest in my studies and, after three years, much to the dismay of my parents, I gave up and returned home. I moped around not knowing what I should do and feeling very unhappy. Eventually, my parents suggested that, as Vinay had enjoyed Michigan, where he did his master's in economics, why not finish my studies there. I settled for industrial engineering which had both management and engineering contents which was the right blend of academics for me. I completed my degree and came home again in 1966.'

Arun's younger brother, Vivek went straight from school to Michigan where he too studied industrial engineering and overlapped for one year with Arun.

'When I came back I went into the family business in 1967. The tradition set by my grandfather was to start at the bottom in the family business. My father told me an interesting story that when he entered the family business at the age of twenty-two, he was packed off to Kanpur to work with one of my grandfather's acquaintances. When he came back after a year, he asked my grandfather where his office was. To this he apparently replied, "You just go to the power plant and shovel coal for a few days into the boiler and then we'll see where your office is." In my time, we did not have to shovel coal but we were expected to go and work the looms and the spinning machines in the mills.'

By the time Arun joined the business it was so large that there were many different companies into which a family member could be placed. 'Let's see,' Arun said, 'at the time I joined, my eldest cousin was in Calcutta running an engineering business and my second oldest cousin was involved in the chemical business in Delhi. My father and older brother decided that it would be best for me to work in the textile business which was run by my brother, Vinay. Looking back now, it was a big mistake because normally brothers do not work together, at least in the initial phase. Traditionally in India family members report to a cousin rather than to a brother. This is not because of sibling rivalry but it does improve family harmony.

'In fact, right around this time my father and his younger brother began their turf battles and I suspect that is probably why I was placed in the textile businesses with my brother rather than in the chemical business where my cousin was working. I could feel the fissures developing at that time. The end result was that all the textile businesses came under my father and all the chemical and sugar businesses, as well as the engineering business in Calcutta, were run by my uncle. This really did not solve the problem because, while at one level there was clarity of management at a corporate level, as the business was still ultimately owned by DCM, the original textile company, the overall management was diffused. Also, the management styles of my father and uncle were so different that it gave confusing signals to employees in the company. You will remember that this was a publicly listed company. The squabbles slowly resulted in eroding the shareholders' value as well as the family's own net worth. 'Then something fortunate happened from my point of view. DCM decided that they wanted to expand and diversify into making nylon tyre cord which was a new generation reinforcement material for tyres. My uncle, and this is where luck came in, for some reason or other, decided that this business should not be part of DCM but should be a new venture partially supported by DCM financially. So we floated SRF in 1970 as a publicly held company to manufacture nylon tyre cord with DCM having a 40 per cent shareholding, the balance being held by the public. It was decided to set up the business in Madras, far from Delhi and I was nominated to run it. I started the business in Madras and lived there for eight years from 1973 and enjoyed every moment of it – the building of the business including the initial trials and tribulations I went through. As an important side benefit, I was lucky to be away from the family's day-to-day squabbles, which centred around Delhi.'

Relations between Arun's father and uncle went from bad to worse. Part of the reason for this was because DCM started to lose its edge and so profits and income for the family fell. Despite the fact my father and uncle talked about both retiring to allow the next generation to run the family business, one would not go without the other going at the same time. They continued this for another decade until they both finally retired in the early 1980s when they were in their mid to late seventies.

'By the mid '80s, things were difficult in DCM and, even after their retirement, it was evident that the structure in DCM was not conducive for its health and sustainability. I came back to Delhi and was invited to join the board of DCM although I was not involved in day-to-day management. I tried very hard to be a mediator between my various cousins and my brothers but relationships had become difficult over almost two decades of sparring and sniping. Eventually, all of us in our generation approached my father and uncle and said that it was time that the family separated. It was neither good for the company nor for the family. Rather than engaging consultants, we decided to give ourselves a month to sit down as often as necessary to reach a solution to separate the businesses. Since there was a "buy in" from all family members I was pleasantly surprised that we actually completed the work of separation within three months. The reason for not using consultants or mediators was that there was already a desire for everyone to go through the process and also as a conservative family we did not want the media to become aware and play up the fact that the family was breaking up. We had seen a number of big joint families splitting their businesses around this time and the media had a field day in writing about the disputes and which – in more than one case – almost certainly led to acrimony within the families and sometimes a failure of the separation process.

'As mentioned, the agreements were reached within three months and we decided to divide "the pie" into three smaller ones. We tried to split the business in such a way, that as far as possible, assets managed by one family remained under the same management so that there was a minimum disruption to the business and any significant value difference could be made good by monetary compensation.'

The three-way split became somewhat complicated by the fact that Arun's two male cousins from his eldest uncle, decided they wanted to separate between themselves. 'So, it finally ended up between a four-way split. Since the families wanted to make sure it was legally binding the agreements were approved by the court. Within five months, the split was all done – court process and all. In retrospect, while it is not good to separate the business as shareholder value is eroded but from the perspective of family harmony it is sometimes essential. Ultimately, one hopes that there would be enough focus on the separated business to flourish and grow faster than they would have in a tense and constricted environment. There was a huge sense of relief in the family once the deal was done.'

I wondered what part Arun's family had received. Was it SRF directly? 'No, our family's share was an interest in DCM which included SRF. I must at this point make a mention of the textile business. Most of the organized textile industry started racking up huge losses and were folding up because of distorted government policy. We also decided to shut down most of our mills (particularly the old ones) as they were no longer viable. This turned into a nightmare because we had decided that the original textile mill in Delhi (where everything started) should also be closed down. Since this mill was located on prime property it became very attractive for its real estate value. To close down the Delhi mill and compensate more than 6,000 workers took us thirteen years as it got bogged down in court cases and disputes with the Delhi administration.

'Somewhere around 1996, my younger brother came to Vinay and complained that we were going nowhere with the property development. He told us he was also concerned about the huge family debt that we were carrying as a result of the earlier splitting of the group. This was because with the real estate of the mills and SRF coming to us we had to compensate the other two families monetarily. He told us that he wanted out. Having just been through one major split, my brother and I tried to persuade him this was not the right thing to do. But, by 1999, things had got to such a stage that we decided that there was not enough "peace of mind" in the family, that we had no alternative but to part ways once again.

'You know, the important lesson all this taught me was that, whilst it is important to resolve business issues, in a family business it is just as important to work to resolve family issues. If you cannot manage your family, and here I'm talking about a larger family, it is very difficult to work together. It became clear that both my brothers were not on the same wave-length as me. I had come to the conclusion that the family should employ professionals to run our companies and that the family should act more like a supervisory board. This was not what they thought.

'So at the end of 1999, we divided our assets. And we again did it very quietly among the three of us. So in a sense within a decade or so,' Arun laughs, 'I went from being a third-generation businessman to being a first-generation businessman. I got SRF, my elder brother got the DCM property assets and my younger brother got cash and real estate.'

SRF by then had expanded far beyond its original business objective of manufacturing nylon tyre cord in 1975. 'Yes, by the early '80s, like most businesses at that time, SRF was in a difficult position because the Indian market was not growing and there were a lot of pressures from the government. And so I decided to diversify into engineering plastics and the manufacture of industrial fabrics based on the nylon tyre cord. Some of these were ideas that were too premature, too early for India, but we've persisted with them, and although we've had our ups and downs, today they've become major businesses for us.

'SRF also diversified in the mid '80s into refrigerant gases because it was very obvious that a country like India would require refrigerants as the economy grew and we became India's largest producer. We had a technical collaboration with what is now Honeywell, but in those early days was known as Allied Signal. Of course, the big issue in this business is CFCs. We were all producing CFCs in the beginning. However, under the Montreal Protocol, all countries, including developing countries, have to phase out the production of CFC by 2009. We are sure we will comply. In any event, all that is really left now is old hardware in developing countries such as old refrigerators and old car air conditioners. In the meantime, we have started our own research programme in our refrigerant gas business to develop a new generation of gases.'

Arun then turned to one of the positive developments the old DCM group had left behind. 'My uncle and Vinay started in DCM what was called, "Senior Management Trainees Scheme". At the time there were only two companies in India that had a programme like this – Tata and DCM; not even Levers had such a programme at the time we introduced it. DCM used to take twenty of the brightest people from every sphere of life. They could be English majors, botanists or from any discipline as long as they had the inherent skills and intelligence to become a "successful person" in life. Importantly, this did not mean they had to have the potential to become a "successful manager"; just a "successful person". Most of the credit for this programme must go to my uncle and to my brother Vinay who worked hard on this scheme. It was, in many ways, the forerunner to the IIMs. The scheme built cadres of young managers who today are amongst the leading businessmen in the country. For example, Shiv Nadar who runs Hindustan Computers and Ashok Soota who runs Mindtree Consulting are products of the programme.'

I learnt that Arun's grandfather was also interested in education. He made sure there were schools for the children of all his employees. 'He was, during his career, the chairman of the governing board of three colleges in Delhi and founded Shriram College of Commerce which, to this day, is recognized as one of India's premier education institutions. Even though he had a very traditional view on the role of women, he believed it was important that women have an equal opportunity to be educated. He founded the Lady Shriram College for women which, I believe, is ranked among the top three colleges in India. 'Perhaps, I am biased,' he laughs, 'as I am currently Chairman of the Board of Governors.' Arun proudly told me he and his wife have continued the family tradition and that the SRF foundation is providing schools for village children and has also started two private high schools in and around Delhi.

Arun then turned the conversation back to family businesses and ways to make sure they survive. 'As you can see I have experienced multiple break-ups of my family's business over three generations and in recent years have been concerned to make sure it does not happen again with my children; my two sons, Ashish and Kartikeya, and my daughter Deeksha.

'As I mentioned earlier, during the '90s there was a trend for large family companies to bring in professional management. I believed in this and appointed a professional to run SRF. Unfortunately, I did not anticipate that my sons, both of whom hold MBAs from Cornell, would see this as some sort of reverse discrimination. Their view was that they too were professionals and should be given a chance to operate businesses. Since the appointment of the professional chief executive I had stepped back and become non-executive chairman. The tensions continued and, earlier this year [2007], I had to take a call on what was in the best interests of the company and my family. I stepped back into SRF as executive chairman and agreed to give my sons an opportunity to run some of the businesses.'

I asked the obvious question as to whether he was not worried that by putting his sons actively into the family businesses he was not perpetuating in his sons' generation exactly the family business issues that surfaced in both his father's and then his generation. Arun replied that he most certainly was worried about this and said he would tell me what they had done to try and prevent any problems from re-occurring.

'I realized that what my family had experienced over the generations must have been experienced in similar family business in other countries and that there must be some things we could learn from them. So, I took my two sons and our chief executive to IMD in Lausanne which conducts a family business programme. John Ward from the Kellogg Business School, probably the leading proponent of family businesses in the world today, and Joachim Schwass were the two leaders of this programme. We spent a week there and it was really an "eye opener" for us. We had families from all over the world such as Spain, Switzerland, Sweden, the US and the Middle East. All these families openly shared with other participants what they had experienced in their families. I can share with you that it was really comforting to know my family was not the exception. We listened to many examples where families have actually stayed together by designing to stay together. They cited examples of the Wallenbergs in Sweden, the Henkel family in Germany, the Barettas in Italy and the Cargills and Hersheys from the US.

'As a result of our experience we decided that we needed to debate amongst ourselves as to how we want to take our family forward from here. We arranged a conclave with my wife, my daughter who wasn't married at that time, my two sons and their wives. We all sat down together and I told them, "Look, this is what we have observed and learnt in Lausanne and it would be wise if you also read some of the literature that we have brought. Once you have read it, let's all sit together and decide if we want to repeat what's been happening in our family over the generations or if there is another way – something that we can work on to minimize the chances of a separation but if it is to happen, it happens in the right way."

'We finally all got together and built our own family constitution which is approximately eighty pages. The emphasis of the constitution is not its language but its intent and spirit. We have tried to think of every possible eventuality and the constitution envisages that it can be continually updated as circumstances change in the family.

'As I now say, in hindsight, had my grandfather worked on managing the family emotions, and not just the business issues, and the conflicts and potential conflicts in a better way, maybe the break-ups my family experienced would not have happened at all or, if they did happen, they would not have almost brought the company down. Processes should be designed and decisions should be made while everything is going well and not when it is at the fag end of a company's life.'

I asked Arun how his family constitution had operated over the last four years. Has it got rid of the "elephant in the room"? 'Certainly there is no "elephant in the room" any more. If conflicts arise we meet and discuss them. I won't say that we have sorted out everything below the surface, but we've gone a long way in doing so and we've had a lot of help from the family adviser, a consigliore if you like. Once every two months, he sits with my sons and their wives and they have long and, hopefully, open discussions on any issues which may be of consequence.

'I think the real problem arises because each family thinks it is different. We learnt from our time in Switzerland that no family is different and that there is much to learn from how other family businesses have handled similar problems. Why try and "re-invent the wheel"? The crunch comes when the family dynamics change such as outsiders coming into the family. You may have grown up together as siblings with common values, but the moment wives and daughters and sons-in-law come in, they bring a lot of outside values into the system. These don't necessarily match your personal values, and they very often don't match the family values. So you're injecting cultures and values from outside, and that's difficult to tackle when it's too late.'

I told Arun that I had found his candour and openness on his family was remarkable and that I felt sure it would galvanize more than one reader of this book to address their family business issues in the way he proposed. As we brought our conversation to a close, I joked that he may well have another career in the offing when he stands down as executive chairman of SRF. He laughed, 'You are right,' he said, 'even now I have people I don't even know calling me up and saying, "Mr Bharat Ram, can you please fly down to Ahmedabad? We have a big problem in our family and we're not seeing eye-to-eye with family members. And we've heard that you've done some work on this. Can you come and help us?"'

With that, I decided it was time to leave Arun to his weekend family commitments and, in particular, to visit his father who had fallen ill the night before and wanted to be hale and hearty for his 72nd wedding anniversary the following week.

Apart from its technical textiles business, in which it enjoys a global leadership position, **SRF** (www.srf.com) is a domestic leader in refrigerants, engineering plastics and industrial yarns as well. The company also enjoys a significant presence among the key domestic manufacturers of polyester films and fluorospecialities.

"I used to play chess with my brothers and they would beat me in seven to eight moves. I was the kid who was always struggling, did not speak English and was not brainy. If I managed to pass in school, it was just barely. I was shy and had a terrible inferiority complex."

CK RANGANATHAN

Founder & CEO
CavinKare

Chinni Krishnan Ranganathan was born on 30 October 1960 in a coastal town called Cuddalore near Pondicherry in Tamil Nadu. His father was a maths teacher turned businessman and his mother a housewife turned secondary school administrator. His grandfather, on his mother's side was a leading lawyer of the time, and on his father's side, was a military doctor. There were six children (four boys and two girls) with Ranganathan being the fourth with a younger brother and sister.

I remarked that it must have been unusual for a maths teacher to become an entrepreneur. 'Yes, he must have been around his late thirties with many of us still at school. He sold a significant portion of the family's property and started re-packaging pharmaceutical products. Why he went into this area he never told us. My father's philosophy was very simple, whatever a rich man enjoys, a common man should be able to afford too.

'As you know, for most Indians at that time, the most important thing in their lives was security. They don't just quit their jobs and sell the family property. Initially, we struggled. He had a single-dose packaging project in which he just repacked pharmaceuticals like Epsom salts, sulphanamide, boric acid – the powder that heals wounds in single dose of five gram sachets. Otherwise, people had to go to the pharmacy and buy 100 grams, a larger quantity. His small sachets, of course, made it affordable for poorer people. To transport the goods around he bought an old van. He was involved in everything from packaging to sales. He was very serious about it and I can vividly remember him spending a lot of time reading technical and chemistry books in order to understand formulations. He then started formulating himself.'

Sadly, after developing the business for about a decade, he died suddenly of a heart attack when he was only forty-eight. 'In memory of my father, whose name was Chinni Krishnan, I named one of my products "Chik" but that is getting ahead of myself in describing my life story.'

A couple of years before his father died, he developed the first small sachet for shampoo. 'Since there was no machine available at the time, he used simple PVC sheets that you will find in any office, a PVC welding machine and a hose to make the first sachet. It was a very crude machine. He developed the product further by turning the PVC folder sealing machines into sachet packing ones. People were taken aback; they had never seen such an innovation before. My father's exact words were, "This innovation will see us through my generation; a rickshaw puller should use my product."

'I was in my second year of university, studying for my bachelor's degree in commerce when he passed away. His death had a huge effect on the family as none of us knew the intricacies of the business as he had not involved any of us. He was a man of few words even with his children. Since we had very little to do with the business, we wanted to sell it but, as my father had taken a loan from the bank to run the business, the only way to pay off the loan was to sell the sole remaining piece of the family property, which was the home where we were living. So my older brothers decided they would run the business.'

Ranganathan then told me he needed to take me back to his childhood. 'All my brothers and sisters had studied in English medium convent schools whereas because I was academically weak my parents had placed me in a local vernacular Tamil medium school. This had a disastrous impact on me and has haunted me for a lot of my life. When you go into smaller towns in India, maybe even in bigger cities, if someone speaks fluent English then people equate it with the capability of delivering results and brilliance. Naturally, this may not be the reality but I felt ashamed and thought that, as I could not cope well with my studies or speak English, I would never succeed in life.

'I used to play chess with my brothers and they would beat me in seven to eight moves. I was the kid who was always struggling, did not speak English and was not brainy. If I managed to pass in school, it was just barely. I was shy and had a terrible inferiority complex.

'As a result, all my friends were people who also did not study. We used to swim a lot in a well in the garden, we used to bait birds with caterpillars, climbed coconut trees and plucked coconut and palm leaves. We also used to fish using local methods like draining all the water out of the pond. I fished so much that I started eating fish and, as my family is vegetarian, this was looked down upon. They were very upset.

'I failed fourth grade at a time when Father Peter was the school principal. Every week, the defaulters had to meet him to get caned. I was a regular in that group. If I was missing a week from the group, Father Peter would be surprised.

'In my tenth grade, I scored eight marks out of 100 in mathematics. My father was furious. He said, "I'm a maths teacher and this is just so embarrassing for me."'

By the time Ranganathan finished school, his father needed chemists for the business and thought he would get Ranganathan to study chemistry and bring him in the business. 'If you look at my background you will find my oldest brother is an ophthalmologist, the next a lawyer, and the one after that, a sister, is a gynaecologist. I was next, and there was no way I was going to follow in their footsteps.'

He did as his father wished and studied chemistry but found it extremely difficult. 'Maths itself was difficult for me and chemistry only made it worse. There was one more complication: the medium of teaching was English, which I hardly spoke!

'Fortunately, I had a close friend who studied very hard and he used me to test his knowledge by explaining everything he had learnt in English to me in Tamil.'

The death of his father while he was in the second year of college proved to be a defining moment in Ranganathan's life. 'I realized that whatever I did from this point on was entirely up to me. There was no one to blame. I was a changed man. Instead of taking his untimely death only negatively, I looked for positives. My father had been my mentor, my guide, someone I could depend upon; the person who was going to shape my career was gone.'

However, I told Ranganathan that I understood it also made him more of a rebel. 'Yes, my family was very orthodox Hindu and God fearing and frequently performed poojas. I told the family that I did not believe in God. My mother was furious and called me crazy.'

Ranganathan managed to complete his degree in 1982 and immediately joined his two older brothers in the business. Despite being qualified in medicine and law, they had left their professions to take charge of the family business in order to pay off the debt.

'But I was not to stay for long. After four months I realized that to succeed in business was not about literary knowledge but common sense. When I started voicing my opinion on what we should or should not do with the business, it was not taken in the right spirit. Traditionally, in a Hindu family, the eldest is always to be looked up to and obeyed and I was not following the custom. I have to say my brothers did run the business very well and took it to far greater heights than where my father had left it but I saw gaps.

'Finally, it became so embarrassing that we couldn't see eye-to-eye on anything. I said enough is enough and we need to take a call. I was also convinced that the way my brother was making decisions, the company would not go far. So I thought it best to leave and do something on my own. I announced to my family that I did not want a stake in the family business or property and that I was moving out.

'As the business was doing well at that time and I had a good salary and even had a company car, I knew I would be leaving all that behind. But I said, "Hey, I'm ready to cycle again." I found it easy to leave because of my new-found self-confidence and, looking back, I was lucky this split came so early because I could have wasted many years being unhappy in the family business.

'It was a very emotional parting because I essentially just walked out of home with the clothes on my back and my savings of Rs 15,000 which I had earned. My mother and grandmother were particularly concerned about what their friends would think as the family was well-known due to my grandfather having been a prominent doctor in the town. All my friends and well wishers said that I was a fool not to insist on a share of the family business and property as it was my right and so on, but I was never swayed by these things.'

I asked what he did first. 'I walked 200 metres from our home and rented a one-room apartment. Then I set about thinking what business I should do. I did not want to compete with my brothers so I thought I would go into the poultry business which I already knew something about from my childhood. But my one-room apartment was not sufficient for me, let alone trying to run a poultry business from there,' he says laughing. 'A week later I thought it was better I start with something I knew – shampoos. As I mentioned earlier, I chose the name "Chik" in honour of my father. I set about acquiring licenses, a factory, equipment and so on.'

I wondered how he could do all that with Rs 15,000. 'The place that I rented, my house-cum-office, cost me just Rs 250 to rent and the deposit was Rs 1000. The factory was Rs 900 advance and Rs 300 rent. The next thing I invested in was a low-cost sealing machine. Thanks to my father, even low-cost sealing machines were quite good then. That machine cost around Rs 3500. I spent around Rs 1000 on licenses, deposits and other miscellaneous things. I did all this in seven days! The suppliers that I used to deal with when working with my family said that since I was now an individual company they could not give me the same credit. I hounded them relentlessly. I told them to give me small quantities and reduce the credit term from 45 days to 15 days to allow me to sell my product. I promised that in 15 days I would settle their bills and, if I didn't then they would never have to supply me again. I convinced the suppliers one by one. I quickly made my shampoo and placed a small advertisement for Rs 250 in the paper, calling for distributors and representatives. People applied and we were able to sell and settle all our bills. But for further operations to move smoothly I had to re-jig my strategy to enable the company to operate like a well-oiled machine.

'But back to the beginning of my company. I realized the importance of communication. You have to write in English, speak it and understand it. I was now in dire straits as English was the basis of communication. Earlier, my brother used to meet suppliers, distributors, technicians, and even when I was interviewing people for the post of general manager, I could not understand what they were saying. I decided that I would do whatever it took to succeed and was willing to pay any price. The first thing I did was stop the vernacular daily paper and weekly magazines. Instead I subscribed to *Hindu* and *Business Week*. At first, I didn't even understand the headlines but I was determined to learn. I had a dictionary that I used to refer to often. It was very tedious but constant reading helped a lot. Every Tuesday *Hindu* had a column, "Know Your English". In that column, they would give the pronunciation using the phonetic symbols of a word and also give its synonyms and usage. I used to also pick five words a day, look up their meanings and write a minimum of half a dozen sentences using them.'

I was amazed that he had this discipline when he was already in his mid-twenties. 'Disciplining myself was not easy but I knew it was fundamental to any success. I had several notebooks full of sentences and I used to review them constantly so that I never forgot any. This improved my vocabulary tremendously as I understood the meaning of words which is most fundamental in communication.'

I asked what was driving him at this point. 'My fundamental driver was survival, the next was to prove to my family that I could not be brushed aside and the third was wanting to achieve something big. Money was not a driving force. I was finally confident and knew I was capable in business. I just wanted all my talents to culminate into something that would not convince just me. There was a dramatic change in me. The discipline, the conviction, and the confidence worked for me. After I learnt English, I started reading a lot of business news and listened to management audio cassettes. I also started reading a lot of management books which helped dramatically. I completely changed from "a frog in the village well" – which is an expression meaning a village boy totally unconnected with the outside world – to someone completely different.

'Initially, I started the business in my mother and grandmother's name. In 1990, I formed a company for the business. It was known as Beauty Cosmetics before its eventual re-naming to CavinKare. I wondered how he chose the name. 'That is quite a story' he said. 'I ran a contest among the employees and two of them came up with the name – "cavin" meaning "beauty" or "grace" in Tamil and "care" in English spelt with a "k". The two initials match my own father's name and were also the initials of mine. Particularly the link to my father means a lot to me but to an outsider it is just a neutral, western sounding name.'

I asked Ranganathan whether there were any particular secrets in the way he built the business. 'Not secrets. However I did do a number of things differently. For example, I chose to distribute my products other than through normal FMCG (Fast Moving Consumer Goods) distributors. Since my product was not familiar in the market place, any established FMCG distributor was asking a minimum of 30 days' credit. As my capital was fully blocked in infrastructure development and I couldn't borrow from the banks as I had no collateral securities to offer, the option of extending credit to the distributors was ruled out. I needed to find an alternative. We needed to innovate. One of my sales representatives came up with the idea of appointing people who don't know FMCG business, but were keen to start something new. Since they are new to the FMCG field and depended on our knowledge and experience to learn the business, they were ready to give advance demand drafts as a payment mode, which were as good as cash. We convinced people who used rented bicycles to run errands, to add us as an extra business customer and be our de facto distributors. It was an upgrade for them as well. They worked to ensure that the stocks moved and collected our money which we again reinvested. Our distributors' names were Golden Cycle Mart, Rajasthan Cycle Mart and so on. We were able to do this comfortably in every town around Cuddalore. With this structure we grew.

'Using bicycle messengers was without doubt the most innovative financial solution we came up with. It worked wonders for us. Even today, I have not tampered with the system. That's why we have negative working capital; we have other people's money. When you start your own business, no matter how much you put in, there are always more requirements – for more equipment, more raw materials and so on. I approached one of my friends and asked him to make products for me. He would need to invest Rs 40,000 which I estimated he would recover in four months. He agreed and made a profit as well. I used this as an example and more people were ready to pump in their money and factories. At one point, I had 150 companies making the products for me. I now had the money, people were working with me and were prepared to invest in me. So, as the next step, I decided to advertise and build.

'Getting banks to lend me money was a different story. It took me three years to get a bank loan. Finally, one bank manager decided to take the risk. When the business started doing well, I told my auditor that the initial struggle was over and I was making a profit. He told me to pay my taxes. I told him that I had no intention of evading them. He would compute my income taxes and I would pay them. As I did not have any collateral to offer the banks against my loan the bank manager who finally decided to give me the Rs 25,000 overdraft was surprised to learn we paid income tax. That was uncommon as small industries generally won't earn beyond the basic tax exemption limits. Even if they earn beyond, they won't declare it and pay taxes. To the bank, it was clear that despite being small, we make profits and therefore can pay interest and service the loan. The manager waived the need for a collateral security and gave me a loan of Rs 25,000. The Rs 25,000 loan turned into a Rs 1 lakh loan, then Rs 5 lakh, then Rs 50 lakh, and so on.

'One day early on, a few of my distributors, the guys on cycles, came and tore up their invoices in front of me. They said instead of paying 20 per cent sales tax to the Exchequer, let's conceal the sales and share the concealed taxes between us. There was no checking by tax authorities and tax evasion was rampant. I told them, "Nothing doing, I'm paying and will continue to pay my taxes". This approach helped me attract and retain professionals.

'People often say, "if only they had money, they would do wonders". When I hear this, I am always reminded of Robert Shuller's statement "nobody has money problems, there are ideas' problems". It's not about not having money, it's about how you raise money. Only when you are small do you have to worry about funds; now money is no problem at all for CavinKare.'

I wondered how Ranganathan's success impacted the family. 'Well, I think they were shocked. For a time we competed head on but I never retaliated. I was clear in my goals. There is no point in using energy to create negative energy. It will just drain you. I was determined not to get distracted.'

With all the struggles, I wondered if he had ever found time to get married. 'Yes, and believe it or not, it was an arranged marriage. My mother always thought I would elope and never come back. By the time I was to be married, my brothers had all moved to Chennai, so my mother and grandmother were left alone at home. They invited me over for lunch one day. While we were eating my mother asked me to get married and I agreed.

'My mother arranged for a "match-maker" who matched my horoscope with one of her other clients. I personally don't believe in all this but it is the tradition here and, in any event, this was all in the hands of my mother. The "match-maker" told my mother it was a perfect match. When I learnt my "match" was from a prominent political family, I was not keen. Her grandfather is currently the chief minister of our state. But my mother, grandmother and uncles pushed me to at least meet her. I went, met and liked her and said, yes I will marry her. We married in 1987, when I was twenty-seven.

'We have two daughters and one son.' I remarked that it would be poetic retribution if he had a rebellious son or daughter. He laughed and said, 'Indeed, my elder daughter is very rebellious. One small argument and she is ready to leave home, just like me.

'Our second daughter is adopted. We love her as our own and all our children get on well together. We made it a point to tell her she had been adopted so she would not be disappointed later in life. I can tell you it took a lot of guts for me to build up the courage to tell her.'

I asked him whether his son and daughters would have the same opportunities. 'I'm not here to force anyone to do something they don't want to do. Actually, I don't want my children to join my business. I expect them to be self-made and independent. They should not expect my money. My daughter always says, "Why should I ask you for money? You have educated us and that's sufficient. I will seek my own business."'

Ranganathan wished to add one more point which he believes is crucial to success. 'That is loyalty. Loyalty is very important, particularly when you are a small proprietary business. I learnt the hard way that both loyalty and competence are essential to run a successful business; it's not one or the other. Many traditional businessmen emphasize loyalty over competence and, as a result, the business suffers. They will hire their brothers or brothers-in-law or friends who will be their business associates. I broke out of that mould. I entrusted work to professionals. Trust comes from the way you go about business and the way you develop and adhere to systems and processes.'

As one final question I asked Ranganathan what his vision was for the future of CavinKare. 'What I want to do is establish a multinational company that is known internationally, not just in India. Money isn't my driving force at all. I would like to suggest to all the youngsters reading this book that they read Paul Meyer's views on success and achievement. He said, "Whatever you vividly imagine, ardently desire, sincerely believe and enthusiastically act upon ... must inevitably come to pass." That is, indeed, how I go about my business.' Passion backed with hard work has no match and we can achieve anything we want in life.'

With that we brought the interview to a close and Ranganathan introduced my colleague, Suresh Iyer, and I to his son and younger daughter who had been waiting outside for the meeting to finish. I could sense in the way he interacted with his children that he was bringing them up with as much love and affection as his mother and grandmother had bestowed upon him.

CavinKare (www.cavinkare.com) is a home-grown Indian leader in personal care (hair care, skin care, home care) and food products. It has now expanded in marketing its products internationally. The company markets ten major brands including Chik, Meera, Spinz, Nyle, Indica, Ruchi and Chinni. Initially, CavinKare relied on contract manufacturing but has now established its own world-class plant at Haridwar to cater to the demand of both domestic and international markets.

> I have decided to give more importance, not only to "corporate" but also to "family" governance. Without family governance, the circle is incomplete.

GM RAO

Founder & Chairman
GMR Group

GM Rao was born on 14 July 1950 into a family of seven children, being the fifth among all, and third among the boys. In all there were four boys and three girls. His father, a gold merchant and trader of agricultural products, owned a shop and a warehouse, where he would sort the pulses and jute that he bought from the farmers, to distribute to the wholesalers. His father had three brothers and they had long since divided the family property among themselves and lived independently.

Rao's boyhood passed as though he did not have a care in the world. When he should have been poring over his books as his heart told him to do, he was with his friends who persuaded him to keep them company. His father and the rest of his family were oblivious of his activities. Not that they were not concerned; for them, education was superfluous in the trading business. The only reason why his parents sent him to school, was because the family expected him to acquire basic knowledge that would help him in doing business – multiplication, subtraction and addition, and to read and write in Telugu. The other brothers had studied up to high school level but had not passed the final exam.

'I can remember well how, if my friends and I heard that a new movie was playing in one of the nearby towns, we would all sneak out at night from our homes, and ride our bikes to watch the movie. Sometimes this involved a sixty kilometre round-trip excursion. No one ever complained. It was idyllic. Incidentally, the reason we did this at night was because usually the movies were shown in open air, on a screen, which was a large white sheet.'

However, these boyish escapades took their toll. Rao flunked his secondary school examination and was shaken. 'I pleaded with my father to allow me to repeat the academic year. He told me that the Rs 50 he would have to pay as fees was a waste. He added that no one in our family had passed the secondary school final examination and that I, too, would not pass, as we were not an intelligent family.' After much persuasion, his father relented. Rao returned to his studies, to top not only in his school in the SSLC (Secondary School Leaving Certificate) exam, but also his entire Mandal (sub-division of a district – comprising a group of villages). 'By this time, all my friends with whom I bunked school had left. Free from these distractions, I was able to focus on my education.' He had vindicated himself.

As anyone would predict, his father was incredulous. No one believed that he stood first. His maternal uncle used to say in jest that Rao must have cheated in the exam. Nonetheless, the community was overjoyed, more so because he was the first in the three generations of his family to have graduated from school. 'To celebrate this, can you believe, they advertised my accomplishment on a village billboard? I am sure this must seem absolutely bizarre to a westerner from the cities and, even to me. Looking back now, it seems unreal that so much importance was given to this.'

Two factors helped Rao to realize his academic karma – a fresh batch of peers who were studious, and his teacher, Venkata Rao, a mentor who always exhorted them to aim higher. 'He told us that we should pursue the science and engineering fields and aspire for a better life. In those days, becoming a doctor or an engineer was like a dream. No one in my village or the surrounding areas had ever done this.'

Rao obtained his family's consent to attend pre-university at RSRK Degree College in Bobbili, a small town, some fifty kilometres from home. He had chosen to study science as he was good at maths and, 'Usually I scored full marks, 100 out of 100 in maths.' He stayed in a small rented room where he cooked his own breakfast and had meals at restaurants in exchange for monthly food coupons. With a newly awakened sense of responsibility, his interest in movies waned. 'Now, all I wanted to do was to come first in class and, believe it or not, I usually did. I came first out of 400 students and won the College Cup. I cannot tell you how much more satisfying this was than wandering around in the village.'

Having completed pre-university, Rao got admission into the most prestigious engineering college in the region – the Andhra University Engineering College. Andhra Pradesh had only three such institutions at that time. 'I chose mechanical engineering for its versatility over other available disciplines in civil, marine, electrical and electronics engineering.'

With little or no help – other than an occasional visit or advice from the odd friend or relative – Rao had to fend for himself. He paid his fees and enrolled himself in college. 'I am thankful today for the confidence and self-reliance that this phase of my life instilled in me. I see how much my daughter and daughter-in-law look out for their children, organizing tuition in the mornings and engaging them in various other activities. I tell them that when I was a child, there was nobody to help me or guide me in any way. My father didn't even know which course I was doing during my engineering college.' Rao believes that when people aspire to improve the lives of their children, they should encourage independence in them. 'My golden rule for raising children is to give them judicious liberty and throw them a few challenges.'

By the third year, Rao ranked fifth in college. He was elected union secretary of the college in his fourth year which he guesses, indicated that, he related well to his fellow students.

Rao was twenty-one when his father arranged his marriage to a girl who happened to be his cousin. Though he was only midway through college, Rao thought to himself that, since the girl belonged to his own family, he would do well to obey his father's wishes. Like other devout Hindus, Rao could only marry within his community. 'These weddings were always arranged by parents. The boy would meet the girl and he would accept her. If not, he would look for another match. Marriages were not so much a union of two individuals as of two families. Each family probed into the other's background and past, as far back as they could.'

By the fifth year of college, he had his first child, a daughter. He returned to his family after completing his graduation. Until then, as his wife lived in Rajam, the couple would meet over weekends either at a small hotel in Vizag or back home, which was a couple of hours away.

In his parents' generation, convention required girls to marry before puberty. 'My mother was barely eight when she was married. People who disregarded this norm were ostracized. At the same time, child marriage was illegal in places which were under British rule. If the girl was married before puberty, the government would punish you; if she wasn't, the community would punish you! The only recourse for people from my community was to sneak away to Yanam, the nearest French colony, get married, and return to their villages.'

He remembers that even during his school days, once a girl had reached puberty, she was removed from school as was the tradition. By the time Rao was married, these practices had stopped. 'Everything has changed now.'

Rao, his wife and child subsisted on the family income. 'I know my father was very proud that I became an engineer, although he would never ever show this to me openly, but I knew. Nobody in our community, stretching across fourteen villages, had even passed their SSLC, let alone engineering.'

Within six months of Rao qualifying as an engineer, his father divided all his property among his four sons. They drew equal shares from a lot of four chits of paper their father tossed up. Rao's draw was Rs 3 lakh in cash, a truck, two acres of land, and a house which had been let out on rent to a bank for Rs 200 a month.

'Given the choice, I would have studied further but my family pulled me in a different direction. My father had wanted me to get a job, my mother saw me as an entrepreneur and my brothers hoped I would join them and start a manufacturing plant. In those days, people looked up to entrepreneurs. It was the time of the "licence raj"; all essential goods – milk, milk cans, sugar, cement – were rationed.' Rao finally settled for a job in a paper mill at Rs 500 per month.

About two years later, his father died of sudden heart failure. With his inheritance, Rao acquired a stake as a partner in the family business run by his brothers and rented his truck to them.

The paper mill in which Rao was working was in Rajamundhry, some 200 kilometres from Rajam. Given this, he stayed with a friend while he looked for a house so that his wife and family could join him. His role was as a shift engineer in charge of a workshop. After three months of working in eight-hour shifts, Rao was bored. He found that his boss was not well disposed towards Rao's community and so he resigned and returned home.

He soon found work on the same salary in the Public Works Department of the state government. 'I used to travel the 40 kilometre distance each day by bus or motor scooter. This job was no better than the previous one as, after six months, the monotony of idling all day set in. I had no work. I would go there in the mornings, sit there all day, do nothing and return home in the evening. So I quit and joined my brothers in the family business.'

Though his father had divided the property, Rao's brothers kept the business running as partners. Every month-end, they would thumb through the accounts and split the profit. His elder brother got the lion's share as he had a larger family with four children. His brothers believed that, being an engineer, Rao would not have any idea about trading. They nagged him, as did others, to find a job suitable to his qualifications. Rao plodded on and continued to add value to the business. An important contribution was to eliminate the middleman from the supply chain and sell directly to large companies in Chennai. When profits improved, he earned his brothers' respect.

After the demise of their father, Rao and his younger brother and their families continued to live together in the same house for some time. The other brothers had moved out with their families even while their father was alive. At about this time, the first rush of entrepreneurship coursed through Rao. In the quest to start a business, Rao visited Visakhapatnam to have a closer look at some small industries. He was lucky to meet someone who had a jute license to sell in Chennai. Jute was a large industry controlled from Calcutta. So exhilarated was Rao at the prospect of starting his own business that he made light of the many bureaucratic obstacles that he encountered in transferring the licence. One-and-a-half years flew by before he was able to complete the work he had started in 1975 – acquire the finance and get approvals for the cement and iron quotas. The procedure for the cement quota was particularly complicated. 'We had to give an estimate to the industries department. They would forward their recommendation based on their own estimates to Visakhapatnam. Then they would allocate.'

In the meantime, he and his brothers continued to jointly manage the traditional trading business. His brothers also recognized the value of being in the jute business; particularly as it would be profitable from day one. Within nine months, Rao had recovered his entire investment and, in a year, the full cost of the project. 'This was a major turning point in my career as an entrepreneur.'

Rao then bought a business which was doing poorly, turned it around and considered expanding it further. While he wanted to reinvest his returns in business, his brothers were averse to taking more risk and preferred to keep the cash. 'It was at this point I realized, our risk profiles were different and that in future, I may need to take these risks by myself, rather than expect my brothers to join me.'

As an example of his new found more independent path from the family, Rao then acquired a sick ferro-alloys plant, at the instance of the district collector who wanted to help rehabilitate the industry.

His next stop and a turning point of fortunes, was banking. Quite by chance, Rao learnt that Bangalore-based Vysya Bank – among India's largest private banks with a network at that time of 200 branches – was scouting for fresh talent to succeed outgoing directors whose tenures were ending. Rao was acquainted with Vysya Bank's CEO and was offered a position on the Board. Rao accepted. It was 1985 and he was thirty-five.

With a capital of Rs 60 lakh, Vysya Bank was under pressure from the Reserve Bank of India to increase its capital base. The bank's efforts to raise finance through a rights' issue had only been partially successful as it was 50 per cent under-subscribed. The chairman and CEO then strongly urged all the directors to invest to help the bank.

As his asset base was growing, Rao did not have any spare cash to invest. However, he felt investing in the bank was an excellent opportunity. So he raised money from every available source he could find, including raising a loan by pledging his wife's jewellery and land as collateral against a loan from Andhra Bank. In the end he was able to invest Rs 5 lakh. After one year, the bank repeated the rights' issue. Once more, they found insufficient takers. Again, Rao chipped in by borrowing more money from friends to invest more in the bank. As a result he became a major shareholder holding around 25 per cent of the bank's shares.

Rao believed that his shareholding was likely to enable him to remain a director of the bank and that this would also help him in his future business activities. 'There is no doubt that whether I was attending a business meeting or social event, those present would look differently at me as a bank director as compared to a mere jute mill owner. People in political and bureaucratic circles were suddenly a lot more attentive to me. For a change, I was on the other side of the table meeting people from different backgrounds, meeting borrowers and defaulters, discussing proposals, handling other aspects of the banking business, and mastering the finer points of management.'

But primarily, the investment in Vysya Bank was one, based on income and potential capital growth. 'Whereas the return on bank deposits was 10 per cent, the 18 per cent dividend at par I received, was much better and, of course, was secure.'

But it was the capital appreciation which would prove spectacular. After the economic reforms in 1993, his Rs 10 share became worth Rs 3000. Rather than cash in immediately, Rao held on to his shares. The bank then had another rights' issue in which Rao and his friends participated, leading to them owning around 40 per cent.

'Banking was the fourth lesson in my career. The first was when I was the secretary of the students' union in college. The second was working with my brothers in the trading business and learning how to work with farmers. The third was the difficult task of running a jute mill in a village where local politicians constantly provoked workers to strike.'

Rao in the early '90s still lived in the village and decided it was time to move to Bangalore with his family – he had three children – and established a small office in the building which he still retains to this day. He also had a Hyderabad office staffed by ten people and managed by a friend.

His main business interests in the mid '90s consisted of his investment in the Vysya bank, the old jute mill and the ferro alloys business. As for the family business, due to the different business philosophies of Rao and his brothers, Rao foresaw a rift looming large and believed he had better separate while he and his brothers still had a cordial relationship. 'Within a week, we worked out an amicable and clear-cut division of assets comprising two jute mills, a rolling mill and a steel mill. I kept the jute mill I had started and acquired the other mill from my brothers. And so by the mid '90s, I was on my own so far as the wider family was concerned.'

Economic liberalization led to the growth of the banking industry. Many new banks sprang up. Vysya Bank Chairman Ramesh Gelli left and opened his own bank – Global Trust Bank – jointly with friends and professionals in Hyderabad. 'The exodus of Ramesh Gelli and other senior executives from Vysya left a vacuum. Now, as the only major shareholder, Rao was left with the onerous task of re-building the bank. 'I retained a professional as chairman and recruited a couple of senior people. Though on paper I controlled the bank, in reality, the Reserve Bank of India was the real one in control and left me little room for manoeuvre. Being little-known in banking circles beyond the state did not help. Without exception, owners of private banks were tarred with the same brush by the authorities and it was usually assumed they were all involved in dubious practices such as lending to related entities and taking "kick backs" for loans. Even when I protested my honesty, the Reserve Bank bureaucrats were reluctant to trust me. So deep was the mistrust in those days that the Reserve Bank always had a director on the board of these banks.'

Having invested most of what he had in the bank, Rao was left with two choices – either of protecting or increasing his investment. 'So I decided to protect the investment by looking for a foreign bank to bring in its financial expertise and systems. This lead to Bank Brussels Limited (BBL) acquiring a stake of 10 per cent.'

Not much later, ING, the global bank, purchased BBL. This transaction introduced him to ING and, in 2001, ING and Vysya established an insurance business together. The following year, ING acquired Rao's interest in Vysya and took over its management. 'ING asked me to stay on as Non-Executive Chairman but I decided to invest the money I had made on the sale of my banking interests in other businesses.'

Rao started several businesses. Two of his major investments were in sugar and breweries. 'In those days, I would enter every possible business where I saw the opportunity to make a profit.' He had already leased his jute mills. He also entered and exited from an export oriented business for manufacturing cotton ear buds from Chennai and as well as from Quintant, an IT company which he founded with Phaneesh Murthy who had previously been a senior executive at Infosys. I could see Rao was not a traditional Indian entrepreneur who builds but never sells. He was a serial entrepreneur.

The next main sector he entered was power. In 1996 he acquired the interests of CMS Energy Corporation of the US which wanted to close down its Indian operations following the US energy giant Enron's debacle in India. Over the following years, GMR has invested in further power plants in Andhra Pradesh and also acquired a 50 per cent stake in Intergen, a Netherlands-based power company which has twelve power plants located across the UK, the Netherlands, Mexico, Australia and Philippines.

Rao was still not finished in seeking out strategic opportunities. The next major initiative came in the area of road infrastructure. He learnt that for the first time the National Highways Authority of India (NHAI) and Infrastructure Development & Finance Company (ID&FC) had called for a tender on six road projects to be done on a public-private partnership basis. 'For some reason I could sense the public-private partnership business model would be big in India and applied for all six. We won two tenders offered in the first round.' But Rao had a hurdle to overcome – NHAI's apprehensions about handing over the projects to a newcomer. 'I met and convinced its chairman by saying something along the following lines, "that it was GMR Group which was putting its money on the block. On the other hand, all NHAI is giving us was the right to extend the road from two lanes to four lanes. If we don't perform, throw us out. Give us a chance."' Whatever he said must have worked because GMR Group got the contracts and completed the roads ahead of time and earned a bonus. After that, Rao securitized and sold the annuity receivables to a consortium of banks. Since then the group has become involved in several more road projects.

One of Rao's most visible recent projects is in Andhra Pradesh. 'Some years ago the then Chief Minister N Chandrababu Naidu embarked on a major infrastructure development campaign to attract global investments into the state. He dreamed of giving Hyderabad an international airport and acquired a 5000 acre plot and floated a global tender. GMR won the tender with its key international airport partner for the project, the Malaysian Airport Authority. As it happens I have been through the airport several times and am impressed with the result, both in terms of design and efficiency. It is a world apart from its predecessor. As a result of this success GMR won the bid in 2006 to redevelop and modernize Delhi's airport. The big challenge,' Rao says, 'is to complete the first phase in time for the Commonwealth Games in 2010.'

GMR Group has also taken over the management of the existing Sabiha Gokcen International Airport in Turkey to develop and operate the airport for a twenty-year period.

Rao spends a lot of time developing a strong relationship with his partners. 'From the start, beginning with ING, I had win-win partnerships for every deal.' He attributes his rapport with partners to being able to 'get into their shoes and know what they want.' The other GMR partners apart from ING, CMS Energy and the Malaysian Airport Authority, mentioned above, include the International Finance Company (part of the World Bank), Fraport of Germany, UEM of Malaysia and Lemark of Turkey.

The latest area of infrastructure that GMR has entered is that of urban development, including Special Economic Zones and commercial and residential property development.

Rao is still very hands-on in major new projects. 'Once my family or I learn the ropes, I let professionals take over. This has been "the rule of thumb" in all the areas the group has ventured into; be that of setting up power plants, constructing roads or building airports.'

Rao is emphatic that family businesses in India walk on 'thin ice.' 'I have decided to give more importance not only to "corporate" but also to "family" governance. Without family governance, the circle is incomplete.' Rao has seen too many families – even in his village – as well as large corporates – destroy themselves by ignoring this. He has observed brothers, who once had the deepest respect for one other, fighting on the streets. 'I am anxious to protect my family from this potential calamity. If it's a well known family, it will be all over the media. I do not want that situation. We are all human beings, we all have our differences.'

In a serious effort to avoid this possible outcome, in 2000, Rao attended a national summit of family business held by the Confederation of Indian Industries at Jaipur with all his family members to learn how successful family businesses survive multiple generations. From what he learnt at the summit and from other similar seminars and experts, he embarked on evolving family agreements and drafting a family constitution involving his wife, daughter, son-in-law, sons and daughters-in-law. The family worked on this over 57 meetings at two-day retreats. 'They cried, fought and argued. It's not so easy for all eight members to come to an understanding. We took a while. Everything was put on the table and then we wrote the family policies and integrated them into a family constitution.'

The family constitution is structured to foster good governance and good communication. The document spells out the process of choosing Rao's successor, conflict resolution, entry of new family members, media policy, political policy, and so on. 'If I want to enter politics, there will be two days of debate. I will have to transfer my entire stake in GMR and my position in the business to the other family members.' The family media policy allows only Rao to talk. 'We have a spokesperson and CEOs. If anybody wants to talk to the media they will have to take the permission of the chairman or the family director who is the Sector Head. In my opinion it is often because of media that families start to fight because it is perceived that one member of the family has more time in the limelight and is thus favoured. Of course, that may not be correct, but it may be so perceived by the public. We want to avoid creating such perceptions.'

Every other month, the family meets for a dialogue to discuss business and family issues in the presence of three facilitators. The meetings foster emotional and spiritual bonding among members. The family constitution deals with any eventuality, be it marital discord or adoption. In case of a divorce, the constitution spells out how the assets will be split. Rao insisted on including the women in family conferences. 'I said, in India or anywhere, I think women play a critical role in the stability of families.

'What use is the money I make, if family members fight over it on the streets? I thought it better to work to build an institution that will endure for generations rather than just creating assets. I am very clear that without family governance, we can't have corporate governance.'

With these prophetic words ringing in my ears, as I could see through the window that night had fallen in Bangalore on a Saturday, I thought it was only fair to draw the meeting to a close and allow Rao to get home and spend some quality time with his family.

GMR Group (www.gmrgroup.in) is a Bangalore-headquartered global infrastructure company with interests in airports, energy, highways and urban infrastructure. In addition, the other focus area of the group is the agri-business with sugar as its main product-line. The group is also actively engaged in the philanthropic activities in the areas of education, health, hygiene and sanitation, empowerment & livelihoods and community-based programmes under its foundation. The group holding company has two subsidiary companies – GMR Infrastructure Limited and GMR Industries Limited, both listed on the Indian Stock Exchanges.

‘Village kids – and I see myself as a typical country boy – will outshine city kids because they are tough, they have the fire in their bellies, and the spirit of sacrifice to chase their dreams. Millions of villagers out there are just waiting to make the most of the minutest opportunity.’

DR K RAVINDRANATH

Founder, Chairman
Global Hospitals

We got our audience with Dr Ravindranath on a busy August afternoon at Global Hospital when he was between operations. Though he owns and runs a number of hospitals, Ravindranath's true love remains surgery. He arrived late for our meeting, directly from the operation theater and still in overalls, after performing a 'particularly complicated' emergency operation. During our interview, he took many calls from colleagues and patients; apparently, everyone was aware that he was outside the operation theatre.

Ravindranath was born in 1954 into a prominent agricultural family in a small village called Chiramana in the Nellore district of Andhra Pradesh. He was third among seven children.

His grandfather was a well-to-do landowner, while Ravindranath's father, for most of his life, was the elected representative of their village. 'He always ran unopposed and spent a lot of his personal funds in serving fellow villagers.' In his time, his father was active in India's fight for freedom against the British and had been jailed for his views. When he was only fifteen, he even ran away to Burma to avoid arrest. 'A man with great ethics and morals, he was closely involved with the top Indian socialists of the day such as Puchapalli Sundarayya and GC Kondaiah. He must have been a great worry to my grandfather, who was an establishment figure.'

His father followed a simple credo: never knowingly cause anyone harm – not even your enemies. He believed there were only two important careers:

teaching and medicine. He never guided them towards law, politics or even the bureaucracy – the Indian Administrative Service was too elitist for him. 'He used to say that the only thing that stays with you until you die is your education; everything else is transient.'

Ravindranath and one of his younger brothers became doctors. His eldest brother, who was not interested in studying, became a builder, much to his father's chagrin. 'He really did not understand that not everyone is cut out for academics.' The youngest brother became an engineer, an acceptable choice as it involved study.

'Sadly, he did not get a single teacher out of the seven of us.'

Did his father place the same emphasis on his sisters' education? 'He was quite positive about that but, unfortunately, in traditional families, girls are married off early. We didn't have the money to send them off to big towns for further education so they married early. All my sisters finished school, though – an achievement in those times.'

Ravindranath found studies easy. Throughout his academics he was in the top few of his class. 'I guess it was my father's influence but I was also very active in all other school activities such as sports and student union politics.' He studied for his MBBS at the Sri Venkateswara Medical College in Tirupati and MS at Madras University. He took up post-graduate work in surgery before leaving, in 1984, for the UK, where he received his FRCS from Edinburgh and Glasgow. He began with the Memorial Hospital, Darlington, and, after that, shuttled between London hospitals such as Hammersmith Hospital, St Mark's Hospital, and King's College Hospital.

After six years in England, Ravindranath was back home in India in 1990. What made him take this step when his career was on the ascendant? 'The main reason was my father. He always used to say that England has enslaved people for centuries and asked me, "Do you want to continue to be part of that?" He urged me to come back to India. He said that many people needed my services here. He used to say, "You are one among many in London but one among few in India." Was his father right to compel him to return? 'Absolutely,' replies Ravindranath. 'Even a few of my British colleagues endorsed my father's views when I discussed this with them. They told me they were confident I would succeed back in India and that, if they were in my position, they would return too.

'It was, nevertheless, a big decision for me as I was on the faculty at the University of London and had offers from Mayo Clinic and Pittsburgh Hospital, which was a global leader in liver surgery. I enjoyed my time in England and learnt a lot about people and, most of all, myself.'

He recalls having a showdown with a consultant in London for being derogatory to one of his colleagues, an Indian, who was a registrar at the hospital. Everybody feared he would be sacked for taking him on. 'As you would appreciate a consultant is at the top of the pile in a hospital. I said to him, "I'm sorry. I've seen my share of British who are bad; if you have anything against one of our colleagues please refer to him by name and do not call him a 'bloody Indian'. I do not refer to you as a 'bloody Englishman'."'

The consultant was furious and an inquiry was ordered. Fortunately, the English nurse who was witness to their argument supported Ravindranath. 'I was exonerated when he was found to be at fault.' This incident restored his faith in the inherent goodness of the British. 'Honesty of its people is one of the things I like about Britain. Leaving aside the way they treated India during the colonial period, I respect them for their discipline, compassion, integrity, seriousness about life, and their sense of "fair play". Without "fair play", I could not have reached the position I did in England. If I was equal to another Briton then they would probably favour their compatriot, but if I was better than him, then I would get the job.'

But professional satisfaction was coupled with unease inside. Ravindranath had seen first-hand the plight of Indians who visited his liver transplant unit at King's College. Under EU regulations, UK nationals were the first in queue for a transplant followed by citizens of EU countries. Only if there were no claims from the UK or EU would other nationals be eligible for a transplant. 'If there were ten Indian patients in wait, one would get a liver, the other nine would die. It was pathetic – I saw a number of filthy rich Indians coming to King's and dying miserably without their family.' This stirred in Ravindranath the first thoughts of making a beginning at home. 'Then, Apollo Hospitals approached me and said they would set up a liver transplant unit if I returned to India.'

Ravindranath spent more than eight years with Apollo Hospitals, Hyderabad, before he left to start a small 60-bed hospital unit at the plush Banjara Hills locality in Hyderabad.

A 'difference of opinion' caused Ravindranath to split with Apollo. 'I was prepared to run the liver transplant unit at a small loss subsidized by other areas of my specialization; they wanted it to be profitable from the outset. I was convinced that, for me to get my liver transplant business up and running, I needed to be in the driver's seat.'

In 2002, he set up Global Hospitals. He now owns eleven hospitals across several Indian cities.

Ravindranath put every rupee he had into the initial 60-bed Hyderabad hospital rather than borrow from his or his wife's family. Wasn't that a great risk? 'Yes, it was, and I know my wife was terrified. She said to me, "What will we do if this fails?" I told her, "There's skill in my hands. I can earn money any day anywhere in the world. As long as I am fit and healthy, I can take care of my family."' For the first time, Ravindranath would straddle the dual role of a surgeon and hospital administrator. 'A lot of people thought I would go bankrupt,' he laughs.

Was Apollo Hospitals wrong about the liver transplant unit? 'Indeed, I proved them wrong, although I have to acknowledge Apollo is the leading private hospital group in India today. There are many areas where you can run a profitable operation even if you were to do liver transplants alone. In this country, be it any disease for that matter, if you do well, there is an opportunity. The margins may be less but the volumes make up for it.'

Ravindranath has tried to instill 'British' values in his hospitals. He has no relatives working in the group. In fact, a couple of them who failed to make the grade were shown the door. 'In this hospital there are no boundaries of caste, creed or nationality. The best get the job.'

Does he make as good an administrator as he is a surgeon? 'I'm probably not as diplomatic an administrator as some others might be, but I believe people will tell you I am straightforward. I believe in quality and I will support whoever delivers that to the end.'

How does Ravindranath manage two full-time careers and still have a personal life? 'You're right; it is very difficult to manage.' What is a typical day like? 'I wake up at 5.30 a.m. I then spend 45 minutes on yoga with an instructor who has been teaching me for the last five years. Then, an hour at the gym, working on the cross trainer and treadmill before doing some weights. By 7.30 a.m., I'm out. Back home, I read the papers for fifteen minutes,' he laughs, 'because they tell me to rest for awhile. By 8.30 a.m., I'm in my car most days and in the office by 9 a.m. I get back home by 9 p.m.'

Often on Sundays, he addresses conferences or visits one of his other hospitals. If he is in Hyderabad, he drops in at the hospital in the morning and makes a round of all his patients. He would then try and get home in time for lunch with his family.

Most of Ravindranath's time in hospital is spent in surgery and patient care. The rest is in administration. 'I am not going to give up being a surgeon for any reason. I believe I have been given the gift of surgical skills and I'm still learning and improving. It would be wrong to give up what I love and am good at.' What about his dream of a liver transplant unit? 'We have done 80 transplants so far [as of June 2009] and have the most successful multi-organ transplant programme in this country. We are comprehensive and provide everything. I have not yet achieved my vision of creating the largest liver surgery and transplant programme in the world.'

Global Hospitals' business model is to cater to everyone – rich, middle class and poor. 'In our country, no hospital can really gain credibility by operating only on the rich. The model of just charging the rich does not work and, even if it did, it is not the right model for this country.'

I suspect this last comment was another inherited trait from his father. 'Absolutely, there are a number of opportunities in India. The deficiency of infrastructure, doctors, nurses, and technicians makes a huge demand on our existing healthcare structure. Some years ago, the population in India was a bane; now it's a boon. Everyone wants good healthcare for themselves, their family, their parents, and their children.'

How does he contribute in overcoming some of these problems? 'Well, Global is obviously investing in infrastructure and we have already started healthcare education, which is critical. We have started super-speciality training in this hospital.' From the day since he was at Apollo Hospitals, Ravindranath has trained the largest number of laparoscopic surgeons in this country – nearly 600 – over the last seventeen years. 'One of my colleagues there asked me why I was training my potential competitors. I told him that if I did not train them, then someone else would. If I trained them then there was a good chance they would send their difficult cases to me, which has actually happened. Believe me, in any "nook and corner" in India, I meet someone I have trained.

'There is so much intelligence in this country. If only urban infrastructure could come to our rural areas! The private sector has to chip in, as the government does not have enough funds. Once I had enough money, I built a high school and hospital for my village and donated money for the poor people from the area to build their own homes. I am proud to say that the school has a 100 per cent pass rate. The school has now produced several doctors and a number of engineers who have gone overseas for further study. Over 100 students have gone on to become teachers, doctors, engineers and other professionals.'

Dr Ravindranath believes that India will become a knowledge source for the rest of the world. 'Whatever China does with manufacturing, India will do with knowledge-based industries.'

He's convinced that rural India will outshine urban India. 'Village kids – and I see myself as a country boy – will outshine city kids because they are tough, they have the fire in their bellies, and the spirit of sacrifice to chase their dreams. Millions of villagers out there are just waiting to make the most of the minutest of opportunities.'

He cites an example from the family. 'Believe it or not I married my cousin, the daughter of my mother's brother. I know that is not scientifically wise but it happens in my society. Anyway, my father-in-law (and uncle) only studied up to his SSLC and speaks little English. After struggling for some time, he started a tiny transport and construction company called "Lanco" after his family name. When the business was underway, he went away to secure a big contract that was of great importance for the financial future of the family. He did not return until three months after his first child was born. His company is now one of the leaders in its field in India. This is the commitment one finds in rural India.'

By now, Ravindranath was getting frequent reminders for his next surgery, so we had to close our meeting. On our way out, I looked around the room and observed several photos of Ravindranath with different dignitaries, including one with the then president of India, Dr Abdul Kalam. 'Well, this was before he was President. One of his friends, Haridwar Singh, in Delhi, had a liver disease. Everybody said that he would die. Dr Kalam called me to see if I could help. I went to see Haridwar and felt he had an 80 per cent chance of survival if he could have a liver transplant; if not, he would die for sure. At that time, in 1993, there was not a single transplant unit in this country. So, I rang my friends in London and they agreed to do the operation for free when it normally would have cost GBP 70,000. Haridwar headed off to London for the operation and came back to India "hale and hearty" three months later. He is still alive and well today. Dr Abdul Kalam and I went to the airport together to receive Haridwar.

'Kalam said to me, "My friend has come back with a British liver. Ravindranath, I am very worried at what is happening to our nation. We are an intelligent race and are putting satellites in space but we can't perform liver transplants? What is it that is stopping you from doing it?" I told him the problems were a lack of infrastructure and no transplant legislation, amongst others. Although he was not president at the time, he was a very influential adviser to the government. He promised me all his support if I set up a transplant unit. Imagine my delight when I approached the government for low cost funding of my first liver transplant unit, only to find he was a member of the board approving the loan! The first slide of my presentation was of Ganesha, the elephant god. I told them that, if we go by Hindu mythology, they were able to do a head transplant which is impossible even as of today. Why then could we not even do a liver transplant in India, though these operations are commonplace in other countries, I challenged. Even today, I often start my presentations with this slide.'

Any parting words of advice for young Indians? 'The first thing is if you really want to follow some career or profession, go all out for it; don't falter no matter what the challenges; in the end you will succeed. Education, discipline and hard work are the keys to that success.'

His last words ring a bell. I've often hear them from successful Indian business people. 'Young people, and in fact everybody, should never forget that they have an obligation to contribute to the well-being of those less fortunate than them.'

With that, he waved 'goodbye' and disappeared into the operating theatre.

Global Hospitals (www.globalhospital.net) is a Hyderabad-based super-speciality corporate hospital founded in 1998. It is one of the leading multi-organ transplant centres in India specializing in liver, heart, bone marrow and kidney transplants. It is also a referral centre for complex surgeries and treatments in the areas of liver, gastroenterology, cardiac, pancreatic and blood disorders. Through a Memorandum of Understanding with King's College Hospital, London, and with Professor Tanaka of Japan, Global Hospitals is able to provide world-class surgical expertise in living and cadaver donor liver transplants.

> One day, I was just walking past the lab [Pfizer] and the thought suddenly struck me: I had to build my own Pfizer one day. The feeling was so powerful that, from that moment on, I looked at chemistry from the point of view of a businessman.

DR ANJI REDDY

Founder & Chairman
Dr Reddy's Laboratories

The outdoor café beside the waterfall at the Hotel Oberoi in Bangalore is one of Dr Anji Reddy's favourite retreats. This is one of the places he stops by when he wants to do strategic thinking. Unfortunately, it was not the best place for recording an interview so we had to move to a less noisy spot inside.

Dr Reddy was born in September 1941 in the village of Tadepalli near the city of Vijayawada in Andhra Pradesh. The village had a population of about 10,000 at that time. 'The village was on the banks of the great river Krishna where nearby a dam had been built by Sir Arthur Cotton many years before. 'A canal flowed through my village all the way up to Madras (now Chennai). It was very picturesque. We would have had to cross the river by train for education or walk all the way into Vijayawada. My parents didn't want to take that risk so I was sent to live with my grandmother who lived about ten miles away in Nutakki. All my memories of village and student life are not of the village where I was born but of my grandmother's village.'

His father's first wife passed away leaving one half-sister from that marriage. His father then married his mother with whom he had six more children – four boys and two girls; Dr Reddy is the eldest.

Dr Reddy's father owned land on which he principally cultivated turmeric. 'The *Financial Times of London*, called me the son of a turmeric farmer and all the Indian papers followed suit. My mother was a house wife.

'My father Venkata Reddy was a visionary, although he did not study much. In fact, he hardly went to school. He did not even complete his SSLC. He must have had five years of schooling. His passion was ayurveda, a system of traditional medicine. He used to buy books on ayurveda, make concoctions using various herbs and treat our cattle.'

I speculate that the pharma industry may well have been in his blood. He laughs and says, 'You could well be right because he did develop concoctions for humans. I don't know how or why, but he developed a medicine for dysmenorrhea which is pain associated with menses in young girls. He would bring home something that looked like dried lemons, which he would peel and then pulp and combine it with some powder and put it in a pill. Indeed, this left a deep imprint on me.'

I asked why he tried to develop this medicine. 'Out of curiosity. It was purely a hobby. He distributed his medicines free to villagers. I was told a story by my mother that one day his medicine helped the daughter of an important government official who wanted to pay my father. He arrogantly left a Rs 10 note on the table. My father was so insulted, he immediately donated the money to his temple.'

Dr Reddy stayed for six years with his grandmother from 5th to 11th standard and topped each year of school. He adds, 'I was lucky that I have a good memory and, even though I often played the fool at school, I did not have to work hard; passing exams came easily to me.

'I remember well my old school near my grandmother's home. It was not far but in the monsoons the path to school turned to absolute slush. I remember well my feet getting stuck in the muck as the school was built on marshy land. I recently revisited my school as they were doing a biography on me. They complained that even to this day there is no compound wall to the school, and buffalo frequently stray into the school property. I immediately agreed to donate the money to build the wall. I have so many happy memories of my time at that school.

'It was a beautiful experience living with my grandmother. In fact, until she passed away, I was more attached to her than to my mother. Once she passed away, the attachment shifted. My grandmother was a spiritual person. She was not literate but she loved Indian classical music and devotional songs. I grew up in a very serene atmosphere. We did not even have electricity in my school and it was very peaceful. Believe it or not, I was only introduced to radio in 1954, the last year of my stay with my grandmother. Before that, there was nothing.'

I learnt that none of Dr Reddy's siblings followed him to stay with their maternal grandmother because by the time they were ready to go to school a bridge had been built over the river so they could easily get to the school on the other side.

In 1955, Dr Reddy moved back to his parents' home and travelled each day to and from Guntur to attend Andhra Christian College. 'Today, it would take 35 minutes, but in those days it took me two hours each way. My cousin wanted to major in history, so I also wanted to follow suit. I had no fascination for science whatsoever, even though I got good marks because of my memory. However, he dissuaded me from history and urged me to take up science. That is how I changed my course.'

I asked why his cousin suggested he do science? 'He felt that I would be wasting my time studying history. Maybe he saw a spark in me. When my sister was interviewed, she said that I was naturally inquisitive. She said I would pluck a flower and dissect it. I don't remember any of this.'

As not many people make it from a village school to become a corporate leader I asked him whether in his case he attributed it to his family, teachers or something else. 'It is true most of my school mates stayed in the village but there are at least two others in my batch who got PhDs. One of them worked alongside me, in due course, at Indian Drugs and Pharmaceuticals. In my case, firstly I attribute my success to that cousin of mine who persuaded me not to study history. Sadly, my science teacher was not very inspiring or I suspect he would have awakened an interest in science. But I do have to make a mention of my chemistry teacher in college, Dr Vardanam. He was a Dalit. Like a number of Dalits, he converted to Christianity, earned a PhD and became head of the chemistry department. He was a very impressive person and definitely sparked an interest in chemistry and his love for organic chemistry was profound. I will exemplify, are you a chemist by any chance?'

I had to let down Dr Reddy by telling my background was sadly the legal profession. He was on a roll and in his element. 'It doesn't matter', he said. 'If you look at the molecular structure of propyl alcohol, it is CH3-CH2-CH2-OH. He would never write propyl alcohol like that. He would always write CH3-OH, which is methyl alcohol, then he would turn the CH3 to CH2, add another CH3, which then made it ethyl alcohol, then he would turn that 3 into a 2 and put another CH2, which now made it propyl alcohol. It would not leave you; his teachings still haunt me. Because of him I developed my own love of organic chemistry.' I had to admit to Dr Reddy this made absolutely no sense to me whatever but would take his word for it that Dr Vardanam was a great teacher!

Upon graduating first in his class, armed with his bachelor's degree in chemistry, young Dr Reddy moved to Bombay to attend Bombay University to do postgraduate study. 'In the beginning, my major was textile chemistry. I found textiles boring and, for some reason, changed over to technology of pharmaceuticals and fine chemicals.

'I studied there for two years. We had a professor by the name of ML Khurana – a very kind man. He used to radiate peace, like my grandmother. Several years ago, I gave the Professor Khurana memorial lecture. In that lecture, I told the audience that Professor Khurana's lab had a very mesmerizing effect on me. His lab was supported by industrialists. The amazing fact was that all the dyes used in the Indian textile industry originated from that small lab. So, anyone who was studying for their BTech in dyes and dye stuff would be sponsored by a company. He or she would then have to develop a process for a particular dye stuff relevant to that sponsor. It was a beautiful symbiosis. Similarly, in pharmaceuticals, Pfizer was one of the companies supporting the chemistry lab work on an anti-tuberculosis drug called INH, Isonicotinic Acid Hydrazide. TB was rampant in India then. One day, I was just walking past the lab and the thought suddenly struck me, I had to build my own Pfizer one day. The feeling was so powerful that, from that moment on, I looked at chemistry from the point of view of a businessman.'

After earning his master's, Dr Reddy moved to the National Chemical Laboratory in Pune to study for his PhD. I was pleased to hear him tell me that he did not stand first in his studies at Bombay University. 'No, I did not this time, although I was in the first division. When I came to Pune I made the transition to almost becoming a pharmaceutical technologist from being just a student under a pure chemical engineering professor. I had to struggle hard but I enjoyed it.

'Papers have been written on my thesis which was based on the kinetics of oxidation. However, I was popular, not for my thesis, but for something my professor, Professor LK Doraiswamy, asked me to do. "Dr Reddy," he said, "you know there is a thermodynamic property called liquid defusivity. It is necessary to estimate this property as it is very important. Even our Atomic Energy Institute and NASA are trying to do this. There are only two equations for this property so you please work on developing an equation for it." I sat in a corner, as there was not much room, with my calculator, which was as big as a typewriter then, and a slide rule that a friend had given me. I arranged all the data and whatever else was necessary, and I cooked up an equation in two days. My professor was stunned. My equation was quite good as it fitted the data he had given me. Professor Doraiswamy then sent my equation to a popular scientific journal, *Industrial and Engineering Chemistry*, saying that they could publish it as a "letter to the editor". They replied, saying that they would not print it as a "letter to the editor" as it was a very important equation. They said I should work on it some more and they would publish that as a main article.'

The paper was published in February 1967. Professor Doraiswamy recently wrote to Dr Reddy to let him know that a book, *100 Years of Chemical Engineering*, has a chapter stating that one of the most important chemical discoveries to come out from Asia was his work on liquid defusivity. 'I was stunned. When my daughter married a chemical engineer, the first question I asked my son-in-law was if he knew my equation!' Dr Reddy says laughing.

Dr Reddy's PhD was actually awarded by Bombay University even though he was studying at the National Chemical Laboratory in Pune. For some bizarre reason, the final hurdle involved passing a German translation. 'I did not prepare but just used the dictionary we were allowed to take into the exam to make sentences even though they did not seem to make much sense to me. Somehow I passed.' I said that was not fair. 'See, passing is not directly proportional to the number of hours you study. Where I put my German to test was six months ago. We bought a German company called Betapharm, for USD 650 million. I went there to address my people and the mayor of Augsburg had a small reception for me. The next day, there was an article on the mayor's party for me. I was about to take the paper to the reception and ask them to translate it for me, when I thought to myself, I have passed a German translation exam; let me see if I can do this myself. I could understand everything.'

I asked Dr Reddy how he saw his personality. 'I think I should answer that with a story. When my first anti-diabetes drug was licensed by Novo Nordisk of Denmark, a world leader in diabetes care, the CEO Lars Rebien Sørenson wanted to meet the people who were behind the new drug. He asked me why I chose to work on an anti-diabetes drug. I was driving him out of my vineyard when he asked me this. I told him that it was because I am a diabetic myself. He was stunned. He was speechless. He said most people in my place would have cooked up some story. In India, nobody wants to say that they are diabetic. They want to hide it under the carpet. I think this shows that I am very straightforward and honest in my dealings with people.

'When someone trusts you, they trust you 100 per cent. There is no compromise. When trust is lost, it is lost completely. When we licensed our first drug to Novo Nordisk, they repeated all the tests. As we continued research, I observed some compounds that were not only reducing the blood glucose but were also reducing lipids like cholesterol and triglyceride as well. I was intrigued. I told my scientists what I had noticed and asked them to investigate further. They thought this a strange request. We had already licensed an anti-diabetes drug and wondered why I wanted them to do more on this. So, I rang up Anker Lundemose who had done a lot of the project work on the first drug and asked him to send a good molecular biologist to us. He sent Patrick Doyle, an Englishman, a very bright man. I told him that I wanted him to have a look at the molecule. Without waiting for our boys to present the molecule, Patrick came with a wish list. He said that they had on their records that 60 per cent of diabetics have high triglycerides. If only he had a drug which reduced both glucose and triglycerides then its ED 50 should be 5 mg, so on and so forth. Then up rises Rajagopalan from Dr Reddy's Research Foundation, who presents Patrick Doyle with a compound whose ED 50 is 1mg. Patrick was stunned. Even today when I meet him he says, "Dr Reddy; I was in a trance for 24 hours."

'We realized that we were on to something big. This was the first drug in its class. Patrick Doyle did a few more experiments and concurred with our findings. The first molecule is called PPAR-alpha-gamma activator which is responsible for lowering sugar and the second one is called gamma alpha. As there is an alpha it was both lowering glucose as well as triglycerides. So we called it dual-PPAR-alpha-gamma activator. Novo Nordisk licensed this and we proceeded with tests. A few years later, they named the drug "Ragaglitazar" – "Raga" for "Reddy Alpha Gamma", in my honour. We had created a new class of drug.'

I asked Dr Reddy to take me back to when he graduated from Bombay University with his doctorate. I learnt by that time he had been married for a year and, his first child, a daughter, had been born a year later and his son, a year after that.

I figured with all these degrees he must have been in high demand. 'No, not at all. I joined a government-owned pharmaceutical company, Indian Drugs and Pharmaceuticals Ltd (IDPL) in Hyderabad, in my Telugu speaking state. IDPL was then setting up a synthetic drug project for the first time in India. There is a twist to the tale in the end. It so happened that that factory was not only producing the drug but was doing research to develop other drugs. This didn't exist in any private sector companies at that time other than probably Tatas. They would never do research. They would not spend even a rupee on research. There was no culture of research.'

I asked what these pharma companies in the private sector did. 'They would import the drug from Italy, have that brand here and prevent others from entering the market and they would make money. That is how they became very rich. However, in the government company where I was working, there was a works' manager with a DSc from Germany who was passionate about research. So, I joined the research team and our job was very strange. We had the lab process where, from the test tube level of production, we would have to take it to a 100-kilo batch to prove it worked. There were always problems in getting the research to that level and, in India, the "blame game" is very common. The factory people would say this is a "humbug" process and the lab people would say that the factory people didn't know how to produce drugs. But in this case the general manager came up with a simple but brilliant idea. He constituted a team of four people and I was one of them. The four of us worked in six hour shifts and each one of us was responsible for all elements in the production from lab to production. There could be no blame game.'

I sensed we were about to enter a crucial stage in his life. 'Yes, this opportunity gave me confidence. The import situation was crazy at that time. If one wanted to import paracetamol or some other drug there was a duty of 150 per cent. But if we were able to make the same drug in India with the same level of efficiency with the same raw materials there was no question of a failure. So I said to myself why should I work here? I got some of my friends together and we started Uniloids in 1973. I named it,' he laughs. 'My friends said it sounded like a billion-dollar company. Why I named it "Uniloids" was because an Indian company, Unichem was one of the most respected companies at that time. There was also another well-known Indian company, Indian Alkaloids. So I combined these two names to name the company.

'I had some money and we took a loan and we started the business. The very first product, metronizadole, a drug for amoebic dysentery, was a hit. There were a couple of snags along the way as we could not get rid of one impurity. One day, it came to me in a flash that the impurity would be soluble in ammonia. So, we washed the product in ammonia until the yellow colour disappeared. In the process, we ended up with a product that was better than the original Italian one,' he laughs.

The company was a great success but, by 1980, Dr Reddy found that he and his fellow shareholders had different philosophies so Dr Reddy withdrew and started a second company, Standard Organics, with a single partner on a 50:50 basis. The partner brought the capital and Dr Reddy the technology.

This company too flourished but again differences between the shareholders led to Dr Reddy leaving in 1984 to found Dr Reddy's. It seems to me that many of the interviewees in this book have faced the challenge of finding long-term time partners with similar philosophies – Narayana Murthy of Infosys being one of the exceptions. Also the separations are often difficult at the personal level. In this case the departure was painless as Dr Reddy's partner made him an offer to buy out his shares for 84 times his original investment. Dr Reddy did not have to think long. He took the money, started Dr Reddy's Laboratories and the rest is history.

Dr Reddy's Laboratories (www.drreddys.com) is one of India's leading pharmaceutical companies and produces medicines which are both affordable and innovative. Headquartered in Hyderabad, the company is now a global player with a presence in more than 100 countries. It has, for instance wholly-owned subsidiaries in the US, UK, Russia, Germany and Brazil; joint ventures in China, South Africa and Australia; representative offices in sixteen countries; and third-party distribution set ups in twenty-one countries. Dr Reddy's Laboratories is listed on the BSE and was the first pharmaceutical company in Asia outside of Japan to be listed on the NYSE.

"I am told that one day, when I was a child, my parents went to a fortune teller. The fortune teller apparently told them about me up to the age of fourteen, and stopped after that saying, "I don't want to say anything more about this child as he will be totally useless.""

GVK REDDY

Founder & Chairman
GVK Group

GVK Reddy's offices in Hyderabad are among the most spectacular of all the office locations where my meetings for this book took place. I have been told that the GVK offices, a two storey well-restored colonial era building earlier housed the relatives of the great nizams of Hyderabad.

The next surprise came when his secretary Sudha introduced me to Gunupati Venkata Krishna Reddy or GVK as he is widely known. I guess I had not thought about what he would look like, but I certainly did not expect a tall well-dressed bespectacled older gentlemen of around 6' 3".

GVK was born on 22 March 1937 in the village of Kothur, about ten kilometres from the town of Nellore not far from Chennai.

I asked GVK what sort of child he was. 'Oh, I was very naughty. I was a very, very difficult child and used to bunk school at every opportunity. I was so naughty my parents tried to keep me on a tight rein and kept a close eye on what I did after I got home from school.'

I asked GVK why he thought he was so naughty. 'Perhaps because I was brought up in an extremely conservative joint family, I was a very aggressive child. My father was the eldest of six brothers which made it a very large joint family. My uncles were into construction business and my father took care of agriculture and local politics. I was probably trying to revolt as there was no freedom to do things which a boy of my age could do. Looking back now, they were right from their point of view. I was too young to understand this.

'I am told that one day, when I was a child, my parents went to a fortune teller. The fortune teller apparently told them about me up to the age of fourteen, and stopped after that saying, "I don't want to say anything more about this child as he will be totally useless."'

By the time GVK was twelve, his parents sent him to a nearby village called Buchireddypalem where one of his uncles stayed, asking him to discipline GVK and to also see that he studied well in the high school. He stayed with his uncle for one year.

On one of the visits from his village to the other village his parents asked the family cook to accompany GVK. To reach Buchireddypalem they had to pass through Nellore, which was not very far away. 'We both decided to stop at Nellore and went to see a movie. We were accompanied by another friend. On the way back we had to pass by the railway station. I heard a train coming and spontaneously said to the friend, "Let's take the train to Madras." We ran and caught the train and went off to Chennai travelling for four hours. The cook returned to my village. We landed in one of my uncles' house in Chennai near the Moore market. He was shocked to see us early in the morning. He immediately called my father who came to Chennai and took us back to Nellore. Looking back, sometimes I laugh at all the foolish things I did.' There was no change and his uncle asked his parents to take him back saying that 'this boy is useless, cannot be disciplined and he will not study.'

By the time GVK was fourteen, his parents were very concerned about his rebelliousness and did not know what to do. GVK's father and uncle had established a high school in the village, and GVK was admitted into that school. The headmaster of the school was asked to control and discipline GVK and to make him study. GVK used to go to the headmaster's house at night to study, sleep there and return to his own house in the morning. 'For six months my behaviour did not change. But I can vividly remember the day it did! One day I was sitting in class and saw one of my classmates being congratulated by the teacher and applauded by the students for coming first in some exam. I asked my friends why we could not do the same thing. They responded, "Why not? Let us try!" So we started reading. When I started reading I hardly understood anything as I was so far behind in my studies. I must admit we had no choice but to mug up on everything from "A to Z". After a year, I ranked first in science. And when everybody started praising me I told myself this was preferable to being naughty and always being in trouble. Then I started working hard. I had proved the fortune teller wrong.

'Until my parents started to see my good results they did not believe the headmaster when he told them that I was a changed boy and was studying hard.' There were other changes in GVK as well. 'When I was naughty, I was loud and boisterous but by the time I transformed myself into being a good student my personality became much quieter and from that time up to now I have always been an introvert.

'Years later after I graduated from high school and came to Nellore for college I was again transformed. I became interested in sport and in my first year I started to play tennis which has become my sport of addiction. In due course I became college champion. You may not believe it but I still play tennis for two hours almost every day when I am in Hyderabad. It is fair to say I absolutely love playing tennis.

'My father was a farmer and became a local politician. It was the expected role of the eldest son in the family. He was a very soft but outspoken person. Once I changed, and he accepted that I had changed, from that point on, my father always supported me 100 per cent. If I said something he would tell people that I never bluff and that I also say what I believe.'

I asked GVK about his mother. 'She is now ninety-six years old (2007) and is unfortunately bedridden. She still lives in the same house in the village I grew up in and refuses to move to Hyderabad to live with me or my siblings. She was a very tough disciplinarian and used to beat me for being naughty. We go to visit her regularly. When I was there recently her nurse jokingly told me my mother had threatened to beat her if she left the room. So when I went in I teased her by saying, "So who are you beating now?" She took the joke well and actually said, "Do you know after beating you for being mischievous and naughty I used to go into another room and cry, 'Why am I beating this child'?"'

GVK completed his intermediate from VR College in Nellore during 1955-57 and then came to Hyderabad to complete his degree – BA in Economics – from Vivek Vardhini College. 'After my exams each year I used to go back to my village to spend time with my family and friends. That was my plan too for when I finished my final exams in my last year and I even thought about studying abroad. Usually I went home by train but after the final year my parents said they would send a car to pick me up. I thought this was very nice of them and a sort of reward for doing well. Instead of going to the village I was taken to Nagarjunasagar, about 100 kilometres from Hyderabad where my uncles were working for family construction business. As soon as I reached the place my father broke the news to me that I was to immediately start work in the construction business.'

GVK and his two brothers worked hard to grow that part of the construction business. They expanded into canal excavations and then got into construction of part of the Nagarjunasagar dam and also took up some more projects like under tunnels. 'After about eight years of working together with my brothers we decided to separate. The main reason was that I was very ambitious and prepared to take big risks. My father was afraid that with such huge risks the family could lose everything that had been built up over the years. After discussions with my father I came to the conclusion that their fears were understandable as we had very different personalities. So we decided to split the business and I suggested that I would start my own construction business in Hyderabad. I told my grandfather, father and brothers that my first project was to build a house in Hyderabad for rent. This did not please my grandfather as he knew it meant that I would more than likely move to Hyderabad and he wanted us all to remain in Nellore. And so I started my own business in 1968 and my brothers continued in their own construction businesses.'

GVK's construction business prospered. But for some reason this was not enough for GVK. 'I don't know what it was but I was not satisfied. Perhaps it was partly that, while I was successful financially, contractors at that time did not have a high social standing. Looking back perhaps I felt this was unfair and that I could succeed just as well in a business which was socially accepted. Whatever the reason, I decided to get involved in manufacturing pre-laminated particle boards in a joint venture with the Andhra Pradesh Industrial Development Corporation (APIDC) using Swiss technology. The company was called "Novopan". Nobody liked the idea; neither my wife nor my parents. "Why do you want to go into an industry you know nothing about?" they kept telling me.'

I too was intrigued why GVK would want to go into such a business. 'Well,' he said, 'that is quite an interesting story. As you would know at that time in India one had to have a licence to manufacture anything. I had decided to expand beyond construction into manufacturing so I went to meet the managing director of APIDC and asked him for a licence to manufacture steel or cement or start a brewery. Licences were not available to start any of these industries. Those days private players were not allowed to start a business without licence from the government. He could see I was getting very frustrated and told me, "Look there is a licence available to manufacture particle board and the person who has the licence currently cannot proceed so you can have it if you wish." So I decided to consider the proposal. Dr Sudhakar Rao, an IFS officer, who had written a thesis on pre-laminated particle board was on deputation to APIDC from the forest department. He convinced me to take up this project as a substitute for wood, a scarce commodity. He travelled with me to Switzerland, Germany, Austria and Italy where he showed me the factories to manufacture pre-laminated particle boards. I was then convinced and went ahead with the project.

'But that was not the end of the story because I needed finance to put up a plant in India. Almost every bank I went to, rejected lending me money because someone else had started a similar factory and had failed. Finally ICICI agreed to finance the project as a lead institution along with others in the consortium as they were convinced about my abilities. With the finance secured I started Novopan Industries Limited, my first manufacturing unit.

'Initially it was difficult to convince the end users and it took some time for the project to become viable and to operate it successfully. As backward integration I set up Nova Resins to manufacture thermoset resins for the pre-laminated particle board with Austrian collaboration. I went into forward integration to manufacture home and office furniture to educate the people on how to use the product with German collaboration. Then I opened show rooms across the country to sell the furniture and invested a lot of money on marketing. By then I had a very large investment in the project but was absolutely convinced despite all the doubters that I would succeed. Slowly demand picked up and Novopan became a market leader and profitable.

'But by this time, around 1985, the "licence raj" was really beginning to annoy me. I decided to stop the construction business and move to the US where I knew I could freely build a business and where my success or failure would depend on my own ability and not on some licence.'

I wondered if money was the main motive for moving to the US. 'Absolutely not,' he said. 'Certainly, my aim was to make a profit but I was already successful from a financial perspective. I am ambitious and love challenges and I wanted to succeed in whatever I did.

'Another key reason for moving to the US was that I knew the federal and state governments in the US actually helped businesses get going. In my case the local county in Montgomery in North Carolina actually gave me 200 acres of land free to build a pre-laminated particle board factory. They also provided me with high pressure water without charge and helped me in getting finance for the project. This was just so different to the situation in India. I am pleased to say the business prospered and we manufactured and marketed our products well.

'But by 1991 there was a "sea change" in India and the "licence raj" started to disappear as the Indian government liberalized. That year the chief minister of Andhra Pradesh, Dr Marri Chenna Reddy came to visit my factory in North Carolina and saw for himself the way the US government encouraged business and how in such a short span of a few years I had become a respected member of the local community and developed excellent relationship, not only with our customers, but also with our employees. He was pleasantly shocked and persuaded me to come back to India and take up infrastructure projects, especially power.'

I asked GVK whether by 'come back' it meant he and his whole family had moved to the US. 'No, that is the funny part as my family did not want to move as they were so settled in Hyderabad and I did most of the "moving". In fact, my wife mostly stayed in India and I shuttled back and forth between India and the US.'

I asked GVK what he focused on after his 'return' to India. 'Power,' he said. 'I could see in liberalized India there was going to be a huge demand for power and had seen from my time in the US how independent power producers operated. We invested in a power project in Jegurupadu in Andhra Pradesh with the support of the International Finance Corporation (IFC) which, as you may know, is part of the World Bank. We went into generation in 1996. This project was launched ahead of time. It has received praise from many quarters including Dr James Wolfensohn who was at that time the president of the World Bank and this plant has gone into the balance sheet of the IFC as one of its half dozen "environmentally and socially responsible private sector investments" in the world. This project provided huge credibility to our group to move on into other major infrastructure projects.'

Now it was time for GVK to realize an older dream going back to his student days of owning a beautiful hotel. 'I suppose it must have had something to do with coming from a family involved in construction. With the success of my businesses, I decided I could make my dream come true and built and owned two hotels in Hyderabad – the Krishna Oberoi (currently Taj Krishna) quickly followed by Holiday Inn Krishna (currently Taj Deccan). The Taj Banjara was earlier constructed by GVK together with another partner which he subsequently sold to the other partner. It has now come back to GVK under a thirty year licence agreement.

As my time with GVK was drawing to a close I decided to turn the discussion back to his family. I was a little surprised to learn that his was an arranged marriage as I had figured that, with his highly independent character, he would not have taken kindly to being told who to marry. 'Historically, in India each family will look at the girl or boy and their families and if there is a match then they will arrange the marriage. Although I may have been rebellious and had a strong independent streak, I actually believed in the discipline of this approach and its success rate. In the time of the British whenever one went for a job they used to ask, "Who is your father? Who is your mother? What do they do?" I guess the theory is that if the parents are ok then the child will be ok. These days you go to a night club, you go out, you travel, you find somebody who looks very smart and who looks very nice and you get married. One would have to admit that neither method is foolproof.

'In my case I got married at twenty-three and my wife Indira was only sixteen. Although we were at the same college we did not know each other due to the age difference but, as she was extremely bright, she was not as far behind me in college as the age difference would suggest,' he says with a laugh. 'We lived for several years in Nagarjunasagar before we moved to Hyderabad when I set up business on my own. As I mentioned earlier that move was strongly opposed by my parents as the village thinking at that time was to keep everyone together and that if anyone moved to the city they never came back to the village. That part is certainly true. If I had stayed in the village I would never have got to where I am today.'

I said I remembered GVK mentioning his wife was appointed as the Managing Director of Novopan while he was in the US and successfully operated the business. 'She's my "speed breaker". Many of the businesses activities I have sought to enter were in her opinion a big risk and her questions forced me to think more clearly about what I was doing. I don't think she has ever stopped me from taking the risk or I would not refer to her as a "breaker" but it is important for me to have someone question me like this. I did take a lot of risks in my early years but, after achieving a certain level of success, I have always told her that if the risk turned ugly and I lost on that risk we would still continue to be what we are today.

'Although you may not believe it from meeting me today but by nature I am quite an introvert. I think this largely comes as a result of the way I was brought up as a child where our views were not welcomed by the adults in the family. I felt quite suppressed. When I first started my business I used to practice speaking aloud by myself as to what I was going to say to this or that person. In fact I remember not long after I went into business my mother heard me in a business meeting talking to a colleague. After the meeting she came up to me and said, "So you really can talk." But I still don't talk so much in meetings and I think that has sometimes made people uncomfortable as they don't know what I am thinking. But it is just my "make up". My wife and son are quite different as they are much more extroverted. The way my personality fits into my management style is that every morning I head straight to the conference room rather than to my office. There I sit with all the heads of department and we discuss what has happened yesterday, what has to be done tomorrow, and a whole range of topics such as what has gone wrong and how we should fix it. I encourage everyone to express their views and then I make the decision. I would say 99 per cent of the time I agree with the consensus or majority view of the meeting and only 1 per cent of the time I would disagree. But even in those few cases where I disagree I am confident to back my own judgement and bear the consequences. Sometimes when I talk I am sure it sounds like a "dictator" but I do listen to the views of others.'

I asked GVK when he looks back on such a long and successful career if he could identify why he feels he succeeded and others failed. 'I think my most important attributes are a vision of the future and the courage to follow my convictions with persistence to achieve that vision. The Novopan business is an example of that. Many people thought that I would give up and fail but I persisted and the business has succeeded.'

GVK Group (www.gvk.com), is a diversified business entity with a predominant focus on infrastructure and urban infrastructure projects where it has taken a lead position in developing and owning projects of national importance in diverse areas ranging from power, airports, and roads. It also has a significant presence in the hospitality services and manufacturing sectors.

> When I look back on those days, it was foolish courage. When I look at how amateurishly I started the company, I don't think I would have been successful today. I think I just had the luxury of a time when India was very primitive and there was the "licence raj" so there wasn't any real pressure on anyone to perform in a big way.

KIRAN MAZUMDAR SHAW

Chairman & Managing Director
Biocon

I met Kiran Mazumdar Shaw late in the evening at the lobby of the beautiful Leela Palace in Bangalore. She had just finished a long day's work in Delhi leaving Bangalore in the early morning and only arriving back in the evening. The capacity of Indian entrepreneurs for hard work never ceases to amaze me. It may not have been so during the time of the 'licence raj' but, in recent years, there is a palpable buzz of energy in the air and I have found Indian businessmen and women of all levels and ages, willing to meet at all hours of the day and night, weekends included. The English proverb of 'all work, no play makes Jacky a dull boy' seems to have no place in modern India and it is almost as if Indian entrepreneurs know they have to make up for the lost years of the 'licence raj'. That, and the fact the Indian market is extremely competitive.

Somehow we found each other in the bustling lobby and seated ourselves at a small table in the corridor outside the bar, as almost every other space was either full or too noisy for the interview. Where we sat becomes relevant as you will read.

Born on 23 March 1953 in Bangalore, Mazumdar had a secure childhood. Her family was relatively well-off 'though not wealthy by any standards' she says. Her father was a brew master and had worked for most of his career with United Breweries. Her mother was content to be the home-maker. Mazumdar is the eldest of three children. Her brother Ravi, is a professor at the University of Waterloo in Canada, and her other brother Dev, is software entrepreneur in Los Angeles. They are younger to her by two years and eleven years, respectively. Her childhood memories are of happy times, foremost among them being the many holidays the family spent in India and close by.

Mazumdar went to Bishop Cotton Girls' School, a Protestant school in Bangalore. Her father was a 'progressive' man who thought well ahead of his time and who believed his children – daughter or son – should have a good education.

Kiran Mazumdar fared well at school. She had an inclination for biology and set her heart on becoming a doctor, but she didn't qualify for medical college. That left her with the option to pursue a bachelor's degree in biology.

After completing her first degree, Mazumdar found herself once again at a turning point. She wanted to go on to applied science, and her father suggested she study for a master's in brewing. Her younger brother was studying computer science and it seemed she was her father's only hope to perpetuate his professional line. The senior Mazumdar reasoned with her: 'The brewing industry is opening up, India needs good brew masters and talent is hard to come by.' 'For me it appeared a good career prospect. I listened to him and decided to follow his advice.'

The master's in brewing programme took her to Ballarat, a small rural town outside Melbourne, Australia. I was surprised, but pleased, to hear her say she enjoyed her time there, as the winters can be bitterly cold and the summers painfully hot. I was also surprised because rural Australia at that time would have been rather conservative and I could not imagine there being too many Indian restaurants or many other foreign students in what, in Indian terms, is a very small town.

Her education in Australia taught her to fend for herself early in life. She had to be 'one of the boys', learn to have a drink with them and enjoy being 'mates' with them. The experience schooled her for a time when she would have to be comfortable in a 'man's world' in India. For this reason, Mazumdar has never felt singled out as the only woman in a room full of men. 'I spent my entire master's being the only woman in the course and, throughout my career, I have often been the only woman in the boardroom. I have become quite comfortable with that.'

She also enjoyed the course. 'I wouldn't say that I knew too much at the time, but I was definitely intrigued by the science of brewing, largely because I was a biologist by training and I enjoyed the whole process of yeast fermentation, how the yeast actually worked, what were the biochemical pathways and so on.'

Mazumdar returned from Ballarat a pioneer, India's only female brew master. She began working for breweries as a consultant. 'I quickly found out that they were very happy to have me as a consultant and were also happy giving me the hardest jobs, but they were not ready to employ me full time.' She was told a woman had no place among the rough and unskilled workmen of a brewery. 'I had no problems, but my employers did.' She argued back that surely a full-time job was not all that inconceivable as, after all, as a consultant did she not keep odd hours for them? 'At the end of the day, I understood where they were coming from; contractually they were not responsible but employed full-time, they were.' It took her a little time to come to terms with the reality that India at that time was not ready for women on the shop floor.

It was on the rebound that Mazumdar started Biocon in India after a fateful meeting with the Irish company's founder, Les Auchincloss thanks to an Australian brewmaster friend, Colin Dowzer. Dowzer had worked for Courage Breweries in Melbourne and then left to start the Australian counterpart of Biocon in 1976. Biocon Australia marketed products developed by the Irish parent company.

In 1977, Dowzer visited India to study its brewing industry. He must have given a favourable report to Biocon headquarters back in Ireland because the following year, Les Auchincloss visited India to meet Mazumdar. At that stage, Biocon's interests in India had been limited to sourcing raw materials, but it was now looking for more. He offered Mazumdar the opportunity to set up Biocon in India and make and market his company's products locally. As it happened, at exactly that time Mazumdar had been offered a job at a brewery in Scotland. She was in a quandary yet again as to which path she should follow. Les Auchincloss talked her out of taking the brewery job. Her fascination at setting up her own company overshadowed the lure of the Scottish offer. Les Auchincloss reassured her that she would continue to be in touch with brewing, since Biocon had a portfolio of products for that industry. She could always return to her brewing assignment in Scotland later if she wished, he said. Mazumdar accepted the challenge and Biocon India was formed in a 70:30 joint venture with the Irish parent.

Biocon India's debut products for the brewing industry were papain and isinglass. 'Isinglass is a form of collagen obtained from the swim bladders of fish and is mainly used for the clarification of wine and beer. Papain, on the other hand, is an enzyme produced by papaya and can break down inert (that is, non-living) proteins. I was soon tired of producing these products as the work was too low-end and I realized that I was not going to get excited if this was all we made.' That was when Mazumdar turned to biotechnology and manufacturing enzymes by fermentation rather than plant extracts.

She went fund hunting to bankers. 'I told the bankers that I would need to invest in R&D and that it would cost me money. The bankers shook their heads as R&D was an alien concept for the '70s Indian banker and, looking back,' she says with a laugh, 'they must have found it strange this was being proposed to them by a twenty-five-year-old woman who ran a strange business of fish entrails and plant extracts.'

Her father was ready to help her in any way he could, but pride held Mazumdar back from accepting his offer, as she was out to prove herself. She also knew that help wouldn't be easy coming, even for an industry veteran like her father.

'My father was very well known in the brewing industry, but, in India, once you retire, people switch off in how they relate to you. In that sense, the best thing my father did was to tell me that he would always be there for me and that, if I needed his help, he was fully behind my decisions and plans. I had his support all the way.'

Biocon's beginnings were in the garage at her rented home that she turned into an office. The first lab and factory came up in a rented 3000 sq ft. As a business neophyte, Mazumdar believes she had the luxury to evolve her business. No one expected her to perform. 'When I think back on those days, it was foolish courage. When I look at how amateurishly I started the company, I don't think I would have been successful today. I think I just had the luxury of a time when India was very primitive and there was the "licence raj" so there wasn't any real pressure on anyone to perform in a big way.'

She created a captive market for the products of her Irish partners but did not seek much assistance from them beyond that. She relished her independence and was determined to build the company and be on her own. 'My Irish partners too realized and appreciated that my pride wouldn't allow me to take too much help from them as well.'

Driven by her vision of pioneering R&D in India, she allowed herself just one indulgence from her Irish partners; Mazumdar asked for and got free rein to use their labs to study enzymes. She went to work in Ireland and sent her people after her. Mazumdar and her Irish partners then discussed opportunities for an R&D collaboration in India. Together, they identified products they would develop and sell to India's brewery and fruit juice industry.

In due course, Biocon's Irish partners sold their stake in the company to Unilever, UK in 1989. Unilever continued to be her partner and was represented on Biocon India's board for ten years. In 1998, Unilever sold its stake to ICI. By this time Mazumdar was tired of the changes in her foreign partner and believed they added little value to the business she wanted to develop. And so she made use of the sale by Unilever to ICI to buy out the foreign shareholding in Biocon India. She had also found some of Unilever's rules stifling and they had continuously blocked her from taking the Indian company into pharmaceutical areas.

'I said, "well, let's part ways". That's how I got back the shares. Of course, I didn't have the money. My husband had to buy those shares. He had a flat in Chelsea which he had to sell to buy those shares for me.' She says her husband jokes that he was the first venture capitalist in Biocon 'but it paid off fantastically because we went public in 1998 and Biocon now (2007) has a market capitalization of over USD 1 billion.'

If Mazumdar's actions had a grand scheme, it was not to make money. 'At that time I just wanted to run a successful company. I was a bit of a rebel. I wanted to prove that a woman was capable of running a business and handling a plant, because some men had said women couldn't do this. I wanted to prove them wrong.'

The gender bias has had its funny moments, though, recounts Mazumdar. The occasions when she advertised for secretarial or accounting help at the time she was starting off in her garage were amongst the best. Candidates would cheerily walk in to the garage, smile at her and say, 'I have an appointment with the managing director.' 'Yes, that's me,' she would tell them. 'That would arouse their suspicion: surely the secretary was pulling a fast one on them? They would end up interviewing me rather than me interviewing them!'

The old sense of gender bias that she suffered has faded away with time. 'In those early days, I had a big complex because I was angry. I wasn't diffident. I wasn't upset about the difficulties. But I was angry: why is it that people look at you differently? The banker looks at you with skepticism. If you are a woman manager, they look at you differently. Financial institutions feel you are high risk.'

Mazumdar sees a world of a difference between the status of women now and in 1978. She meets many counterparts in other businesses. 'It's nice to know that there are so many women in leadership roles. Look at ICICI bank with all its women managers and, of course, my dear friend Naina Lal Kidwai, who is the head of HSBC.' Also in the same league are Vinita Bali of Britannia Industries and Sangeetha Reddy of Apollo Hospitals Group. There's no women's group or network, but 'we all know each other very well.'

On the contrary, Mazumdar feels that a woman's life is no easier in Australia. 'I think Australia is also quite a chauvinistic society in many ways.' She observes that Australia has many career women, but 'I do not see a lot of women heading businesses.'

Mazumdar has met Meg Whitman, president and CEO, E-bay – 'She was brilliant' – and Carly Fiorina, the former CEO of HP. 'We can see that all of us in our own way are very confident women. We do not suffer from a gender complex in any way. In the business world we are able to equate on a one-to-one because you need to do that. I never wanted favours on the basis of being a woman.'

Women have a special place in Biocon. Mazumdar is pleased that a third of her scientific team comprises women. Appointments, though, are based on merit, not reverse discrimination. Her male colleagues often recommend women for a position if the applicant is competent. 'I guess it happens naturally. Also, because I'm a woman, heading my own company, it does attract a lot of women to join us.'

Part of her confidence and fight comes from the school she attended. 'We were encouraged to pursue different paths.' Mazumdar had a large number of friends who got married at their families' bidding. She considers herself fortunate to have a father who rubbished the convention. 'Poor mother was always under pressure to get me married off. But my father was firm. He told me, "I am not spending all this money educating you just to have you get married." He was a great influence on my life, so ahead of his times.'

When Mazumdar's father passed away in 1993, her mother was shattered. Mazumdar helped her to pull herself together. 'I told my mother that here were two alternatives: keep yourself really busy and active or feel sorry for yourself. I encouraged her to be independent and suggested different ways in which she could be busy.' And so in her mid 60s her mother became an entrepreneur. She now owns an organic farm and runs a successful automatic laundry and dry cleaning business. Customers for the laundry service include some large airlines such as Lufthansa, Jet Airways and Kingfisher Airlines.

'Setting up the laundry business was quite an ordeal. My mother needed a loan and went to the bank. The bank official apparently said to her, "Madam, you're such an old lady why do you want to run a laundry?" My mother's response to him was classic, as she told him, "If any eighty-year-old can run this country, why can't I run this factory?" You see at that time, Atal Behari Vajpayee, our Prime Minister was around eighty.

'I always say that I got my entrepreneurial genes from my mother, and not my dad,' quips Mazumdar. 'My father was a good manager; I'm not so sure he was a good entrepreneur.'

I asked Mazumdar about how she ended up marrying a Scotsman. 'John headed Coats' operations in Bangalore for many years and was a confirmed bachelor. We met and had a lot of things in common, right from our appreciation of art and golf. But the marriage took some time coming. I was married to my job and I could think of nothing else. It was quite a commitment and marriage was the last thing on my mind.' Their seven-year-old friendship eventually ended up in marriage in 1998. John Shaw was by that time based in Europe. Mazumdar was categorical: if one of them had to quit, it was not to be her. 'I said I wasn't going to give up my business but he could give up his,' she chuckles. Shaw is now Vice-Chairman at Biocon. Their responsibilities are clearly marked: she looks after research, he after finance.

Like many of the interviewees in this book, Mazumdar believes her biggest strength is a 'good eye' for an opportunity. 'I have picked opportunities when no one could see them. I have taken some bold risks, but I converted them to successes by looking at the opportunities differently.' For example, during a visit to Cuba in 2000, she spotted a couple of novel products which she in-licensed, further developed, trialled, registered and brought to the Indian market. 'A lot of companies ask me how I did this. I tell them that it's because they are not looking for the right opportunity: they are usually just looking for me-too products, whereas I have always wanted to innovate.

'I have always stood out – as a woman, to begin with. I was always looking to start a business that is unique. If we want to be a success then we need to stand out. My strategy has always been to keep looking for ways to be different. Innovation is a great way to differentiate.'

But back to the relevance of where Mazumdar and I met for this interview and which I mentioned at the beginning of this chapter. As our meeting place was at a table in the hallway outside the main bar, many people passed in front of us as we sat deep in conversation. At some point in our meeting I felt someone looking at us. I looked up and saw a well dressed young man, probably in his late 20s, standing several paces from us. I pointed this out to Mazumdar who beckoned the young man over. He said to Mazumdar, 'India is so proud of you Dr Mazumdar. Thank you for what you have done.' With that he withdrew. Both of us were, needless to say a little surprised but quickly got back into our conversation. Thirty minutes later I felt those eyes on us again and this time it was the same young man, together with a colleague. This time when she beckoned them over we noted he was holding a book in one hand and a small package in the other. He said, 'Dr Mazumdar, will you please accept my present and sign this book for me?' While Mazumdar was signing the book, he again repeated, 'India is so proud of what you have done, Dr Mazumdar, for which we thank you.' Mazumdar asked him, 'Do I know you?' to which he replied, 'Not really, but two years ago I was at Bangalore airport and I saw you waiting for your luggage to come off a carousel and so I came up and introduced myself to you. You were very gracious to me, even though you had come off a long flight from Germany. I admire so much what you have done for Indian biotechnology, Dr Mazumdar. Thank you.' If I ever wanted independent support from the Indian 'man in the street' as to why Mazumdar's story is in this book – this is it!

Biocon (www.biocon.com) is a research-driven, global healthcare company with a strong matrix of capabilities along the biopharmaceutical value chain. Focusing on unmet medical needs in cancer, diabetes and inflammatory diseases, it offers novel therapies on a platform of affordable innovation.

‘In one sense, I was delighted to be on my own at last; at the ripe old age of twenty-nine. But it was very tough as I had no financial support. I often had to avoid calls from creditors while I chased debtors to pay. I built up running accounts at the local restaurant just so I could eat!’

SHASHI KIRAN SHETTY

Founder & Chairman
Allcargo Global Logistics

I met Shashi Kiran Shetty at his office near the Mumbai airport. The meeting proved to be one of the most emotional of the book, as Shashi relived many of his life struggles which he had possibly not thought about for many years.

Shashi was born on 7 June 1957 in Bantwal, near the port city of Mangalore, in Karnataka. Like a number of other people in this book it was a joint family with father and mother, three uncles and aunts plus many children living in two houses which were side-by-side. 'Actually, the numbers often shot up for long periods as one of my father's brothers had died young and so his wife, being my aunt and her children used to come and stay for long periods. I believe there were often over twenty people living in the two houses.' Shashi's immediate family consisted of four sisters and a brother, Shashi being the second eldest.

The joint family owned a large retail shop, an oil mill and a rice mill. 'My uncles ran it, while my father, a prominent member of the Indian National Congress' local chapter, was an active but humble politician. He had neither studied much nor specialized in any profession or trade but he was known for being a wonderful orator.'

I remarked that, with so many children in the joint family, the other school children must have been scared of crossing the Shetty clan. Shashi laughed and said, 'Exactly. Going to school was quite an experience. Actually I was teased quite a bit at that time.' I asked how that affected him. 'At that time it used to bother me. I used to get back and fight anybody who teased me. However, I loved my cousins and we always had great fun playing together before and after school. It was a very simple life. We used to go to the river to swim and played lots of sports like badminton and with cricket we could almost make up a team by ourselves.'

All of Shashi's primary and secondary education took place in Bantwal, with the exception of one year. 'Around the time I was in 9th standard, I decided to shift to a school which was renowned for its discipline.' I asked why he went there. 'Well as you have probably picked up, I was reasonably rebellious and I knew two of my cousins who had been doing poorly at school were sent there by my uncles. I was not failing at school, but felt myself I needed to get away and that the regimen would suit me. What a shock I got. I felt like I was in a jail. We had to get up at 5.30 a.m. each morning and immediately study for an hour before we washed for breakfast. All the food was simple vegetarian. The school was owned and run by Brahmins. The main owner was an unmarried gentleman who was a devotee of Sri Sathya Sai Baba of Puttaparthi. We had to pray at least twice a day. It was a very regimented life and, whilst I hated it at the beginning, I decided to stick it out as I had pestered my parents to send me there. It would have been embarrassing to suddenly say I wanted to come home. My time there calmed me and the discipline I learnt there has stayed with me ever since.'

I wondered if this was a big sacrifice for his parents to send him off to this boarding school. 'No, at that time we could afford it. A few years later, as you will hear, it would have been a different story.'

As a lead in to that part of his life I asked Shashi to tell me a little about his family. 'The joint family owned a large retail shop in our village. My uncles ran it, whereas my father's job was to look after local politics and make sure no decisions were taken locally which would affect the family business. You see, my father was "adding value" to the business with his connections. We had a reputation in the business because of my father's name. My father was a member of the All India Congress Committee. At some point when I was in high school, the political career of my father came under strain. At election time, my father was overlooked and he wasn't given the ticket by his party to contest elections to the state's legislative assembly. This made him very bitter.

He resigned from the party in protest. Looking back, this was a major strategic error as the Congress in those years was extremely powerful. His career as a politician was effectively over.'

At the same time, the family business was also heading for tough times. 'My uncles had expanded the retail business to include oil and rice mills. Unfortunately, they did not put in the necessary systems or financial controls. There was no cheating of anyone; just bad management.'

The combined effect of the loss of my father's political protection and business failure was catastrophic on the family for many reasons. 'For a start everyone started to blame each other for the failure – my uncles blamed my father and vice versa.'

That was around 1974. Shashi was in his first year of studying for a three-year commerce degree at SVS College outside Mangalore. 'By the time I finished my degree, the business had collapsed, other than the retail shop.'

The once-thriving Shetty clan was being reduced to near penury. 'My father had no job. All he could muster for himself was some work acting as an unofficial arbitrator in land disputes. Virtually no income came into the joint family, other than a small amount from the shop.

'Excluding the shop, all of the other family properties had been mortgaged to secure large loans. The banks had commenced litigation. It seemed none of my cousins wanted to sort out the mess. Finally, one of my cousins took over the shop and another moved to the Middle East to earn moneys to send home.

'I felt huge pressure as I was the oldest male child in my family and I believed it was my duty to earn enough money to pay for the weddings of my three younger sisters. For Indian families, this is a matter of honour.

'On graduation my cousin in the Middle East offered to find me a job out there. I waited for a year without anything happening, I could wait no longer and decided to try and find a job in my village or somewhere around. The situation of the family made that difficult. Before the collapse, the family was respected whereas now, many people avoided us.'

With no work in or around his village, Bombay beckoned. 'Two of my older cousins had moved to Bombay as had my older sister. They sent me the money for the journey to Bombay. It took over twenty-four hours in a bus. I got a trainee's job in a shipping company which had two shipping agencies. I had never seen a ship, let alone a port. My task was basically to handle supplies for ships when they arrived in Bombay. I had to meet the ship's Master and find out what he needed and then get it for him.'

With experience, Shashi got involved with the storage of the cargo, sorting out warehouse issues as well as helping the Master and crew with customs and immigration. 'I had been progressing rapidly during my time with the company and one day a couple of years after I started, I was called to meet my boss. He told me I was dismissed. Needless to say I was shocked and have never learnt to this day why I was dismissed, other than I suspect jealousy of one of my work colleagues was behind it.

'I was so ashamed, I did not even tell my sister with whom I was staying.' Fortunately for Shashi, two of his former colleagues, KP Dalvi and Arun Chaudankar, had moved to another agency. They gave him a job.

'I was only out of work for fifteen days. When I went out in the mornings, my sister thought I was still going to my old job, whereas I was pounding the footpaths trying to get a new job.'

It was at this point, as with the lives of many other interviewees in this book, fate or luck or whatever you want to call it, played a hand. Not long after he joined the new job, KP Dalvi left and joined another company. One month later Arun Chaudankar joined him.

'This, in effect, left me as the sole person in the agency.' The promoters of the company tried to find senior staff to replace my colleagues but, for some reason, they could not find anyone.

'Here, I was with only two years' experience running everything. I took this as a challenge and worked hard. For two years I successfully ran the agency and became very close to the promoters. But they definitely saw a gap in my management experience because I was still only in my mid 20s. So they employed another person to head the agency. He was only five or so years older than me and the first thing he did when he started, was to change everything I had been doing for the last two years. He brought in his own people who were sycophantic towards him. I found this too much to bear. I had to get out.'

The new job came in the form of Gokak Patel Volkart (now called Forbes Gokak), a Tata company. 'The main attraction was that the company was the agency for a number of large shipping lines and was run professionally, like all Tata companies. I knew I would learn a lot; the money, needless to say, was a bonus.'

It didn't take long for Shashi to realize that this wasn't the job for him. 'My job was as an operations executive. I felt like a "fish out of water". For the previous two years at the earlier company, I had run everything and I was responsible for everything. At Patel, I was a corporate executive with a clearly defined role and little else. I quickly came to the conclusion that I had to run my own show.'

From his work as a ship's agent, Shashi smelt an opportunity in moving goods at the ports. 'I could see the problem ship owners had with this. So I set about establishing a small company. But I had little money and no equipment. I went to a few transport companies who knew me well and asked them to support me with selling me some of their second-hand equipment on an installment payment basis. They agreed but said I would need to find a certain sum of money. I then went to potential clients and asked if they would support the business. A few of them agreed. But I still needed some more money. So I put in all of my savings from my four years' work which totaled Rs 25,000 and found a partner to put in the same amount. I borrowed Rs 60,000 from relatives, but I made a point of not worrying my parents who were still having a tough time. This was around 1982.'

Shashi and his partner formed a company and named it Trans India and bought one fork-lift truck. 'My role was to bring in the clients and my partner focused on operations and maintenance of the equipment.' The business went well but Shashi felt that something wasn't quite right. 'My partner was a very dear friend from my community and who I met some years before, as his family used to run a restaurant next to one of my earlier jobs. He was just a couple of years younger and we got on well. However, I was tainted by the experience of the collapse of my family's business which I largely put down to my father and uncles' taking their eyes off the financial side of the business. This made me obsessed with financial management making sure invoices were issued on time and pursued for payment, minimizing costs, paying taxes and generally making sure all the records of the company disclosed the true financial position of the business. My partner had not had the same family experience as me and was much more relaxed about the financial health of the business. Whilst we had fun together, I felt if we continued as we were, we would eventually have a fight which would damage our friendship.

'So, I suggested to my friend that we split the business equally between us. A couple of days later my friend came back to me and said that if I gave him two of our forklifts I could keep the company and our other two forklifts. The only problem with this offer was that he wanted his two forklifts to be free of any debt whereas I would carry all the debts of the business including his two forklifts. Despite this, I agreed to his counter proposal.

'In one sense, I was delighted to be on my own at last, at the ripe old age of twenty-nine. But I had no financial support. I often had to avoid calls from creditors while I chased debtors to pay. I built up running accounts at the local restaurant just so I could eat!'

As Shashi doggedly persisted, the business began to fall into place. 'Our reputation for reliability grew and, with the increased business, I was able to borrow money from the banks and buy some trucks. Borrowing money at that time was not a simple affair so I was very lucky.'

In 1988, Shashi took the step of getting married and, at the same time, brought his younger brother into the company to help him. A year later, his brother-in-law, his wife's older brother, joined him. Wasn't he repeating his earlier not-so-pleasant joint family experience, I asked? 'Actually I really wanted to minimize the number of family members in my business. I was wary after what had happened to my father and uncles' family business. My brother-in-law came into the business in an unintended way. I had seen the mushrooming of leasing companies and suggested he start a business using leased trailers and trucks. We started to contract his trucks and trailers for Trans India's business which was growing rapidly. Eventually, as almost all of his business was through Trans India, it just made more sense he join Trans India.

I asked Shashi whether Trans India eventually morphed into Allcargo. 'No, they are two quite different business in the same sector. Trans India is a surface transport business – receiving containers from the ship, moving them into the back-lying areas and into the out-lying areas within Mumbai city and Nhava Sheva, after that opened; Allcargo is a multi-modal transport business. It was in 1992 that I got the opportunity to start Allcargo. The story begins with CMB Transport, a Belgian shipping line, now acquired by the Maersk shipping group. They were the first company in India to start a joint venture to run their agency business headed by Dinesh Lal, who I knew well. After becoming successful in India, CMB wanted to bring into India its subsidiary AMI International – a freight forwarding company. This led them to me. Almost all the companies they met in freight forwarding were tied up with competitors. Although Trans India was a transport company in the shipping business, AMI was confident about working with me on a non-exclusive basis. So I tied up with AMI and we formed the company Allcargo Movers India.'

With the support of Dinesh Lal and their principal, AMI International, Allcargo Movers set up services running between India and Europe and Africa. 'We used CMB's ships and containers for the clients of AMI. Our focus was "LCL" cargo which means "Less than a Container Load". Shipping lines did not really care about what was in a container. Whether it was empty or full you paid the same price. Clearly if one could consolidate what was to be shipped and pack the containers full to the brim, one could save lots of money for those wishing to transport goods by ship and, at the same time, make good money for the handlers who pulled it all together. We were the first to start this market in India. Initially, we met with a lot of resistance from potential clients who were skeptical because they noted that, not only did Allcargo Movers not own a ship, but it did not even own containers. There was a lot of convincing to do but we built up a good team of people, so that after about a year or so, this business started to get traction. Once we got that, we were able to grow very quickly.

'The next thing that happened was that due to the rapid success of Allcargo Movers, the AMI senior executives in the head office in Antwerp called me for discussions. They said, "Look, we need to be in India and we would like to convert our agency with you into a joint venture under which we will hold 70 per cent and you hold 30 per cent." They gave me all the reasons why they should have a majority but I reminded them that I was generating all the business and the only thing they provided was handing services in some ports in Europe and Africa. Our negotiating went back and forth over a six-month period with neither party willing to give in. I was convinced that AMI would come to India whether it was with me or someone else. So I began looking for alternative principals for Allcargo.'

The search led to a company called Eculine. 'I met them and showcased the volume of exports from India that we were responsible for. This was naturally very attractive to them and they appointed Allcargo to be their Indian agent. The switch proved all for the better and the relationship between Eculine and Allcargo developed quickly and profitably for both parties.'

I asked Shashi if the establishment of the relationship with Eculine had brought us up to date. 'Goodness, no,' he said. 'As my agency business with them grew strongly, I proposed to Eculine that we establish some offices together in third world countries. They agreed and we established joint venture offices in UAE and Singapore where I held a minority. Because they were joint venture offices this put me in touch with the owners of Eculine. What happened then is a long story but it is again one I experienced with my own family. A successful business loses its way and lax financial management propels it into decline. Private equity investors came into Eculine after the family failed, but they too were unable to turn it around. The situation reached the point that if the private equity investors dumped their investment to get out, it could mean the original promoters of Eculine would be left with nothing. I knew the basic Eculine business was sound and it had become very important to Allcargo. I went to the private equity investors and said that I could raise money for Allcargo in India for investing in Eculine. At first, they laughed at me as they just did not believe an Indian company could go global like this. Of course, this is no longer news with the giants of Indian business such as Tata and Arcelor Mittal buying major Western businesses, but it was very unusual when I proposed the idea. When the private equity people did their numbers they could see merit in the idea. The upshot was through Allcargo we invested USD 12 million into Eculine in exchange for a 33 per cent stake with the right to take the investment up to 50 per cent if I felt comfortable at any time during the first three years. But I had a condition for my investment which was that I had the right to put the management policies in place. Fortunately, they agreed. Over the next couple of years we closed down unprofitable offices and put in place systems that cut costs significantly. The business started to perform better and I increased Allcargo's share to 50 per cent. But that was not the end of it, as I discovered that even with taking our investment up to 50 per cent, the original promoters who held a lot of the balance of 50 per cent still had large debts quite separate from the Eculine business. They agreed to sell their remaining shareholding so that now Allcargo owns 100 per cent of Eculine. This coincided with Allcargo going public in June 2006.'

While his business life was going well, I asked Shashi how things were going with his personal life. 'As you know I married a couple of years after I founded Allcargo. It was a matter of succumbing to the pressure from my parents. They knew my business was doing well and believed I should settle down. They also knew that, if they did not find me a wife, I would have probably continued to live the life of a Bombay bachelor,' he says laughing, 'though I have some fond memories of a few great friends during those bachelor days.'

I asked Shashi if he believed arranged marriages would still be appropriate for his children. 'I don't have any issues if my children marry for love. At the time of my parents it was different and particularly different for my family. If I had married outside the Bunts community before my younger sisters got married, it could have damaged their prospects of finding a spouse.'

With the hardship he had experienced during his early life, I wondered how he tried to communicate this to his children. 'It is extremely difficult. I am always telling my children the problems I had to overcome, but I don't think they really understand. Naturally, I don't want them to experience what I did and I guess my wife and I can do is to encourage them to work hard and to always do their best. I always look at it like this. If it comes to a test of survival and you survive, then you know you can survive anything. I always thank my "lucky star" that it put me into that position so that it could get the best out of me. And once you do your best then it becomes a habit.'

As I mentioned at the beginning of this chapter, conducting this interview proved to be one of the most emotional in the book. Talking about his life story clearly provoked deep and painful memories for Shashi. Perhaps some of this lies in his own character but I suspect Shashi's life story is indeed different from many others in the book. It is different in the sense that many of the interviewees in the book came from nothing to build businesses, whereas a number of others came from wealth or relative wealth and built upon it. Shashi experienced the trauma of being born into a family of relative wealth and high reputation, only to see both frittered away by the time he finished high school. So, he started his business life, not with nothing, not with something, but with a negative net worth and the belief he had an obligation to do well for the honour of his family.

Allcargo Global Logistics (www.allcargoglobal.com) provides logistic services to the trading community worldwide. It is primarily involved in multi-modal transport operations, container freight stations, project and ODC cargo handling, airfreight, transport logistics, equipment hiring and oil rig and supply vessels management. The company is headquartered in Mumbai.

"When the body is so tired that it feels no pain, when the mind is so exhausted it feels no anguish, something beyond the mind and body makes you endure the journey you have decided to embark upon. This incomprehensible, intangible something is what Gita, the Hindu book of scriptures and philosophy, calls "Atman" – the Self. I call it the spirit of man. We all possess it deep within us. It need only be ignited to experience our true potential."

(Dr Vijaypat Singhania's speech of thanks at a public reception in New Delhi after the completion of his record-breaking micro-light flight from Britain to India in 1988.)

VIJAYPAT SINGHANIA

Chairman Emeritus (Retired Chairman & CEO)
Raymond

VPS, as he is known, started our interview with a much needed lesson for me on Indian history and the area from which his family is descended. The Singhanias, he told me, come from Rajasthan, which is famous for its fierce inhabitants; most of whom have lived hand to mouth in its arid and unforgiving lands for centuries. Rajasthan is peopled by two distinct groups; the Marwaris who occupy almost three quarters of the land area and who live principally in the north, west and central Rajasthan, and the Mewaris who mainly hailed from the south/eastern part of the state. The Marwaris are an even mix of the warrior caste Kshatriyas and of the merchant traders, the Banias. The Mewaris, on the other hand, are predominantly Kshatriyas and staunch defenders of the land and caste. These two groups have clashed over the centuries.

Inside the Marwari area, the most fertile region is called Shekhawati in which is located a village called Singhana. This is where VPS's family originally came from. The principality of Shekhawati is still famed for its wall paintings and frescoes that adorn its homes and as a record of life there. Shekhawati is quite small in area; less than a hundred square miles, but it has been the origin of almost all of the successful Marwari business houses in India.

VPS's great-grandfather Lala Juggilal Singhania moved in the late nineteenth century from the village of Singhana with not much more than the clothes on his back and settled in Kanpur in Uttar Pradesh. There he made a living carrying bales of cloth on his head and selling it in the streets. During WWI – Lala Juggilal and his eldest son and VPS's grandfather, Lala Kamlapat branched out from selling cloth by the yard into money lending. They dealt in *hundis* – bills of exchange or commercial papers and acted as a discount house for the Imperial Bank of India, now the State Bank. This business flourished and the business expanded under the name 'JK' (a combination of father and son's initials) to having offices in Kanpur and Calcutta.

Great-grandfather and son thought about going into the brewing business but, as Lala Juggilal was a member of Mahatma Gandhi's Swadeshi Movement they decided against doing so and instead in 1917 built a small cotton textile mill in Kanpur. Their timing was perfect. Not only did they supply clothing manufacturers in India but they fed, as VPS says in his book *An Angel in the Cockpit,*[1] 'the hundreds of thousands of soldiers fighting and dying in all parts of the world'. J.K. Cotton Spinning & Weaving Mills Ltd. became the 'mother lode' company for the Singhania family.

VPS's great-grandfather Lala Juggilal died in 1922 and his son Lala Kamlapat in 1937. Lala Kamlapat had three sons, Sir Padampat, Lala Kailashpat (Vijaypat's father) and Lala Lakshmipat. The Singhania family business continued to expand and WW II again contributed to the coffers of the family when they supplied not only textiles but everything from cashew nuts to tents to the British Army. As a result of their war efforts Lala Padampat was knighted and VPS's father and uncle, Lala Sohanlal Singhania were recommended for knighthoods in 1947 but by then independence had come to India and the recommendations did not proceed.

VPS said there was a bit of a story behind these knighthoods. I asked him to tell me. 'Well, I am told one of my uncles, Lala Sohanlal Singhania became secretary to my father. He was older than my father and helped him with all the defence supplies. My uncle had to deal with the Indian-based officers all the way up to generals in relation to the acquisitions the British Army made from our family companies. Believe it or not but I am told bribes were a common part of doing business with the British Army in those days. My father wanted nothing to do with this and so poor old Sohanlalji handled it all. Most other families had similar 'front men' to deal with the generals. Needless to say my father became close friends with a number of important generals. One of them got together with Lala Sohanlalji and, after the war, proposed to London that my father be given a knighthood. My father came to hear of this and told the general he could never accept a knighthood if his elder brother did not have one. So the general changed the name in his proposal from my father to his elder brother who was duly awarded a knighthood by King George V.'

It seems VPS's father was a 'happy-go-lucky' individual. Not only is a famous Indian golf tournament named after him (implying he must have played more than a round or two – surely unusual at that time) but it is said he collected everything under the sun. He is said to have accumulated what was the second largest private collection in the world of jade and more than 6000 antique pocket watches. 'However,' says VPS, 'he was not just an antique collector. He was the least serious of the three brothers in matters of industry, but it was his work that got the contracts to supply the British Army and this was where the real fortune was made for the family in those early years. There is no doubt, like many Marwaris, he had a very good eye for business opportunities. One of the first businesses my father acquired in Bombay in the 1940s was a small blanket mill. The mill used to make very inferior cheap blankets called a "Loi" and which were branded "Raymond" after the son-in-law of the owner. A "loi" is a cross between a shawl and a blanket, a very thick shawl which poor people use to cover themselves when cold. The owner from whom my father bought the company was a very famous Englishman, Sir David Sassoon. In those days Sir David Sassoon owned maybe half of Bombay. In fact, one of the docks in Bombay is named after him, the Sassoon Docks. This acquisition was called Raymond Woolen Mills Company Limited and became the foundation of our family's Raymond Group which makes and sells suits and clothes throughout the world and has many other businesses.

'There are a couple of family stories about the beginnings of Raymond after we bought it. My brother-in-law (married to my elder sister) ran the company when we first took it over. In the mid '50s Gopal Krishna Singhania, one of my cousins had just returned from a tour of England and said to my father he would like to make men's suitings at Raymond. The sales manager told my father, 'Your son has gone berserk, he wants to make suitings in India. Suitings are made in England, not in India. He's mad and I'm a blanket salesman.' So, he resigned and said, 'I won't work for your company because you have got a mad chief executive.' With all this drama my cousin took over Raymond as its CEO. He was Sir Padampatji's eldest son. We used to call him "GKS". Under him Raymond made the first suiting material in India in the late '50s.'

You would think for VPS to be born into this world would have been wonderful but, as you will read, that was not to be. VPS was born on 4 October 1938 in Kanpur, the third child after two elder sisters. Three years later his younger brother, Ajaypat was born.

'In the first of the major upheavals in my life, I lost my mother when I was four and Ajaypat was only a year old. She died during pregnancy. My mother's death brought about an aching vacuum in my life and began at an early age the "loneliness" that I have lived with in later years. I only have a couple of memories of my mother. I remember once I got bitten by a honey-bee and was lying in her lap. She used her sari to apply a warm pack with her breath on my eyes.

'My father remarried and my stepmother was not a kind woman. She used to beat me and my brother three to four times a day, "regular as clockwork". Stepmothers do not have a great reputation in India, and like other children, I hated mine. Shuttling between Kanpur and Bombay or wherever else my father chose to take us, I felt like an orphan. Both my sisters married early and were reluctant to revisit the family home.

'My stepmother would often fly into a rage at the schools where Ajaypat and I were attending and remove us to somewhere else to show how serious she was. The effect was, of course, to make it hard for us to make friends and my grades suffered. For long periods Ajaypat and I would be left with my eldest aunt, Lady Anusuya Devi, Sir Padampatji's wife. My paternal grandmother, Lady Ram Piyari Devi, a stern and dominating woman was my only anchor in an otherwise unstable childhood, despite her aloofness and the lack of any physical displays of affection.'

I asked him what other memories he had of his early childhood. 'I can remember the many trips we took from Kanpur to Bombay before we moved there. From Kanpur we used to change our train at a station called Jhansi and we had to wait there for about five hours. It was about 28 to 30 hours to Kanpur from Bombay. Later on I remember we used to travel by a private airline called Jam Air which was run by the Jam Saab of Jamnagar. Nawab Saheb was the local Raja equivalent. He used DC-3 Dakotas. It used to take about five hours to travel on that. Some days it stopped en-route in Bhopal and some days in Gwalior. Sometimes we travelled by train, sometimes by plane. My brother and I got very used to travelling.

'Other memories of those trips were the fact that most of the trains were not air-conditioned. From Kanpur to Jhansi takes five to eight hours so we had to carry big ice boxes in the compartments in which we used to put some fruit and other things to eat. But the moment we reached Jhansi we used to be so thrilled because the Punjab Mail used to have air conditioned coaches. Of course, in those days, the air conditioning was not great, but anything was good in the 40-45 degree centigrade temperatures during the day. Going from Bombay to Kanpur we usually left in the evening and around 8 a.m. the next morning we arrived in Bhopal where my Calcutta uncle had a factory. He used to arrange for people from the factory to bring fresh milk in earthenware pots. I can vividly remember how delicious we found that milk and used to gulp it down.'

While VPS was still a small boy his father and his uncles spread out – Sir Padampat ran the overall business from Kanpur, Vijaypat's father moved to Bombay and Lala Lakshmipat moved to Calcutta. 'My uncle who settled in Calcutta started the first bauxite mine in India to produce aluminium, then moved into jute production and then into producing engineering products like wire ropes. All these businesses were part of the joint family business and both my father and Lala Laskhmipatji reported to their elder brother, my uncle, Sir Padampatji.

'My father and my mother travelled to UK with me. The first time I went overseas I was less than one. My parents travelled on Queen Elizabeth I. There is a photo I cherish and have kept of me in a basket underneath a dining table on the ship. There is a story in my family that on that trip I was going to be kidnapped for ransom when we reached Paris. I don't know why they thought this but they did and it has now gone into folklore in the family. There are many other interesting stories of my family's travels. Believe it or not my uncle once took sacks full of coal from India when he travelled by ship as he was worried his cook would not be able to find coal to cook his food. It is said that once when his bags were being unloaded in England, one of the porters got filthy carrying the coal bags and threw them in the sea saying, "I refuse to carry this junk". So, the story goes.'

I said to VPS that his brother Ajaypat seemed to feature in lots of his stories but not his two older sisters. I wondered why. 'Well, my eldest sister was six years older than me and the second was four years older. My eldest sister was married off when she was fifteen and the other when she was twelve. My family married young. Don't you know what happened to me with my marriage?' I said that I did not and asked him to enlighten me.

'It was at a wedding of one of my cousins in Calcutta on 18 February 1951 that my father happened to see a girl from some distance playing with her siblings. Three days later he embraced a person who became my father-in-law. On 21 February, 1951, at the age of twelve, I was engaged to Asha, then nine years old. She was from the illustrious Jalan family of Calcutta. She was brought to my home for the first time on the pretext of being given chocolates. Five years later when I was seventeen and she was fourteen we were married. We had our first child, a son in the following year. He is the father of my beloved first grandchild, Ananya who is the one whose photo I put in the cockpit when I made the first micro-light flight from England to India. One positive event around the time of my marriage was that my father divorced my stepmother who had been such a source of unpleasantness for my brother and me.'

When he was very young VPS went to St Mary's Convent in Kanpur and after that, due to his stepmother's continually moving him and his brother around, he went to so many schools he can hardly remember them all. 'However, my father finally saw all the damage it was causing and allowed me to finish the last four years of my secondary education at the Gur Narain Khatri High School in Kanpur where I topped the Allahabad School Board in maths and science, to which my school was affiliated. I was packed off to Bombay to join Sydenham College of Commerce and Economics, much against my will, at the behest of my father. He said I was to be a businessman and businessmen must learn commerce. Naturally, I protested but his word was law. When I left the college I had failed the degree exam and for a long time did not understand or enjoy commerce or economics. It was only years later when I started teaching post-graduate management students that I had a change of mind.'

I asked him if he did not want to become a businessman what did he want to become – an engineer or a pilot? 'I was actually pretty hopeless at the liberal arts and probably a science or engineering career would have suited me more. I remember one year getting 7 out of 100 for history, 6 out of 100 for geography and 6 out of 100 for art. In maths and science I did very well as my final results at high school showed. So commerce or economics was not a natural fit.'

I said to VPS he had painted a very unhappy childhood. He said, 'I have to tell you something else to understand how we used to think and why we thought that way. Kanpur was a very small town; I think the population of Kanpur in my early days was well under a million. We were a very orthodox and conservative family. We never visited friends and friends never visited us. We had to remain at home. A watchman used to go with us to school and come back with us. So, we never saw anything besides our house and in the evenings we had to go to the family temple. That's all we saw. It was impossible for us to dream of going to a movie, to a restaurant, to a friend's house or to a party. This was unheard of in the whole family, for both the boys and the girls. We had no access to any information or exposure to the outside world. This was typical of conservative Marwari families in the 1940s.'

I remarked to VPS that surely some of his school friends would ask him to come and play at their homes after school. 'In school nobody dared to say that because they knew that we were from one of the leading families of Kanpur. Everybody would think that since we were from such a noble family we were unapproachable, and they couldn't invite us. The class distinction could actually be felt. I can't remember whether we felt about it in a good or a bad way. It was not very perceptible but I think it was there and even the teachers in the school used to treat us differently, "Oh, this is the Singhania family you must treat them reverentially".'

I imagined, that could make the Singhania and other well-to-do families arrogant, but VPS disagreed. 'None of us knew what the word meant. Although we may have been treated differently by the teachers we were still caned and made to stand on the benches. My uncle was a tough guy and very short tempered and he used to scream at all the children. Even when I used to meet my father I had to be careful because he too had a very short temper.'

This reminded me that initially VPS lived in a joint family in Kanpur before his father and younger brother moved to Bombay and Calcutta. 'That's so,' he said, 'and it reminds me of one story. After we got home from school, the children of all the three families would wash and then sit together with guardian teachers and tutors to do our homework and more schooling. We would often refer to children from the other families as our "cousins" which of course they were. However, our teachers and tutors would get very angry if we did that and told us, "You are all brothers, don't you dare use that word cousin." The teachers and tutors were almost like family and, in their own way, they tried to cement our family relationship, to remain united, to be a strong joint family.'

I asked VPS to tell me more about his bizarre, for me, betrothal and wedding. 'Well, firstly my father never told me that I was engaged. My cousins used to tease me about it. "Vijju," that's my nickname, "you're getting engaged. Apparently what happened was, I learnt this from my elder sister many years later, my father saw this girl who reminded him of my late mother and he said, "I want that girl." If you see some of her pictures at the time of my marriage and put them next to my mother's early photos the likeness is uncanny. After my so-called engagement the only time I saw my wife-to-be was when her family came to Bombay for dinner. There we sat at the same dinner table but we never spoke.'

So what happened next I asked. 'One day I was told sit here and do this. It was the start of the wedding ceremony which started on 14 April 1956 and ended sixteen days later on 29 April 1956. My father never warned me that I was about to get married. Believe it or not but I never really ever had a friendly relaxed chat with my father. My uncle from Kanpur was the same with his children although the one in Calcutta did communicate with his children.'

I wondered what impact this had on VPS's parenting of his own children. He told me, 'I am afraid to say it has been the same. I feel very sorry that I neglected my children because I didn't know anything. I didn't know how else to deal with them. I've never seen anybody being treated differently. That was the done thing. In retrospect, I know that was a very unfortunate thing and I truly regret it. I never gave my children the love they deserved, for I never knew what it meant.

'With the knowledge of my failings with my own children I think that is why I fell in love with my first grandchild, Ananya. I think the first time I understood the meaning of the four letter word "love" was when I first saw her. Something happened to me, which never happened before. I couldn't live without her. I couldn't live without seeing her, without being with her. She was, I believe, also very fond of me. Sadly my elder son and I fell out and he moved to Singapore and I did not see Ananya for many years.

'I think in recent years I have made a very serious attempt at changing my relationship with my children but I think with age, change becomes much more difficult, and of course one's children grow up and become independent. What's gone is gone and you cannot bring it back. So one tries to make attempts to do whatever is possible to fill those missing moments. Nevertheless, I'm trying very hard but sadly the relationship will never be what it could have been thirty years ago.'

I now turned our discussion to the thorny issue of how successful joint families managed to handle generational change. I told him that Arun Bharat Ram had spoken at length on this issue. I asked him about the Singhanias.

'During my father's time, the family stayed together and I remember both the younger brothers, my father and my uncle had great respect, and were totally subjugated, to their elder brother, Sir Padampatji. He was the boss and not just a brother. I can remember some senior executives in the company ask my father why he did not seek a monetary settlement from Sir Padampatji over some event. My father replied, "Don't you dare question his authority, whatever he says is final." Unfortunately, I have to say I do not believe my uncle behaved correctly or fairly with respect to his younger brothers or the joint family. But my father was never willing to think this could be the case. Even after the death of the three brothers, whilst the next generation lived in different parts of the country, we still lived as a joint family. But about twenty-five years ago the businesses were split up between the families of the three brothers. Unfortunately, it was not an amicable split and legal action was commenced by cousin against cousin. The law suits continue to this day. I really didn't want to be part of it but have been pulled in as a defendant.'

I remarked a twenty-five year family law dispute seemed quite long while not to resolve things amongst the heirs. VPS laughed and said, 'The Marwaris can be incredibly litigious over such things. I am told that in my home town of Kanpur there is one family dispute which has made it into the *Guinness Book of World Records* as the dispute has been ongoing for seventeen generations! I have been telling my cousins "for god's sake" stop this fighting. In our family's case I guess it boils down to a change in the influence and wealth of the three families. The Kanpur family was the heart of the Singhania family in earlier generations and still probably has the most assets. However, in terms of respectability and success of the various businesses, the Bombay businesses of my family would be number one, the Calcutta businesses would be second and Kanpur would now be a distant third.'

I asked whether these problems arose immediately on the death of his father and uncles or whether it took time to surface. VPS laughed and said, 'My youngest uncle died first and then my father died five years later in 1969. The problems arose when my eldest uncle died in November 1979 shortly followed five weeks later in January by his eldest son, GK Singhania who had become chairman of Raymond after my father died. When GK Singhania died we all went to Kanpur for the final rites and ceremonies which involved a thirteen day mourning period. But my family did not wait for the mourning period to finish. On the third or fourth day all talk turned to who would take over Raymond which was considered the "plum pudding" of the group. Most people thought "VPS", that's what I was known as, that I was going to put the first claim as it was my father's company. I told them, "Listen, I'm not going to make any claims. This is a family company, let the family decide who they want to run it." I was quite happily running a chemical company at the time and did not care one way or the other.

'Now the hierarchy of who became the senior member of the family is quite interesting. Although in my father's generation Sir Padampatji was the oldest and thus head of the family in my generation, as GKS, the eldest son of Sir Padampatji had died, the next surviving eldest was my cousin who was the eldest son of Lakshmipat Singhania of Calcutta. His name was Hari Shankar Singhania. We used to call him "HSS". He decided he wanted to take over

Raymond and called a meeting of the senior executives of Raymond in Kanpur where most of them had been attending the funeral and various ceremonies. He told them, "I have decided to take over Raymond." All these senior people had been employed by my father and worked with him for many years. I am told they responded, "Hari Shankar Ji, you are the boss and can take over the company whenever you want, but you should know that all the senior executives of Raymond will quit. We are not willing to work for anybody other than KPS's eldest son," who, of course, was me. HSS then came and told the family that he did not lay a claim to take over Raymond. The Kanpur family then said they did not lay claim to Raymond. And so I was asked to take over as chairman of Raymond. All of this, I might add took place during the mourning period when, of course for sentimental reasons, no business is meant to be done!'

I knew Raymond had grown immensely during his twenty or so years of chairing Raymond but it struck me that he was not a classical businessman. To this he replied, 'Let me put it this way. I was a very hard working industrialist. Sure, what came in between was a very stupid thing called flying. This took priority over everything. So, to that extent I did neglect my business. But the business grew hugely during my term.'

Finally, VPS had mentioned flying, his passion and for which he is famous in India and beyond. I asked him to tell me about how it all happened.

'I cannot remember the exact moment when my love of flying began or from where it came. However, I can remember my fascination of seeing aircraft take off and land. Once when a Dakota was readying itself for take-off, I watched in awe the small guy behind the cockpit lifting this huge piece of metal off the ground. That could have been the day when the seeds were sown for what later became an "addiction", or perhaps a better word, is an "obsession".

'In flying maybe I was seeking to escape the reality of the broken home where I was growing up. I know when I was in the sky that I found temporary solace that allowed me to reconcile myself to the life I led on the ground. When I was in the air and looking down, what I saw seemed so illusory. Part of me perversely encouraged this escapist attitude, grabbing any chance to take off and forget who I was and who, more importantly, I was expected to be, for an hour or two of abandon.

'In those days you had to be at least twenty-one to legally fly an aircraft and so eleven days after my 21st birthday on 15 October 1959 I took my first flying lesson from the Bombay Flying Club. It took me a long while to become a member of the club as it was a very snooty outfit. I got my first Private Pilot's Licence from the Hind Provincial Flying Club in Kanpur with three aircraft endorsed on it – a Pipercub J3C, a Chipmunk and a Piper L5.

'Over the intervening years I have flown almost every civilian aircraft that India has. I even had a few attempts at owning an airline. It was far too early. For example, in 1970 I bought three old DC-3 Dakotas from Indian Airlines and founded a little airline called Safari Airways. It had to be a "non-scheduled" airline because Indian Airlines had a monopoly. Three years later after pumping a lot of money into it I closed the business – the red tape and bureaucracy were just too much for me.

'The book, *An Angel in the Cockpit*,[2] was written about my flight in August/ September 1988 in a microlight from England to India in twenty-four days from Biggin Hill in England to New Delhi in India. That was a wonderful challenge and experience but I would not want to repeat as there were many close calls which could have resulted in my death. It got me into the *Guinness Book of World Records*, since I had beaten a long distance speed record set by a Englishman, Brian Milton a few years earlier.

'A couple of years later my good friend, Captain Raman Kapoor who was then a senior check pilot, instructor and examiner on Boeing 737's flown by Indian Airlines asked me to join him on a flight from Delhi to Srinagar via Amritsar. After we took off from Delhi he asked me to join him in the cockpit and to take the jump seat. I was fascinated by the complex controls compared to the other smaller aircraft I had flown; not to mention the comparison with a microlight! Shortly after we left Amritsar for the short flight to Srinagar he asked his co-pilot to swap seats with me and then, believe it or not, asked me to take the controls and, not only fly the plane, but to land it at Srinagar. I was terrified and my heart began to thump violently. But he calmed me down and I made a feather touch landing. I was smitten and the seeds of self destruction had been sown. I now wanted to fly Boeings!

'I could not get a licence to fly Boeing 737s in India as the only training facility was owned by Indian Airlines and so I went to a training school in Miami in the US where I studied for a "conversion". I then obtained an American ATP licence (their highest category of Air Transport Pilot licence issued under FAR 121) with a Boeing 737 endorsement and a Captain's rating. When I came back to India I asked the then Indian Director General of Civil Aviation to recognize my US licence. Being the "licence raj" era he naturally thought up a reason as to why it should not be recognized and told me I would have to do the training and exams in India which, of course, was a sheer waste of time. I put my foot down and a "battle royale" ensued. I worked out a way to thwart the director general. If he would not recognize a US licence then perhaps the Americans could be persuaded not to recognize Indian licences. This meant that Air India would not be able to fly to the US without getting all of its pilots to convert to US licences. My bluff worked. Maybe, I was correct in my analysis and so the DGCA backed off.

'I joined East West Airlines in India as a co-pilot for starters. Remember this is while I was still Chairman of Raymond. So I used to choose flights which interfered as little as possible with my corporate role. It was a period of very little sleep and I am embarrassed to say I can remember more than once nodding off to sleep during corporate meetings at the office. East West eventually folded up not long after its founder, Mr Takiyuddin Wahid was gunned down in front of his office. Apparently there was some sort of gang warfare. That was not the end of my career as a commercial pilot as I then joined Damania Airways, then Alliance Airways, a subsidiary of Indian Airlines and finally, Sahara Airways. I then had to stop as, according to the then law one could not fly as a commercial pilot after the age of sixty, which I turned in 1998.

'I am proud to say during this period I won the Arc en Ciel round the world race from and to Montreal in 1994 in a Cessna Conquest, a twin engine turbo prop. There was one terrifying moment on that trip when both engines failed between Canada and Morocco and the plane nose dived towards the Atlantic Ocean. I panicked and looked at my co-pilot, Dan who smiled and calmly advised that since we had run out of fuel in the main tank perhaps we should switch to the auxiliary tank!

'My co-pilot and I went to the prize ceremony wearing tiger costumes and, as we went up to collect the prize with our tails in our hands, they played the "Pink Panther" music in the background. It was great fun as my family flew in from India for the ceremony and I was awarded the Federation of Aeronautique Internationale's coveted gold medal. As the only Indian to have one, having won the race, once again got me into the *Guinness Book of World Records.*

'Having done just about everything else with aircraft I decided that there was one form I had not really done much of. That was hot air ballooning. I had a little fun flying in East Africa but decided to set myself the goal of doing the world's highest hot air balloon ascent. I started training for it in 2005 by going to Cuneo in Italy to see how I handled sub-freezing temperatures. In June of that year I did a test run in Ahmedabad and, in November of that year, achieved my goal taking off from Bombay Racecourse in the largest balloon ever built. It had an envelope volume of over 1.6 million cubic feet. Having beaten a Brit's record by going to 70,000 feet above sea level, this got me once again into the *Guinness Book of World Records* for a third time.'

As I am sure a reader of this chapter will have noticed – I had got VPS onto a topic which he loved and which did not contain a lot of the sadness and regrets exhibited in other parts of his life. I closed our meeting by saying that I hoped he would be able to reconcile with his elder son and for his immediate family to be re-united. 'Mr Church,' he said, 'I can assure you that is my fondest hope and I shall pray to God to make it happen.'

Raymond Limited (www.raymondindia.com) is the largest integrated manufacturer of woollen & worsted fabrics in the world. The company comprises the following divisions: textiles – with a capacity of 33 million metres in wool & wool-blended fabrics, Raymond commands over 60 per cent market share in worsted suiting in India and ranks amongst the first three fully integrated manufacturers of worsted suiting in the world; engineering – JK Files & Tools and Ring Plus Aqua Ltd. are the group companies that are engaged in the manufacture of precision engineering products such as steel files, cutting tools, hand tools, agri tools and auto components; and aviation – was one of the first private sector companies in India to launch Air Charter and commercial flights.

1 *An Angel in the Cockpit* by Dr Vijaypat Singhania, Roli Books, Delhi 2005 p. 14

2 Ananya is the 'angel' in his cockpit referred to in Dr Vijaypat's book on the trip, *An Angel in the Cockpit.* A photo of the cockpit showing the picture of Ananya is on the cover of the book.

‘For me, it was blindingly clear that the most important thing for India after WWII was going to be food.’

PROFESSOR MS SWAMINATHAN

Founder
The MS Swaminathan Research Foundation

Professor MS Swaminathan, widely known as the 'father of India's green revolution', is the one exception to the rule in this book otherwise devoted to business entrepreneurs. I feel that without the work of Professor Swaminathan, not only would many of these entrepreneurs not be where they are today, but India as we know it may not even exist due to the possible inability to feed its people. Indeed, *Time* magazine in its August 1999 edition included Professor Swaminathan along with Mahatma Gandhi and Rabindranath Tagore (Nobel Laureate in Literature) as the three most influential Indians among the twenty leading Asians of the twentieth century. It is said of Professor Swaminathan that he 'used his skills in genetic engineering and his powers of persuasion to make famine an unfamiliar word in Asia'.

I met Professor Swaminathan at his Delhi apartment on a beautiful December afternoon (2007). When he opened the door to greet me I was surprised to find that he looked far younger than his eighty years and radiated peace and contentment. As my interview proceeded, I could clearly see that here was someone who was still in command of all his intellectual faculties. I was also amazed by his memory for names and events far in the past.

Professor Swaminathan was born on 7 August 1925, in the town of Kumbakonam in Tamil Nadu. His grandfather, Krishna Iyer, also came from a town not far away called Monkumbu which, incidentally, is his first name and of his father and many of the males in the family. He had six sons. His grandfather was a farmer. He owned large agricultural farms on which he grew rice, coconuts and mangoes. His grandmother was a devout Hindu who visited the temple of Bhagavati every day with all grandchildren in tow. 'It was she who taught all of us that faith in God requires a strong ethical value system.'

Professor Swaminathan's father, Monkumbu Krishna Sambasivam was a doctor. 'He was a famous surgeon who had done some of his studies in Vienna, which had at that time the world's leading medical faculty. He was not only the most popular doctor of his times but he had a deep social consciousness. This is best illustrated by his work with elephantiasis/filariasis for which our village was unfortunately known. Every third person had the disease. My father was sure he could eradicate the disease with a social awareness programme. So he stood for chairman of our municipality and won easily given his high profile. I am not sure if you know that elephantiasis is carried by mosquitoes and so my father, upon election, immediately arranged for a map to be done of where the mosquitoes bred. He then organized meetings in every street with the residents and told them "mosquitoes are breeding in your street" pointing out the water areas where they were breeding. "If you don't need that water then please remove it. If you need it then please pour crude oil on it." At that time you see we did not have DDT which only became available shortly before WW II and the treatment before that was crude oil emulsion. This prevented mosquito larvae from surfacing. Within one year all the mosquitoes were gone and incidences of elephantiasis diminished significantly. Even today, people in the village talk about it,' he laughs.

The lesson the young Swaminathan learnt from this, he says, was the power of the people to get seemingly impossible tasks done.

His father was a follower of Mahatma Gandhi and Swaminathan can remember Gandhi staying at their home several times when he was young. 'My father was at the forefront of several movements started by Gandhi such as "self-reliance" which we called the "swadeshi" movement and also the abolition of untouchability and opening the temples – the Hindu temples – to all people.

'I can remember one occasion when Gandhi came to stay. I must have been around eight at the time. My mother warned me that Gandhi was likely to ask me to give him my gold bracelet and that I should do so. Most middle-class boys like me had some sort of bracelet and Gandhi collected these from his supporters to melt down and fund his campaign. This seemed rather strange to me but sure enough he did ask for my bracelet and I did give it to him,' he laughs. 'I can remember Gandhi was accompanied by a forbidding English woman, I think her name was Meera Slade. She tried to keep all the children away from Gandhi but he welcomed us to sit with him.'

Swaminathan had his early education at a high school in Kumbakonam and, after completing middle school, he was admitted to the Little Flower High School. This institution was run by Catholic missionaries who emphasized moral education and strict discipline.

Unfortunately, when Swaminathan was only eleven his father passed away suddenly at the very young age of thirty-six. 'It was a joint family and my father and his brother, Monkumbu Krishna Narayanaswami and their families lived in the same house in the town. As was the custom, my father's brother took over the responsibility of caring for my mother and her children as well as his own wife and his four children. It must have been very tough for him to do this.'

Swaminathan graduated from high school at the young age of fifteen. He immediately left Kumbakonam for Trivandrum (now Thiruvananthapuram) to live with his father's elder brother, Monkumbu Krishna Neelakantan. This gave him the opportunity to study in the Maharaja's college which was affiliated with Travancore University, then part of the princely state of Travancore and now Kerala.

Professor Swaminathan decided to study zoology, although his interest had been in agriculture since he was a small boy. While studying, in 1942 the Great Bengal Famine occurred in undivided Bengal, then part of India. Everyday, he read stories about people dying of starvation. This had a significant impact on him, as did Gandhi's movements emphasizing nationalism and self-sufficiency which were at their peak then. 'I knew my mother was hoping I would do medicine as my elder brother had not followed in our father's footsteps but had decided on a career in the pharmaceutical industry. She had hoped at least one of us would become a doctor and return home to run the very good hospital my father had built.

'For me it was blindingly clear that the most important thing for India after WW II was going to be food.' So, on graduation with a bachelor's degree in zoology, Swaminathan moved to the agricultural college in Coimbatore in Tamil Nadu which was affiliated with the University of Madras. He completed a second bachelor's degree in science in 1947 but this time specializing in agriculture. He topped the course.

'I had lots of offers to become a plantation crop manager where one had a high social status but it was clear in my mind I had not taken the degree to become a farmer but to help farmers. In other words, a scientist who can help not one farmer but many farmers,' he laughs. 'So, I decided to go on with my studies and for some reason thought the science of genetics and breeding might be the one area where I could do the maximum good because one might be able to develop a variety which everybody can grow ... a high yield one.'

Swaminathan moved to Delhi in 1947 to the Indian Agriculture Research Institute, the largest of its kind in India. It was here in 1949 he earned a master's in agriculture with a distinction in cytogenetics which is the study of inheritance with reference to cells. He was awarded a UNESCO fellowship to the Wageningen Agricultural University in the Netherlands to conduct research on potatoes.

He only stayed one year at Wageningen. 'I found that to do a doctorate in Holland would take me six years and I would have to produce a book. This was too long for me and not what I wanted to do. My short stay at Wageningen was of huge value to me in setting my life's goals. I learnt that the university's mission statement was to "develop and disseminate scientific knowledge needed to sustainably supply society's demand for sufficient, healthy food and a good environment for humans, animals and plants". That became the cornerstone of my own mission statement in agricultural research in improving India's food stocks for the masses.'

Fortunately, Swaminathan's professor at Wageningen, Professor Dorst understood what he wanted to do and recommended he move to the Plant Breeding Institute at Cambridge University. He did so in September 1950. Two years later, he was awarded his PhD for his work on the breeding and genetics of potatoes and, in particular, their resistance to golden nematode which destroyed many crops in Europe during WW II. It made him understand the importance of potatoes as a basic food stuff in European cultures.

'When I was in Cambridge in 1952, I published a paper in a journal *The American Potato Journal.* That attracted the attention of the people in the US and I got a request from the University of Wisconsin to join them. It appeared they were setting up a new institution to study potatoes. They had collected a lot of potato material from South America which, as you may know, is the home of the potato and, in particular, the Lake Titicaca region in Bolivia and Chiloé Island off Southern Chile, from where the white potato or *solanum tuberosum* came to Europe.

'My time in the US was both enjoyable as well as interesting. You may be interested to know one experience I had there. In the US in the '50s there was a lot of anti-communism sentiment and one senator in particular, Joseph

Raymond McCarthy, was responsible for a huge witch-hunt against those he thought had communist leanings. Each year the US Department of Agriculture publishes what it calls the *Yearbook of Agriculture*. Each senator gets around 300 copies. My friends suggested I call McCarthy up and ask for a copy which I did. A lady in his office called back to say that the senator wanted to give me the copy personally. Naturally, I was a bit surprised but went to meet him. I guessed what his aim was. He was very much against Nehru – Nehru was our prime minister – and there was another leading politician called VK Krishna Menon. He was very much against him too because he felt they were doing the wrong thing with respect to the Korean War, which was in full swing at the time. So, when I met Senator McCarthy, I had to listen to his diatribe on the evils of communism. He then asked me to convey his feelings to Mr Nehru and Mr Menon when I returned to India. Being a scientist and not a politician, I could not see much point in getting into a debate with him so I just thanked him for the book and took my leave. It was a very strange meeting,' he laughs.

'After eighteen months, I was offered a full-time position at the university – an immediate associate professorship. This was an excellent opportunity but I wanted to get back to India. Two days before I left, the president of the university invited me for breakfast and said, "I appreciate your sentiment, but if by any chance, when you get back you don't get a proper position, you are always welcome here." He wrote to me also with the same offer to avoid procedural delays I would undoubtedly have to face if I chose to return to the US.

'I returned to India in January 1954. January came and went, February came and went, March came and went and I heard nothing from anybody on job offers. There was absolutely nothing on the horizon. Everyone said they would look out for me but there seemed to be nothing around.'

Somehow, with the help of his former teacher, Professor N Parthasarathy, he landed a temporary job as an assistant botanist at the Central Rice Research Institute at Cuttack in Orissa. His role was to develop a hybrid between two strains of rice which would be responsive to fertilizer. 'That was a very interesting, challenging job because all our earlier varieties of rice were not developed for fertilizer response, you see. They were for a single purpose – one for straw for animal feed and another for grain to eat.'

After nine months in Cuttack a full-time role came through at his alma mater of the Indian Agricultural Research Institute in New Delhi where he was offered the position of assistant cytogeneticist working on wheat. 'I joined there at the end of 1954 and ceased my involvement eighteen years later in 1972.

'From my work on rice at the Central Rice Research Institute I decided we must do the same thing with wheat; namely develop fertilizer responsive wheat. That meant we needed a dwarf variety. So I started looking at all the available dwarfs and found nothing. Then, one day in the mid '50s, I read a report from Washington State University by Orville Vogel explaining how he had worked on a Japanese wheat variety brought to the US by General MacArthur and converted it into one of the most successful winter wheat varieties called "Gaines". I wrote to Vogel asking him to send me some seeds which he kindly agreed to do. However, he said, "I must warn you it's a winter wheat; it will not flower under your conditions. You require long days and I suggest you contact Norman Borlaug who has developed spring wheat from the genes I have given him from my wheat."

Borlaug was at that time working in Mexico in a Rockefeller programme and responded warmly to Swaminathan's letter asking for seeds of the spring wheat he had developed. Borlaug wrote back to say he would be happy to send the seeds but he would have to visit India to see the growing conditions because he had already planted seeds in Pakistan.

'Given the bureaucracy of India in those days and as I was a very junior scientist it took more than a year to get permission for Borlaug to come. He arrived in March 1963 and together we travelled for one month all over the wheat belt of India in a car. At the end, Borlaug concluded that the seeds would work in India but that he wanted to first check their progress in Lahore, Pakistan. On his return to Mexico, Borlaug wrote to Swaminathan recommending semi-dwarf wheat varieties like Lerma Rojo and Sonora 64 which he thought would do well in India. He promised that Swaminathan would have the seeds by September in time for November planting. 'That's how we started our programme. Within two years it was clear that some of his material was doing very well directly. In order to save time, I proposed to the government that we should start a national demonstration programme directly by scientists in farmers' fields. It was important for me to get a validation of whatever we were observing in a researcher's field. Almost all of the farmers in 500 demonstrations produced five to six tonnes of wheat instead of the standard one and a half.

'I was astounded and showed it. That's why it was called a "wheat revolution" not an "evolution". It produced a 200 to 300 per cent increase, not just a couple of per cent. As news of the success spread like "wild fire", farmers began clamoring for seeds. We did not have enough and had to import seed from Mexico, along with food grain from many countries including the US, Canada and Australia, to tide over the food crisis in India.'

The increase in production cause unexpected problems. All of India's storage had been at the docks as grain traditionally had been imported.

There was little storage in the areas where the wheat was being grown. India was moving from a period of total dependence on imported food to one of self-sufficiency. This objective was in harmony with the objectives of India's then government under Prime Minister Indira Gandhi.

'Indira Gandhi was a very proud person and told me, "We must safeguard food security for national sovereignty; otherwise, I will have to surrender my foreign policy if I need to feed my people with imported food". I think she felt President Lyndon Johnson behaved patronizingly in providing India with wheat. The wheat revolution enabled us to move in 1973 to having a surplus of about 18 million tonnes of grain.

'Food production had been much neglected during the colonial period. The British concentrated mainly on plantation crops like tea, coffee, rubber or pepper. They were also interested to some extent in cotton, not cotton mills for India, but in sending the cotton raw material to mills in England. That is why Gandhi started this "charkha" – the spinning wheel – as a symbol of self-reliance. "Why do you want to send the cotton far away and get the cloth back?" His thinking was that we can spin it ourselves, even if we don't have modern spinning mills.

'Food is first among the hierarchical needs of the human being, therefore, it is a very vulnerable tool in political decision making. That is why Indira Gandhi was very keen to have a very strong food security base, a base of self-reliance, if you like.'

Swaminathan left the Indian Agricultural Research Institute in 1972 to become Head of the Indian Council of Agricultural Research, to which all of India's agricultural research institutes reported. He remained in that role until 1978 when there was a change of government. Indira Gandhi had put India under Emergency Rule which was disliked intensely by the voters and her party – the Congress. The government fell, to be replaced by another party headed by Morarji Desai.

'Desai told me, "I want a secretary who knows agriculture" and I was made Secretary of the Ministry of Agriculture. It was as simple as that. This was a significant change in the way things were done as until my appointment all of the secretaries who headed ministries were members of the Indian Administrative Service. So this was quite a change. It was an interesting but short-lived experience as Indira Gandhi came back to power in 1980.

'She called me and told me she wanted me to become Deputy Chairman of the Planning Commission because she said, "You can think and visualize what I want, and I want planning to be rooted in agriculture."

'I have to say, this was not a role I wanted. It meant attending meeting after meeting and dealing with the allocation of resources rather than doing. After my role as secretary of agriculture, where I could make decisions which

I felt made a difference to the lives of farmers, this seemed much less satisfying.' He told her he was not keen on the job. She relented but after a month she called him again to a meeting and instructed him, "I want you to take the role. We will find another person soon, but right now I don't want to delay setting up the commission."

'The prime minister's problem was that she knew she had many enemies from the Emergency Rule period and did not trust many, if any, politicians. She had only a handful of people she could entrust with roles such as at the Planning Commission. So, there were three of us. The present prime minister, Dr Manmohan Singh, was the member secretary, I was the acting deputy chairman, and Mohamad Fazal was the third member.'

After two years, in December 1981, Clarence Gray, who was Chairman of the International Rice Research Institute (IRRI) in the Philippines, came to visit Swaminathan. Mr Gray invited him to join IRRI as its director general. Swaminathan was well aware of the institute. He had been involved in one of its five-year reviews. It was his dream role. 'Basically, I was a scientist and I was looking to go back to research. I knew that Prime Minister Indira Gandhi wouldn't agree, but anyway I went to meet her hesitantly and told her of my invitation. I told her that it was a leading institution and the work I could do there would be relevant to rice production in India. I told her I would like to accept the role if at all possible.'

'What took place then was something I will remember for the rest of my life. First, she said, "No, you cannot" and then, after a pause, she added, "you are indispensable". I am not good at thinking on my feet but somehow the following words leapt from my mouth. "Prime Minister," I said, "since you say I am indispensable, then I must leave." She looked perplexed and said, "What did I say … did I hurt you?" I replied, "You said I am indispensable and I feel that I must go. I must go when I am wanted, not when I am not wanted." And you know something clicked in her mind somewhere. She repeated my words, "You must go when you are wanted, not when you are not wanted." She then stood up and said, "You have my blessings." Truly,' he laughs, 'that has to rate as one of my most fascinating meetings.'

It took Swaminathan five months to clear his work in Delhi before he could take up the top job at the IRRI. He had to hand over chairmanship of many committees ranging from the Planning Commission to others such as the leprosy and blindness committees.

He left for the Philippines in April 1982 to commence a six-year term at the IRRI. At the end of this period, the Board extended his tenure for another term. 'One of the reasons I was keen to leave was that I had won the inaugural World Food Prize[1] in 1987 which carried a cash component of USD 2,00,000, a lot of money in those days. I wished to use this as seed money to establish my own research institute which had long been my dream. As luck would have it, in the following years, I received more prizes such as the Tyler, the Honda and the Sasakawa, the last being from the United Nations endowed by a Japanese with that family name.'

I must interrupt my narrative at this point to advise that I am sure I have never interviewed anyone who has received more awards or honorary degrees than Swaminathan – well over 50 honorary doctorates according to my rough count.

With the money from these prizes – and the many that followed – Swaminathan was able to establish the MS Swaminathan Research Foundation in 1989 with its head office in Chennai and now with branches throughout India. The foundation focuses on anticipatory research and participatory research.

When Swaminathan came back to India, he became increasingly concerned with the environment. 'I could see many negative things happening in farming such as farmers applying more fertilizer than they should and exploiting the ground water more than they should. All of these things concerned me. That is why I am called the "Father of Economical Ecology" and the "Father of Sustainable Agriculture". As far back as January 1968, I had given a lecture in which I warned farmers on these matters. This lecture was widely quoted long before the negative consequences of the green revolution became known.

'Then I coined the term "ever-green revolution" in order to emphasize the need for enhancing productivity in perpetuity without associated ecological harm. What population rich countries like India need is higher productivity per units of land and water, since both arable land and irrigation water are shrinking resources for agriculture. The green-revolution was criticized by environmentalist because of potential adverse impact on the life support systems of land, water and biodiversity. Ever-green revolution in contrast involves mainstreaming ecology in technology development and dissemination.

'We also have another problem where people over-exploit the land for resources such as minerals and water. I call this "the greed revolution". When people are critical, I say "don't attack the green revolution because green is the colour of chlorophyll; it is a good thing, otherwise we would not be alive today".

The first project for his foundation was to prepare to meet the challenge of rising sea levels. I remarked that this was back in the late '80s long before we all started talking about global warming.

'Yes, many people thought I was off the mark when I told them sea levels are going to rise. I told people you cannot do anything on the day the sea rises but perhaps you could do something if you anticipated it. Back in 1989, I was invited to speak at a conference on climate change in Tokyo. It was attended by the then Japanese foreign minister. He heard what I had to say and offered to provide support of USD 500,000. Not a bad return from one speech, was it?' he laughs.

'My project was on mangroves, what we call the bioshield. It also saved lots of lives during the tsunami because it acts like a speed breaker but we did more than increase mangrove planting along the coast. We also took the genes from mangroves and introduced them into rice and other crops along the coast to make them sea water tolerant. If you come to our fields now near Mahabalipuram in Chennai you will see that new rice variety is growing in a combination of sea and fresh water. The rice is very salt tolerant as a result of genetic engineering.'

With such a schedule I wondered if he ever found time to get married? 'Yes, I got married in 1955 to Mina. We had not thought about marrying at the time we met in Cambridge. She is from Delhi and was studying economics at Newnham College. It was some time until we went back together as I headed off to the US to do my post-doctoral work. When I came back to Delhi, we met up again and decided to get married.'

The Swaminathans have three daughters. The eldest, Soumya is a medical doctor, now deputy director of the Tuberculosis Research Center in Chennai, and one of India's leading experts in HIV, AIDS and TB. Their second daughter Madhura was the first female Rhodes Scholar from India. She did her PhD in Economics at Oxford and is now a Professor of Economics at the Indian Statistical Institute in Kolkata whereas the youngest daughter, Nitya is a rural sociologist having done her PhD at the University of East Anglia in Norwich.'

I learnt something quite unusual about his daughters and which is, I would think, the result of the values with which they were raised. Each daughter has decided when she marries and decides to have children she will, if she is able, have one biological child and, given India's population problems, if they want more children will do so by adopting.

I knew Swaminathan was due to shortly attend a meeting with some of his parliamentary colleagues so I popped one last question asking whether he enjoyed being a member of the Upper House. 'Yes, I am an appointed member of our Rajya Sabha. When Prime Minister Dr Manmohan Singh called me up – as I told you we worked together as members of the Planning Commission – he prevailed on me to join the Rajya Sabha. I replied that if he thought I should join, I would do so. When I discussed this with Mina, she remarked that we left Delhi in 1988 and here we are returning after twenty-seven years.

'One thing I have certainly noticed is that time management of parliamentary process is very poor. Serious issues get sidetracked and peripheral issues take center stage. This week, for example, we spent two full days discussing whether the Indian government should give asylum to the Bangladeshi author Taslima Nasreen. Round and around the discussion went. It is interesting but frustrating.'

As we walked to the door, Swaminathan said to me that everyone should have a mission in life. 'When I was young I used to read many philosophical books, like Swami Vivekananda, in particular. Some 100 years ago he said, "This life is short, its vanity is transient; one day you may be here and another day you may be gone." I have frequently seen this in my long life. Take our cricketers, poor fellows, when they lose one match people are shouting at them and when they have done well, people cheer. Once, I saw them hiding in the airport from people after they had lost a match,' he laughs. 'So vanities are transient. "He alone lives who lives for others."' I must admit it took me until I reached my car to appreciate the depth of these few words.

Professor Swaminathan is one of India's leading scientists. Javier Perez de Cuellar, Secretary General of the United Nations, said of him when awarding him the first World Food Prize, 'Dr MS Swaminathan is a living legend. His contributions to agricultural science have made an indelible mark on food production in India and elsewhere in the developing world. By any standards, he will go into the annals of history as a world scientist of rare distinction.' Much of his current efforts are focused at the **MS Swaminathan Research Foundation** (www.mssrf.org).